About the Author

Patrick McGilligan served as editor-in-chief and fine arts editor of *The Daily Cardinal,* the University of Wisconsin student newspaper, while he was an undergraduate there. He has also been a correspondent for the *Madison Capital Times* and the *New York Times.* He is currently on the theatre and arts staff of the *Boston Globe.*

Mr. McGilligan's plans include writing a study of Karl Armstrong, who is currently jailed in Wisconsin for blowing up the Army Mathematics Research Center in 1969 (the explosion killed a researcher).

CAGNEY

CAGNEY

The Actor As Auteur

Patrick McGilligan

SOUTH BRUNSWICK AND NEW YORK:
A. S. BARNES AND COMPANY
LONDON: THE TANTIVY PRESS

A. S. Barnes and Co., Inc.
Cranbury, New Jersey 08512

The Tantivy Press
108 New Bond St.
London W1Y OQX, England

Library of Congress Cataloging in Publication Data

McGilligan, Patrick.
    Cagney: the actor as auteur

    Filmography: p.
    Bibliography: p.
    1. Cagney, James, 1899–
PN2287.C23M3   791.43′028′0924 [B]   73-14028
ISBN 0-498-01462-2

SBN 0-904208-45-1   (U.K)
PRINTED IN THE UNITED STATES OF AMERICA

This book is for Debra Carol Weiner,
with love

Contents

Acknowledgements

To: Films Inc. and Frank Pedi; United Artists and Donald Krim; Richard Feiner and Company; WBBM-TV in Chicago; United States Department of Defense; United States Department of Agriculture; and, particularly, Elizabeth Dalton and the Wisconsin Center for Theatre Research at the University of Wisconsin in Madison. Also: Ian Mills, Russell Campbell, Mike Drocewski, Joyce Steward, Gordon Douglas, Joseph Pevney, Joseph McBride, Dix Bruce and Emma.

Special thanks to Gerald Peary, and Mr. William Anthony and Mrs. Marion E. McGilligan.

Portions of this book are reprinted from "The Velvet Light Trap," "Take One," and film notes for the Cagney Retrospective at the New York Cultural Center, Spring 1973.

As George M. Cohan in YANKEE DOODLE DANDY (1942)

Introduction

*"The movies have not produced any Hamlet parts for us, but
they have raised a crop of people whose movie legend and
cumulative work are almost of that stature. James Cagney
is one of them, and it is hard to say what our impression of
the total American character would have been without him.
He is all crust and speed and snap on the surface, a gutter-
fighter with the grace of dancing, a boy who knows all the
answers and won't even wait for them, a very fast one. But
underneath the fable: the quick generosity and the reckless
drive—everything everybody would like to be, if he had the
time sometime. But always this, always: if as a low type he
is wrong, you are going to see why. In spite of writers,
directors, and decency legions, you are going to see the
world and what it does to its people through his subtle
understanding of it."*
OTIS FERGUSON

But for a wayward grapefruit early in his career, James Cagney
might be remembered today as an actor, also as a song-and-
dance man, both of which he is. Instead, Cagney is immortalised as the cinema's prototype "tough guy." That is his simpli-
fied public legacy, a testament that neglects his enigmatic and
individual aspects: his long, bitter struggle against Hollywood
tradition for artistic independence and his intriguingly contrary
off-screen character—the soft-spoken amateur artist, poet and
gentleman farmer. A few moments as *The Public Enemy* in
1931, buttressed by other memorable gangster roles through
the years, created an image that dies hard. Nearly forgotten
are the talents of a performing artist whose range—from *The
Public Enemy* to *A Midsummer Night's Dream* (1935) to *Yankee Doodle Dandy* (1942) to *White Heat* (1949) to *One, Two
Three* (1961) — is perhaps the most impressive of all American film actors, and whose contribution to the style and character of the American sound cinema is unique and beyond dis-
pute.

Cagney expressed a broad mix of human qualities that made
him one of the most popular and fascinating stars in film history. He was physically tough—that was his identifying trademark—"All India-rubber muscle, steel-faced," in Pat O'Brien's
colourful description. His gestures—such as the jabbing finger-

11

In 1961 while making ONE, TWO, THREE

point—and his poised stance—rump extended, arms dangling
monkey-like and ready—became as familiar as his clipped, self-
confident voice. Both became fertile copy for mimics who
screwed up their faces to hiss, "You dirty rat," a phrase Cagney himself never uttered. He was short but, though his height
was an implicit factor of his popularity (everyone cheers the
underdog), his size diplomatically was never mentioned in his
whole career until his last feature film, *One, Two, Three* (there
C. P. MacNamara wears elevator shoes.) His unique physicality translated readily into a sensuality and even sexuality about
his person. By the entire manner in which he walked and talked,
one knew—foremost—that Cagney was "a man"—that is, by
the classic American cinematic definition: he abused women
and talked big, he lived by his wits and also by his fists.

Cagney performed at triple-speed: he talked and moved in

a staccato, jittery flow and much of the fascination for his character is the hypnotic consequence; he was urban but not urbane; he was ethnic but not exclusive; he was often Irish or New Yorkese but frequently, especially in his Thirties films, he was the symbolic representative of the working class. Sometimes he wasn't so school-smart; sometimes he wasn't worldly-wise. He made mistakes; he was occasionally cruel. But he was ultimately sympathetic—always. Even as a villain. Cagney was one of the few Hollywood stars who consistently debunked his own glamour, in roles such as the coward in *The Fighting 69th* (1940) or the crippled, small-rackets hood in *Love Me or Leave Me* (1955). He was simultaneously babyish and mannish. With his deep, inset eyes and puffed, etched face, he could resemble a child and he was given to tantrums, wild rages and disconsolate sulks. Intrinsically, he invited the mother instinct; nevertheless, as a man he was complete. Cagney delivered the full spectrum of emotions convincingly, from laughing to crying; he outdistanced other lover-boy Hollywood types by his sheer breadth of feeling. He was, simply, an actor's actor.

He was much more too (there are endless analyses pertinent to Cagney, from Robert Warshow's insightful essay on the gangster type to Doris Day's succinct, personal estimate: "He's the most professional actor I've ever known") but there is a relevant capsule analogy. He was the Chaplin of the Talkies, as precisely fitted to the requirements and demands of the sound era as Charles Chaplin was so beautifully suited to the silent era. For the sound film, Cagney expertly utilised speed and motion and gesture and noise, including the chatterbox jabber of his non-stop voice; Chaplin commandeered quiet and leisureliness. Chaplin was a comedian and Cagney played drama mostly but Chaplin was also a tragedian and Cagney, with excuse, could be very funny. There are other connections. Both were, at times, sometimes at the oddest moments, graceful, ballet-like dancers (Cagney as he spins a quick sidewalk step after meeting Jean Harlow in *The Public Enemy*). Both created enduring cinematic personas with associated meaning. This is obvious not only in *Johnny Come Lately* (1943), Cagney's mysterious crusading tramp film, but in most of their work. They were thematic cousins—the Thirties Cagney and the Twenties Chaplin. By implication, they were champions of the little guy and the hope of the world; and in Chaplin's exile to Europe and Cagney's own abandonment of Hollywood in the Sixties, there is the same element of—not simply retirement—but disenchantment, resignation and retreat from the world.

1
Early Biography

From Manhattan to Vaudeville to Hollywood

"Acting and fighting are often a short cut to importance for boys from poor neighbourhoods. Read the Rocky Graziano story? That's the way it was, and still is."

JAMES CAGNEY

"My philosophy has always been to do anything that comes my way seeking to be done. This willingness astonishes producers. When they ask tentatively, 'How about doing so-and-so?' and I say, 'Why not?' they look at me funny. 'What do you prefer to do?' they ask. 'I don't prefer to do anything,' I tell them, 'If a good musical comes along, I'll do a musical. If a good comedy comes along, I'll do comedy. If a good heavy drama comes my way, I'll do heavy drama. Back where I came from, if there was a buck to be made, you didn't ask questions. You just went ahead and made it.'"

JAMES CAGNEY

James Francis Cagney Jr. (later known familiarly to all as Jimmy Cagney even though he was formally billed as James Cagney) was born on July 17, 1899. Studio publicists eventually changed the date to 1904 but kept intact the other essential and correct facts of his birth. Cagney was born in New York City, above his father's saloon near the corner of Avenue D and 8th Street in the area of the metropolis known as the East Village. His father was James Francis Cagney Sr., a bartender who traced his Irish ancestry back to the O'Caignes of County Leitrim in Ireland, and his mother was Carolyn Nelson Cagney, half-Irish and half-Norwegian. Jimmy Cagney was the second of five children in the Cagney brood. Harry was older, and, in time, the two brothers were joined by Edward, William, and Jeanne, the only girl.

The details of Cagney's youth are clouded by a maze of stories, some contradictory, which began to appear in fan magazines and newspapers with increasing regularity soon after Cagney's first film in 1930. Some of the stories were unquestionably planted by press agents; others were false accounts by well-intentioned writers; sometimes the principals (including Cagney) offered obscure or conflicting versions. One magazine which promised Cagney's "True-Life Story" gave a typically glowing rendition of Cagney's childhood. "He was quiet and well-behaved," the periodical reported. "He seemed to be born with gentle manners. He learned his lessons well and earned good marks. He never played hookey nor 'sassed' the teacher. He was never told to 'see the principal.' He was never a problem child."

Maybe so; and maybe not. But certain data seems to be sure: Cagney's family moved at least twice within New York City during Cagney's childhood, finally settling down between Third Avenue and Lexington, near 96th Street in the Yorkville section of town, when Cagney was eight. Cagney graduated from Stuyvesant High School and got a job as a junior architect, one of the many employments he held during his youth. At age fourteen, he was a copy boy for the "New York Sun." At age sixteen, he worked at the New York Public Library as a book custodian for a salary of approximately 12½ cents an hour (about $17.50 per month). He also served as a bellhop at the Friar's Club, a ticket-taker on a Hudson River excursion boat, a draughtsman at a waterworks and a night doorman at the Lenox Hill Settlement House. He was constantly working and feeding his meagre earnings into a co-operative family fund.

"During one vacation, I wrapped bundles for Wanamaker's Department Store during the day," he later remembered. "At night I was a switchboard operator and an attendant at a pool hall. On Sunday, my day off, I sold tickets for the Hudson River Day Line. It was good for me. I feel sorry for the kid who has too cushy a time of it. Suddenly he has to come face-to-face with the realities of life without any papa or mama to do his thinking for him."

As a child he liked to draw, according to one magazine. He was called "Cellar-Door Cagney" by friends because of his ability to tap dance on slanting cellar doors, according to another. He belonged to a gang of neighbourhood kids and he was known as a good street fighter. In fact, he was an amateur boxer who was the runner-up for the New York State lightweight title. He played semi-professional baseball with the Original Nut Club of Yorkville (including exhibition games at prisons and reformatories). At an early age, a soil conservation lecture

influenced him to such a degree that it directed him towards
his impassioned interest in farming in later life. As a youth
(and as an adult), Cagney was an avid reader—one of his
youthful favourites was Romain Rolland's "Jean Christophe."
His first encounter with the movies was casual—a boyhood ad-
venture. He used to visit an aunt in Brooklyn whose house
was opposite the old Vitagraph Studios, which were making
John Bunny comedies at the time. Cagney would sneak over
the fence to watch the action. After high school, he enrolled
at Columbia University and joined the Students Army Training Corps (the precursor of the ROTC) to help pay expenses.
He took German from Professor Frank Mankiewicz, the father
of film director Joseph L. Mankiewicz. He intended to major
in Art.

But, in the fall of 1918, a Spanish influenza epidemic swept
the Eastern seaboard and Cagney's father, in his early forties,
died. The family tragedy forced Cagney to drop out of Columbia and return to odd-jobbing. Mother Carolyn Nelson Cagney,
the dominant force of Cagney's childhood, became the guiding
spirit of the Cagney family.

"And she was a mother twenty-four hours of the day," Cagney recalled. "That was her job, and she did it full time, over
time. She pitted herself firmly against the forces of our environment—the streets, the schools, the boys we met, the things
we were bound to hear, the influences we couldn't wholly escape. She talked with us, not at us. She told us that what you
give in this life you also get back in kind. She taught us that
what you do is done again, to you. She showed us clearly that
ugliness, crime and vulgarity pay their own dividends in ugliness, crime and vulgarity."

The Cagney family was close-knit, owing to mother Cagney,
and the closeness of the Cagneys remained strong throughout their lives. Brothers Harry and Ed eventually became doc-
tors, and Cagney too once aspired to the medical profession.
When brother James formed Cagney Productions later in the
Forties, Harry became the company physician. Ed temporarily
exchanged trades and signed on as business manager and, later,
story editor. Sister Jeanne, the youngest of the clan, became
an actress, initially against the wishes of her brothers. But
Jeanne, a graduate of Hunter College, made her own reputation in summer stock (in plays such as "Brother Rat") and radio plays (such as "Ceiling Zero"). She eventually appeared
in four films with brother Jimmy—*Yankee Doodle Dandy*
(1942), *The Time of Your Life* (1948), *A Lion Is in*

On the set of THE OKLAHOMA KID (1939) with William
Cagney, mother Mrs. Caroline Nelson Cagney and Jeanne Cagney

the Streets (1953) and *Man of a Thousand Faces* (1957).
Bill Cagney, Jimmy's virtual look-alike (though heavier), jour-
neyed to Hollywood also and, advised by brother Jimmy, he
embarked on a brief acting career in films of the early Thirties.
His few film appearances include *Palooka* (1934) for Reliance
Pictures and Paramount's *Stolen Harmony* (1935). However,
Bill decided that it was unfair for two Cagneys with similar
looks to be working Hollywood simultaneously, so he quit acting to become Cagney's most influential behind-the-scenes advisor. First an assistant producer at Warners (by the terms of
Cagney's contract), Bill later was the producer and president
of Cagney Productions, his brother's closest confidante and
counsel through the years.

"Our motto was united we stand, divided we fall," Cagney
once told a reporter. "I can't remember a time when, if any
one of us had three bucks, he didn't throw it immediately into
the kitty. We never thought of doing anything else. Boys who
worked for their own pocket merely were beyond our understanding. And doing things together, as Mother drummed into our heads, sharing everything, working for the common end,

instead of each going off in separate directions, gave us the feeling we were strong. The trouble with most poor families is that they don't have that community feeling and alone they're helpless in a tough world."

In his youth, Cagney mingled with the amateur theatre world. He did scenery for a Chinese pantomime at the London Hill Settlement House and he substituted one night for brother Harry, who had a role in the production. He later said, "I had leanings toward art and Mom thought that I could learn to paint by working on the scenery used by the theatrical group, while I earned bring-home pay by racking up pool balls and acting as doorman." He joined the Acting Society of the Settlement House and began picking up other parts. He played another Oriental in a Japanese musical comedy called "What, for Why?" He performed in an Italian harlequinade. He executed the first leading role in Lord Dunsany's one-act play, "The Lost Silk Hat." He essayed the part of Picard in "The Two Orphans," a period costume melodrama produced by the Dramatic Society of Hunter College, which borrowed Settlement House boys as actors for the male parts because Hunter was then an all-girl's school.

One of his most distinctive young roles was in a two-act play called "The Faun" produced by the Settlement House. "I was the faun," he told the "Saturday Evening Post" twenty-some years later. "I had my hair in ringlets and a goatskin around my middle, and I pranced around the stage speaking lines like this: 'Nay, sweet, give it to me,' and 'Spring is running through the fields chased by the wynd.' 'The wayward wynd ran its fingers through the pine tree's hair.'" He wrote elsewhere: "It was a touchy project in our East Side neighbourhood and I expected to be attacked on the way home and have my ears chewed by characters of my own age who were outraged by my own riot curls."

In the fall of 1919, after his father's death, Cagney worked at Wanamaker's Department Store. There he learned of a chorus role opening up in a revue at Keith's 86th Street Theater. The story was "Every Sailor," based on "Every Woman," a wartime entertainment featuring a chorus of service men dressed as women. "Every Woman" had played before President Woodrow Wilson in France during the Peace Conference talks and producer Phil Dunning had hired the troupe and converted it into a vaudeville act upon its return home. Cagney auditioned for a part as a "chorus girl." "There was nothing to the audition," he later said. "The stage manager showed me the steps and said 'Do this.' I watched his feet and, being a good mimic, I did what he did. But I quit that act after two months. The high heels I wore on stage gave me a quick jerky walk—a kind of occupational sea legs—and I got tired of my pals saying to me, 'Lengthen it out, Red,' to remind me how to walk properly." Thus, as has been related in countless magazine stories about Cagney, the "tough guy's" first legitimate stage role was as a female impersonator.

"It was a knockabout act, purely burlesque," Cagney later remembered. "We had a lot of fun and it never occurred to any of us to be ashamed of it. It might seem strange and unbelievable taking into account my habitual desire to go unnoticed. But again, this illustrates what I mean when I say that I am not shy or self-conscious when I am on the stage or screen. For there I am not myself. I am not that fellow, Jim Cagney, at all. I certainly lost all consciousness of him when I put on skirts, wig, paint, powder, feathers and spangles. Besides, that was the time, right after the war, when service acts were still fresh in mind, when female impersonators were the vogue."

After "Every Sailor," Cagney's mother, hesitant about show business, urged him to abandon his fledgling theatrical career. "To her, it was no way to use what education I had." But Cagney auditioned for the chorus of "Pitter Patter," a musical comedy adapted from the farce "Caught in the Rain" by William Collier and Grant Stuart, and he earned a role—beginning a decade-long association with vaudeville and Broadway. "Pitter Patter" opened at the Longacre Theater in New York on September 29, 1920. In the chorus was Allen Jenkins, later a longtime crony at Warner Brothers. For Cagney's role, which included the extra duties of laying out clothes for the leading man and keeping track of luggage during the road tour, he received over $50 weekly, a substantial raise from the $25 weekly he had earned in "Every Sailor." He also understudied the leading role.

"Pitter Patter" was not a phenomenal success but "Variety," which scoffed at the programme generally, praised the chorus for its enthusiasm and talent. And, among the chorus women, Cagney met his future and only wife, a small-town Iowan who had run away from home to break into show business in New York. Her name was Frances Willard Vernon (nicknamed "Billie") and she, like Cagney, was also a dancer, with "an instinctive gift of rhythm" in Cagney's words. They were married in 1921 and stayed happily married thereafter—with never so much

With Mrs. "Billie" Cagney while making RUN FOR COVER (1955)

as a hint of scandal or divorce (a rare circumstance among Hollywood couples). For a while in the Twenties, they teamed together in various vaudeville acts.

"Pitter Patter" closed in 1921 after thirty-two weeks and Cagney joined the vaudeville circuit, touring often through Eastern Pennsylvania, with a number of different acts. He worked in "Dot's My Boy," the story of a Jewish actor working on stage under an Irish name, written, directed, produced and originally acted by Hugh Herbert (later another member of the Warners troupe). Cagney toured for a while with the Jaffe troupe of players, headed by Ada Jaffe, mother of actor Sam Jaffe. Meanwhile, Billie Vernon joined a "sister" act—her sister was Wynne Gibson, later a Paramount actress. Billie and Cagney then worked together as "Vernon and Nye"; they did simple comedy routines and musical numbers. "My wife was much better known than I was; her name meant something, mine didn't," Cagney remembered. "The name of Nye was a rearrangement of the last syllable of my name." In 1922, they both worked in a Shubert revue of acts called "Lew Fields' Ritz Girls" which brought the Jaffe troupe and the "sister" act under the same bill.

When "Lew Fields' Ritz Girls" folded, Billie and Cagney set out for California to visit Frances's mother and to explore the opportunities of breaking into the movies. He tried opening a dance studio in California but few students applied. He and a partner, Harry Gribbon, introduced a vaudeville routine in San Pedro; the act flopped. Cagney made the rounds of Hollywood producers but found no takers. "For thirty-five dollars a month, we rented a tiny house in Los Angeles, and Billie cooked on a next-to-nothing budget," he remembered. "I don't know how she did it, but we gained weight. We hit all the movie studios but we found nothing. We couldn't even get past the front gate. Then we began to get hints from some of Billie's 'well wishers' that she'd made a mistake in marrying a hoofer who couldn't even earn a thin dime, and gradually I became aware of a question hanging above me in the air: 'Why don't you go back East where you came from? You're not doing yourself or anybody else any good here in California.'"

Cagney and Billie borrowed money and wended their way back to New York and the vaudeville circuit. For five years, between 1920 and 1925, Cagney worked primarily in vaudeville. Of one of the acts—Parker, Rand and Cagney—"Variety" wrote: "Two boys and a girl with a skit idea that gets nowhere. It is a turn without the semblance of a punch. There are no laughs and the songs mean little. One of the boys (Cagney) can dance. Small time is its only chance. Trio gets $275 tops." Another of the routines, called "Out-of-Town Papers," featured Billie as a small town girl and Cagney as a city slicker. Cagney sells newspapers on a make-believe street corner where he meets Billie. As the skit evolves, city sophisticate Cagney reveals that he too is actually from the same small town, a place called Kokomo, and Billie is joyous. The act ended with a song in duet, Billie singing "Home, Sweet Home" and Cagney belting out a New York tune: "Well, there's no doubt about it/I cannot live without it/I surely want to shout about it night and day/ There's just one place I want to be/And that's the place that's haunting me/And that's Broadway."

"We toured the South with this act and we laid a seven-tier cake," Cagney later wrote. "With my thick New York accent and my fast talk, nobody south of Washington, D. C., could understand what I said. Thank goodness they understood it when we danced."

In 1925, Cagney secured his first important part, as the roughneck in "Outside Looking In," a three-act play written by Maxwell Anderson based on Jim Tully's story of hobo life, "Beggars of Life." Charles Bickford was cast as Oklahoma Red and Cagney played Little Red—for a salary of $150 weekly

($200 weekly after the play opened). Significantly, in his first major theatrical role, he played a young tough, the first departure from his vaudeville hoofer background. "Outside Looking In" opened in September, 1925 at the Village Theater, an experimental house, and Cagney's performance was critically acclaimed.

Robert Benchley, then drama critic for "Life" magazine, wrote: "Wherever Mr. MacGowan [director] found two redheads like Charles Bickford and James Cagney, who were evidently born to play Oklahoma Red and Little Red, he was guided by the hand of the casting God. Mr. Bickford's characterisation is the first important one of the year and is likely to remain at the top for some time, while Mr. Cagney, in a less spectacular role, makes a few minutes silence during his mock-trial scene something that many a more established actor might watch with profit." Critic Percy Hammond agreed: "John Barrymore's Hamlet would be a mere feat of elocution compared to Cagney's characterisation." Burns Mantle wrote that the play contained "the most honest acting now to be seen in New York."

When "Outside Looking In" folded, Cagney was asked to join the London company of "Broadway," a popular gangster melodrama playing in New York at the time. Produced by Phil Dunning (also producer of "Every Sailor") and George Abbott, "Broadway" was the story of a dancer who gets involved with mobsters; Cagney was offered the lead part of Roy Lane. Billie was cast as a dancer. After four weeks of rehearsal, a farewell party was thrown by the New York cast for the London company. But, shortly before the cast was supposed to sail, Cagney was informed that he had been replaced by Lee Tracy, the actor who was playing Roy Lane in the New York company. Cagney was instead given the assignment of understudying the part of Roy Lane in New York; and eventually he replaced Roy R. Lloyd in another role in mid-1927. "We had Equity run-of-the-play contracts," Cagney later recalled, "so they had to keep paying us and they put us in as understudies in the New York company of 'Broadway,' but all the actors in town knew of my being fired and my confidence drained out of my toes."

But Cagney's fortunes took another rise when he landed a part in Daniel N. Rubin's "Women Go On Forever," a melodrama directed by John Cromwell (later the Hollywood director) which opened at the Forrest Theatre in New York on September 7, 1927, and ran for 117 performances. The show starred Mary Boland and received mixed reviews. Mary Boland "had

decided to abandon comic roles and return to serious dramas,"
Cagney later wrote. "On opening night, Mary's first word was
'hummph!' and the audience broke up. That was the end of
that play. We ran for eighteen weeks but it wasn't the play we
started with." To fill in the time, Cagney performed in stock,
in Cleveland and in Stockbridge, Mass. He also briefly opened
the Cagné School of the Dance in nearby Elizabeth, New Jersey. Meanwhile, Billie retired in the mid-Twenties and Cagney
continued his career solo.

Then followed two productions which, while only mild successes themselves, enhanced Cagney's growing Broadway reputation—the "Grand Street Follies of 1928" and the "Grand Street
Follies of 1929." The 1928 version was the greater triumph,
for Cagney staged many of the clever dance numbers (with
Michel Fokine) and he received widespread critical praise for
his own dancing, especially a tango tap finale. The second "Follies" followed one year after the first, also at the Booth Theatre, but to less enthusiastic applause. The freshness of the show
had diminished with the passage of time, and the format (the
original "Follies" was a "topical revue of the season") was ex-
panded to add several historical parodies which were disliked
by many reviewers. One critic wrote: "It has all the sophisti-
cation and verve of an 1884 almanac of a rainy afternoon in
the Louvre." Cagney performed in all eight skits; in one, "A.B.
C. of Traffic," he played a dancing cop.

His stage credits brought him to the attention of successful playwright George Kelly ("The Torchbearers," "The Show-
off"), who was casting his new play,"Maggie the Magnificent."
Cagney was cast as Elwood and, though the play only ran for
32 performances, receiving bad notices, it was, as Cagney himself later characterised the play, the "turning point" of his career. Since Kelly was one of the leading dramatists of the era,
critics carefully scrutinised the production—and, although they
disliked the play, they unanimously liked Cagney. Also in the
cast was a young vaudeville hoofer named Joan Blondell who,
like Cagney, was possessed of higher show business aspirations.
In a match that was to become classic, Blondell played a wise-
cracking floozie and Cagney was her boy-friend.

"She chews gum with menacing virtuosity, struts up and
down before the mirror and wriggles across to the drug store
for a 'pineapple temptation,'" wrote Brooks Atkinson in the
"Times" about Blondell's performance. "If she were given her
head, she might alter the design of the play completely . . ."
Robert Littell, critic for the "New York World," added: "Ex-

cept for the tantalisingly brief appearance of Joan Blondell, a sympathetic young lover by Frank Rowan, and the perfect gas-house lingo of James Cagney, the acting was, to say the least, hard and graceless."

Blondell and Cagney were re-united several months later, on the strength of their considerable performances in "Maggie the Magnificent," for "Penny Arcade" by Marie Baumer, a sombre tale about bootlegging and murder in a carnival setting. Cagney played Harry Delano, the bad-seed son of Ma Delano, who runs the Penny Arcade. Blondell played Myrtle, his gal; she is his paid alibi after Harry murders his bootleg boss in a fit of passion. Though "Penny Arcade," directed and co-produced by William Keighley (later Cagney's director for many Warners films), was dissected pretty harshly by most critics for its conventional melodramatics, Cagney and Blondell were painstakingly singled out for flattery. Wrote "Theatre" magazine: "Mr. Cagney is giving an excellent performance as the weak, amoral son and his confession of the crime to his mother stands out as the high point of the play." Brooks Atkinson concurred: "The play contains an excellent performance by James Cagney as the weakling." Blondell was adjudged "better than acceptable."

Singer Al Jolson, rightly suspecting a lucrative film property, bought the play for $20,000 and re-sold the film rights to Warner Brothers, stipulating as part of the deal that stars Cagney and Blondell go along with the sale. Warners was reluctant to guarantee their old roles to the two unknown players until after a screen test, but Cagney was assured of $400 weekly for three weeks (the time necessary to shoot the film) and train fare to California besides. Billie, mindful of the last California visit, stayed in New York until certain word of a long-term contract was received. Both Blondell and Cagney were tested for the lead roles in *Penny Arcade* but they performed best in the character roles they had created on Broadway.*

Retitled *Sinner's Holiday*, it opened in October, 1930. It was an auspicious if minor debut: even reviewers who damned the film were careful to cite Cagney. Mordaunt Hall of the "New York Times" wrote that "the most impressive acting is done by James Cagney in the role of Harry Delano. His fretful tenseness during the closing scenes is conveyed with sin-

---

* In his autobiography, "Take One: Mervyn LeRoy," Warners director Mervyn LeRoy claims to have directed Cagney in the 1929 First National production of *Hot Stuff* with Louise Fazenda. There is no evidence in the cast lists or anywhere else in Cagney's voluminous biographical material to indicate that the actor ever appeared in *Hot Stuff*.

cerity." The "Exhibitor's Herald-World" commented that "Cagney has by no means an easy role in his portrayal of a highly nervous youth who by nature cannot go straight. It is the type of part which can be spoiled by the slightest shade of overacting, but Cagney carries his characterisation in each sequence just far enough."

Seen today, *Sinner's Holiday* is an odd, revealing document, under sixty minutes long but tidily constructed. Cagney's first film role is that of a gangster, but he is not the professional sort. Instead, Harry Delano is a young punk, a happy-go-lucky bootlegger who can't see the evil of crime, who hasn't yet been through the school of hard knocks. He murders and is arrested and learns his lesson. But he deserves our compassion, according to the story, because his deceased father was an irresponsible alcoholic whose condition infected the no-good son. Thus sympathy—always a Cagneyesque condition—is introduced from the beginning of the actor's screen career. Myrtle (Joan Blondell) is Harry Delano's flawed trump card. Raucous, independent, she nearly trips him up by blackmailing her way to higher stakes but Delano is ultimately exposed by the confession of his eye-witness sister (one of the few violations of the family ethic in Cagney's films). Only Delano's mother (in the first of the Cagney-mother alliances) is unswervingly faithful; a sour, hard-bitten woman, she attempts unsuccessfully to pin the murder on her daughter's innocent ex-con *fiancé* (Grant Withers). "If you're in a jam, let me help you," she pleads. "Ain't I always been your pal?" Cagney asks rhetorically in reply, serious and bluffing. He coddles and fusses his mother and the bond between them is warm though she suspects that he is lying. When she finally fathoms his deed, he sobs in her lap, reduced to infantilism in a terrifyingly pathetic scene, and he is forgiven. Jaunty and brave at the end, he is arrested and led away handcuffed by a cop. He halts briefly to hug his mother. "Forget it, sweetheart," he says in his offhand manner. "Don't cry. You know I love you." Pure-faced, high-voiced, younger than he'd ever be again in films, Cagney delivered the immaculate vision of overgrown juvenile delinquency.

After *Sinner's Holiday*, Cagney promptly signed for *Doorway to Hell*, directed by Archie Mayo, a second gangster role without the manifest overtones of innocence. Cagney played the second lead, Mileaway, the friend of a big-shot hoodlum named Louis Ricarno (Lew Ayres) who is trying to quit the rackets. Mileaway (Cagney) succeeds Ricarno when the gangster departs for a southern vacation (based on Al Capone's

DOORWAY TO HELL

trips away from Chicago to his Florida retreat). *Doorway to Hell* is memorable particularly for a scene, virulent in its social criticism, in which Ricarno visits the slums of his birth before leaving New York, and points to the hovel where milk was sold. His brother and sister, he says bitterly, died of typhoid. As Ricarno, Lew Ayres is sombre. Cagney is a gay contrast—but their relationship is a one-way friendship. Mileaway's friendship with Ricarno is exposed as a sham when Mileaway cheats on the sly with Ricarno's girl. But Mileaway is jailed and Ricarno is murdered by rivals at the end, setting the stage for the melodramatic final legend: "The Doorway to Hell is a one-way door."

Though the film is completely forgotten today, *Doorway to Hell* was a financial hit which helped to solidify Cagney's standing at the box-office. And, because it was his second gangster role, it prepared the way for *The Public Enemy* and Cagney's subsequent fame as a gangster type. The most outstanding acting scene in the film is Cagney's and it occurs when Mileaway is given the third degree by the cops. Worried, in a near-sweaty panic, the young criminal confesses in an outburst of apprehension. Like the confession of *Sinner's Holiday,* the scene is keenly acted and intensely drawn—a highpoint of the film.

William Wellman's *Other Men's Women,* also in 1930, was less distinguished and Cagney's part was small. He played a sidekick-friend to fellow railroad worker Bill (Grant Withers—who also appeared in *Sinner's Holiday*) in a rather tepid story about a love triangle between friends. Most of the film is predictable; the excitement is saved for a momentary thrill at the climax when Jack (Regis Toomey), who is blinded, rides a railroad engine to his suicide over a faulty bridge into a river. Joan Blondell has an equally (equal to Cagney) small role as Marie, a waitress. Cagney is loud and noticeable in his short travels before the camera. During a dance hall scene, he whirls off a few flashy dance steps before the camera cuts away. His brief characterisation is vulgar, lower-class and devil-may-care.

For *The Millionaire* in 1931, it seemed as if Cagney had won another bit part of no consequence—he was present within the frame for less than five minutes—but his role was not without impact. George Arliss, who played the millionaire (one of the top Warners stars of the time, he had casting authority for his films), describes in his autobiography how Cagney impressed him at their first meeting. "Just now and then I can feel sure of my man by one brief interview, in the casting office," Arliss wrote. "There was a small but important part in *The Millionaire*—the part of an insurance agent. The scene was entirely with me, and [it] was the turning point in the story. I knew it depended largely on the actor of this small part whether my change of mental attitude would appear convincing. I saw several promising young men without being much impressed, one way or the other, but there was one more waiting to be seen; he was a lithe, smallish man. I knew at once he was right; as I talked to him, I was sure he could give me everything I wanted. He wasn't acting to me now; he wasn't trying to impress me; he was just being natural and, I thought, a trifle independent for a bit actor; there was a suggestion of 'Here I am; take me or leave me; and hurry up.' As I came to my decision, I remember saying 'Let him come just as he is—those clothes—and no make-up stuff. Just as he is.' The man was James Cagney. I was lucky!"

Despite the brevity of the role, *The Millionaire* is Cagney's first exceptional showcase. Arliss, wedded to the silent film, was slow, silky and gentlemanly as he went through the paces of his retired millionaire act. Arliss's style has its own charm but it is a style of calm and measurement. At the point in which Cagney enters the storyline, as an insurance salesman urging the millionaire to forego retirement and be active, the film leaps forward into an entirely new pacing. Cagney is like adrenalin injected into the deliberate movements of the Arliss vehicle. He is brusque and outgoing. He is noisy and speedy. Smoking a pipe, but moving it to whistle between his teeth, clinching his eyes sharply and disbelievingly, he urges the millionaire in a torrent of friendly advice to stop loafing. "If I was a man like

you, you know what I would do?" he tells Arliss in a mock con-
fidential tone. "Well, I wouldn't sit around and wait for an
undertaker." That said, and having shaken the film like a bolt
of lightning, Cagney exits. Arliss sits as though stunned. It is
the comparison of two styles of acting: the one, older, and more
dignified, representing a quieter age past; the other, vibrant
and hectic, representing the future. To put it simply: in a five
minute exchange, the Thirties supplant the Twenties.

Cagney was slowly acquiring a stable of fans, enthusiasts
and critics who appreciated his style—and producers began to
take notice of this actor who could even steal the show from
veteran George Arliss in such a brief sequence. Among Cagney's admirers were two Chicago writers named Kubec Glasmon and John Bright, and director William Wellman. They
were preparing a story for filming called *Beer and Blood* and
they wanted Cagney to play one of the major roles. The immortality of James Cagney was only a gat and a grapefruit away.

With writer Kubec Glasmon

2

'Just a Dancer
Gone Wrong'

Seminal Years: From *The Public Enemy* to *Yankee Doodle Dandy*

"With Babe Ruth, Jack Dempsey, F. Scott Fitzgerald, the early Stutz Bearcat car, the last of the beaded speakeasy hostesses, he was an image in the American scheme of things; of the Roaring Twenties and the Tepid Thirties, of the dust bowls and the bread lines and gang wars. He is the saga maker of the hard kid who couldn't be pushed too far. In real life, Jimmy is a gentle man, who draws and paints, reads, raises prize cattle, farms, is happily married, has much family. He still grins that crooked mick grin that made him famous. He'll even lift his fists at you for a mock blow, but he was never the Jimmy Cagney he imprinted on so much film stock—just a dancer gone wrong."

PAT O'BRIEN

April, 1930. Four months after the grand opening of *Little Caesar* to mobs and near-rioting at Warner's Strand Theatre, *The Public Enemy* arrived, without advance fanfare, in New York City. "Just another gangster film," wrote the reviewer for the "New York Times," "weaker than most in its story, stronger than most in its acting . . ."

Although it took critics years, and even decades, to fully appreciate the bizarre, disjointed structuring of William Wellman's storytelling, the star of *Public Enemy*, though equally strange and unorthodox, caught their eye immediately.

Edward G. Robinson had been simply brilliant as *Little Caesar*, alias Rico, alias Cesare Bandello, and had received unanimous accolades from the press. Now the same critics were quick to make comparisons and split compliments between Robinson's performance and that of the young, relatively unknown actor who played Tom Powers, the "Public Enemy," with such fiery deliverance: James Cagney.

His rise to fame was almost automatic and practically over-night, as Cagney somehow avoided the problem of identity which would plague Edward G. Robinson for the rest of his half-a-century career. Robinson was always remembered as "Lit-tle Caesar," even off the screen. The character dominated the man, the fiction absorbed the actor.

But *The Public Enemy* encouraged an opposite effect. Who can ever recall the name of "The Public Enemy"—Tom Pow-ers—that awfully plain, forgettable moniker? Who can remem-ber anything about the film without thinking of "James Cag-ney"? One year after *Public Enemy*, Cagney was a top box-office draw. Studio publicists began to crank out material on Hollywood's premier "tough guy." Fan magazines paid close, complimentary attention.

Ironically, the part of Tom Powers had almost eluded him. Screenwriters Kubec Glasmon and John Bright, who based the *Public Enemy* script on their own unpublished novel, "Beer and Blood," demanded Cagney for the lead role, on the basis of his gangster performance in *Doorway to Hell*, according to legend. Only after early shooting did director Wellman agree with his writers. Cagney switched parts with intended-lead Ed-die Woods. "We gambled that Cagney, who was sort of a bo-nus rookie, could deliver when the pressure was on," Jack Warner later recalled.

(Cagney himself remembered later that it was Wellman who thought the casting was "ass backwards" and suggested the switch, contributing one of many versions to the host of con-flicting recollections that have failed to satisfactorily explain the mysterious, therefore mythic, origins of Cagney's most con-sequential part.)

Unlike *Little Caesar* or the later *Scarface*, which concern in their respective stories the sagas of particular, peculiar out-laws, *The Public Enemy* is, in a sense, the story of an every-man. Even the ordinary name "Tom Powers" implies that much. This is the film's greatest strength—the feeling that the hero of *The Public Enemy* is, by extension, the average, urban Amer-ican male who, somehow squeezed by an unscrupulous metro-politan jungle environment, must compete wantonly for a de-cent existence. Lest the implication be misinterpreted, a post-script narration to the film explicitly warns audiences that Cag-ney's Tom Powers is an average person, and further that crime is not the recommended escape from a dull average existence (a sop to the Hays Office).

Tom Powers is a nervy slum kid who graduates from juvenile delinquency to gangland rum-running, partnered with easy-going pal Matt Doyle (Edward Woods). Tom's mother (Beryl Mercer) implores him to give up his life of crime, brother Mike (Donald Cook) openly breaks with him but Tom is obstinate: the rewards are greater than life within the law. Only suckers live legally, Tom sneers at his brother. When rival gangsters murder Matt, a burning, vengeful Tom invades the headquarters of the warring mob, and is himself wounded badly in a wild shoot-out.

Hospitalised, near death, Tom is reconciled with his family. Soon, Ma Powers is humming cheerfully as she tidies up Tom's bedroom, gaily awaiting his return home. Mike, however, is waiting anxiously for Tom's arrival, unnerved by the news that a faction of gangsters are out to "get" Tom in retaliation. A knock on the door signals the dramatic *dénouement*. Dead, the bandaged figure of Tom falls face forward into the camera.

Even today, *The Public Enemy* is an outstanding film, a grim and insightful parable of life under the thumb of big city corruption. Director William Wellman fashioned the production with a promise for genius that he never quite fulfilled later in his erratic career. He constructed the era patiently, almost painstakingly slow, with meticulous attention to the principal characters of the story—the spectacular rain dance of wounded Tom Powers, as he trips and stumbles in the gutter after the ill-fated shootout during a pouring curtain of rain, is a

With Donald Cook, Beryl Mercer and Rita Flynn in THE PUBLIC ENEMY

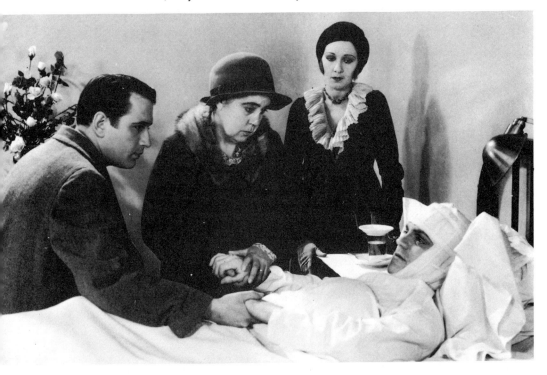

highlight, as spine-tingling a moment as has ever been recorded in the American cinema. The cast is uniformly bittersweet
—including mild Eddie Woods, the saccharine Beryl Mercer,
and Jean Harlow in a small, early role who, though she was
lambasted by contemporary critics, gives a performance as moll
Gwen Allen that is soft and earnest, providing a welcome res-
pite from Cagney's lightning energy.

Above all its many virtues, *The Public Enemy* gave birth
to Cagney, the "tough guy," whose portrayal of Tom Powers
was described by Richard Watts Jr. of the "New York Herald
Tribune" as "the most ruthless, unsentimental appraisal of the
meanness of a petty killer that the cinema has yet devised."

Ruthless, unsentimental—all true. But also strangely appealing. Given the chance to explode his talents, Cagney scored.
After Broadway and vaudeville and obscure parts in obscure
movies, the *cliché* mingled with truth: a star was born. Cagney brought a kind of raw stamina to his portrayal of Tom Powers that gave his smiles the same sort of electric charm as his
snarls.

As critic Kenneth Tynan later explained, with considerable
perception, "In *Public Enemy*, he [Cagney] presented for the
first time, a hero who was callous and evil, while being
simultaneously equipped with charm, courage and a sense of
fun . . . the result was that in one stroke Cagney abolished
both the convention of the pure hero and that of approximate
equipoise between vice and virtue." Thus Cagney, according to
Tynan, "invented a new screen character," one which "morally
and psychologically" would dominate the whole era. The "Cagney code and manners" were fitted ideally for the Thirties, that
most desperate age of Hoovervilles and bread lines. Through
all the horrors, Cagney was resilient. He fought back. He would
screw up his face and smile. Always smile.

All film gangster figures are mysteriously engaging, as Robert Warshow has amply demonstrated in his famous essay,
"The Gangster as Tragic Hero." And were it not for the historical conditions created by the Depression, the rampant national mood of cynicism and despair, *The Public Enemy* would
surely have been less popular than it was, as many critics (most
notably the writers of "The Velvet Light Trap" film quarterly)
have argued persuasively. But neither outlook is able to explain
completely the film's phenomenal popularity and, looking back,
its longevity. The secret ingredient, of course, is Cagney, who
captured the imagination of America in *The Public Enemy* as
few actors ever have before or since, commandeering still

With Mae Clarke in THE PUBLIC ENEMY

inexplicable qualities of attraction that all but mystified the hearts of millions. Cagney, that is, with a little help from half a grapefruit.

The most famous scene of the film—in fact, one of the most famous scenes of all film history—the scene which, more than any other, came to comprise the Cagney stereotype—occurs when Cagney pushes the handy citrus into the face of Kitty (Mae Clarke). Though the equally famous still shot of the crash, grapefruit to cheek, really does not occur in the film, since the encounter is shot from a dispassionate angle, the image of that scene is a permanent monument to the Cagney persona. From all accounts, that scene, so critical to Cagney's later career, was added almost as an afterthought. As with the discovery of Cagney himself, each of the major artisans of *The Public Enemy* have their own version of the inception of the sequence.

"It was my idea, the grapefruit," claimed producer Darryl Zanuck years later. "I think I thought of it in a script conference. When I made *Public Enemy*, I was way ahead in thinking. No love story but loaded with sex and violence." The writers, Glasmon and Bright, insisted that the grapefruit scene was based on an actual episode in the life of a petty gangster named Hymie Weiss who (and Cagney himself later quoted this version) pasted his moll in the face with an omelette.

However, despite the loud claims of producer and scenarists, it seems most likely that director Wellman invented the grapefruit business, probably spontaneously. "We needed something big right there in the picture," Wellman explained in a contemporary interview. "Well, that grapefruit on the table looked inviting—and I didn't like the dame much anyhow. So I told Jimmy to try socking her with it—but hard. He did." Wellman conceded in a later interview that the idea sprang from a deep-seated urge on his part to smash his own wife in the face during breakfast, just for a joke.

(Mae Clarke, later television's Marge Brown of "General Hospital," confirmed Wellman's recollections in an interview published three decades after the film's release. Complaining about her personal type-casting problems stemming from the incident, she told a reporter, "I'm sorry I ever agreed to do the grapefruit bit. I never dreamed it would be shown in the movie. Director Bill Wellman thought of the idea suddenly. It wasn't even written into the script." As for Cagney, he "is an old pro." She added, "He knows how to pull his punches. The grapefruit just glanced off my face. We needed just one take for the scene.")

Wellman's frank confession—"and I didn't like the dame much anyhow"—seems the key to the scene, indeed the very core of Cagney's character in *The Public Enemy* (that cool suspicion towards all humanity) because the sequence is openly anti-woman (anti-women) in conception, tone and effect. The moment is just an instant, so quickly accomplished that a casual turn of the eyes might miss it. Yet, it was one of the most important and influential moments of the cinema's short lifetime, because it defined Cagney to himself and generations of moviegoers, and because his treatment of Clarke swelled a tradition of male-dominated filmdom that still thrives. Wrote Bosley Crowther: "This was and remains one of the cruellest, most startling acts ever committed on film—not because it is especially painful (except to the woman's smidge of pride), but because it shows such a hideous debasement of regard for another human being."

In marked contrast to hostile reactions such as Crowther's are the observations of studio head Jack Warner who, in his autobiography, predictably viewed the grim implications of the scene lightly, like many of the principals involved in the project. "This brutal bit of business," he wrote, "achieved a kind of grisly immortality, aroused endless resentment among militant feminists and made 'Czar' Will Hays stew in the office where he was being paid a huge salary to protect the movies from that sort of attack. I have no doubt that innumerable young lovers, discovering that their sweeties got a masochistic delight watching this rough stuff, adopted the grapefruit technique to get what they wanted. It may have been hard on Hollywood in particular and stubborn girls in general, but it sure was great for the grapefruit business."

Also, Warner might have continued, great for the movie business, because the grapefruit incident exerted a distant but perceptible impact, reverberating far ahead into the future of the American "hard-boiled" cinema. When Lee Marvin tosses scalding hot coffee into the face of Gloria Grahame twenty years later in Fritz Lang's *The Big Heat*, his impulse is inherited from Tom Powers in *The Public Enemy*. When Richard Widmark shoves an old lady down the stairs in Henry Hathaway's *Kiss of Death* in 1947, his cruelty can be traced to the subversive influence of Tom Powers. The brief, harsh deed, which only highlighted the less striking anti-woman currents of the tale (including, for example, the mysterious resentment nursed by young Tom Powers for Molly Doyle in the opening childhood scenes), corrupted the filmic relationship of men to women in the American cinema for years of future movie production, its influence still continuing.

The sequence is so insidious (if entertaining) from the implicit suggestion, mostly obtained from Cagney's fresh demeanour, that the action is somehow moral and that, for whatever reasons, Kitty truly deserves the crude treatment she receives.

Cagney later recalled: "The thing that the public remembers about *The Public Enemy* is the scene in which I shoved half a grapefruit into Mae's face. That half grapefruit was to become a piece of Americana. It was just about the first time, if not the very first, that a woman had been treated like a broad on the screen, instead of like a delicate flower . . . That bit of business became so identified with me that years afterward when I'd go into a restaurant, people would send me half grapefruits with their compliments and I got so tired of that deal I began to duck eating in public. It was hard for me to get used to the idea that, in *Public Enemy*, I had hit the jackpot overnight."

(Elsewhere, in the Fifties, Cagney discouraged his reputation as the ground-breaker for a tradition of callous movie men. "No, I refuse to accept responsibility," Cagney told the "Boston Globe" in 1955. "Six months earlier, Clark Gable slapped

Barbara Stanwyck in the face and after that the public
couldn't get enough of hard-boiled heroes. Before that, heroes
were sweet and tender to their heroines.")

The "jackpot overnight," in Cagney's words, was quickly
grasped by Warner executives who realised the actor's potential at the box-office. Cagney was promptly teamed with Edward G. Robinson, the studio's other top gangster star, for *Smart
Money* (1930), a film which allied Warners' two fastest rising stars in their only joint appearance ever, indeed a fore-
gone conclusion for smart money. However, Cagney's prestige
on the Warners lot did not yet rival Robinson's, as evidenced
by the relative importance of their roles. Though the film may
have been shot concurrently with *The Public Enemy*, as was
often the case in the hectic world of Warners during the Thirties, Cagney is nevertheless second-billed, henchman to "Little
Caesar." While Robinson stars, and dominates the film, Cagney joins the movie, except for a bit at the beginning, in the
middle—and departs as a dead body before the end.

The story was commonplace: Nick Venizelos (Robinson),
a friendly, countrified barber with an appetite, luck and pen-
chant for gambling, sojourns to the metropolis with visions of
gambling his way to grandiose fortunes. By a shrewd combination of stealth and talent, Venizelos succeeds, becoming a
famous and wealthy games-player under the apprehensive eye
of the police. Jack (Cagney), Nick's assistant barber and old
friend from back home, joins Venizelos in the big city as his
confidante and aide. Things go smoothly until Nick rescues a
young woman named Irene (Evalyn Knapp) from the act of
suicide and the ever-suspicious Jack begins to wonder if the
melancholy dame isn't a stool pigeon in the pay of local police.
And he is right: the district attorney has promised not to pros-
ecute the woman on a murder rap if she can pin Nick on false
gambling charges. Nick is framed, betrayed, and Jack exposes
the befriended one as the Judas. "You dirty little stool pigeon,"
Jack screams, slapping her in a brief but savage instant of violence. Unable to believe Irene's treachery, Nick strikes back,
slugging Jack to the floor in her defence, and accidentally
killing his buddy. The police arrive, Nick learns the truth and,
in due time, he is dispatched to prison—but not before he wa-
gers "two to one" with his customary good humour that he will
be freed in five years instead of ten.

Smart Money is a plodding, rather ordinary film, uninspired
by Alfred E. Green's direction, and distinguished only by frequent flashes of brilliant acting from the two principals, Rob-

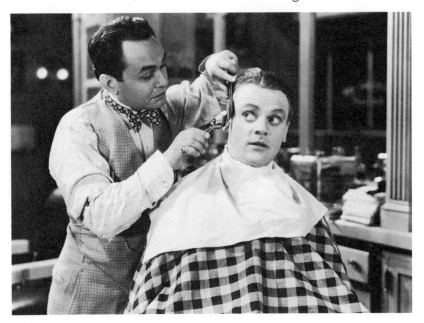

With Edward G. Robinson in SMART MONEY

inson and Cagney. Robinson is a calm, smooth actor who lends an almost aristocratic quality to his role, sweeping the narrative gently along in his bronze style, ignoring if not belittling the otherwise turtle-slow pace of the movie. Cagney is his opposite: brisk, solid, demanding, and he lurks in the shadows with his minor role like a tomcat ready to pounce. But for all its drawbacks, *Smart Money* is an important, transitional film in Cagney's career. By co-starring the young performer with Robinson so soon after the respective successes of *Little Caesar* and *Public Enemy*, Warner Brothers reinforced Cagney's growing public reputation as a "tough guy," firmed his box-office stature via the coupling, and cemented his image in the mind's eye of fans as a uniquely criminal sort by a short, seemingly insignificant moment in the final minutes of the film. When Cagney smacks Evalyn Knapp, only the second time in movies that he had physically assaulted a woman, it was a plain signal from Warner Brothers that, after the relative ambiguity of his first films, the gangsterly road to meteoric stardom had been plotted for the actor.

The four films which immediately followed *Smart Money*—*Blonde Crazy* in 1931, and *Taxi!*, *The Crowd Roars* and *Winner Take All* in 1932—mark the upsurge, the tidal wave of Cagney's career. Cast in the mould of "The Public Enemy," though softened and glamourised, his fame as a law-defying ball of fire spread and grew, greatly assisted by the promotion department of Warners which vigorously marketed the "tough guy" theme. Advertisements for *Taxi!* (1932), for example, billed Cagney as "the fighting-est, loving-est redhead that ever skipped a stop light." Publicity for *Mayor of Hell* (1933) claimed "with Jimmy setting new standards of male behaviour, no maiden's jaw is safe. When he notices them, their hearts beat pitter-patter and their teeth rattle." It was a pattern that was to continue throughout Cagney's career. Even his independent features were to succumb; the build-up eventually reached surreal proportions with *Blood on the Sun* in 1943, a Cagney production which capitalised on Second World War anti-Japanese sentiment *vis à vis* the actor's standing. Patriotic advertisements for the film announced hysterically that "now you can see battling Jimmy in the mightiest feat of his career—beating the Japs at their own ju-jitsu game." From his quintessential films of the Thirties to exaggeration in later years was but a small leap once the mould was set, by promotion and by the films themselves.

In film after film in the Thirties, Cagney was cast as the rogue, the genial villain, a con man with considerably more good within than bad. Yet the violence of the Cagney persona, sometimes inexplicable because it often functioned as a contrivance of plot, worried many film critics—as, indeed, it eventually came to bother the actor himself. Because most of the film critics of the time were male, predictably they delighted in at least one aspect of his image—woman-tamer. "When this department arrived," reported B. R. Criskler of the "New York Times" from a 1936 press reception hosted by Grand National Pictures, "it found the guest of honour—who is said to have been Warners' greatest drawing card in the smaller, tougher theatres of the land—tamely backed into a corner, and completely hemmed in by a throng of admiring women"—and here one can almost taste the envy— "all apparently just dying to have grapefruits thrust into their pretty faces."

Another male critic wrote that "in a world given to suggestions of chivalry, he has made the punch to a woman's jaw one of the bright features of the cinema's social activities." In a slightly more intellectual, if still implicitly male viewpoint, well-known critic Lincoln Kirstein observed that "no one expresses more clearly in terms of pictorial action, the delights of violence, the overtones of a semi-conscious sadism, the tendency toward destruction, toward anarchy, which is the base of American sex appeal."

There were sour notes, too, but of course the detractors (again, predominantly male) criticised Cagney less for his treatment of women than for his general, anti-social demeanour. One magazine scolded Cagney's *Jimmy the Gent* (1934): "The influence of James Cagney on the great American Cinema may possibly be open to considerable debate . . . Mr. Cagney has made a specialty of subversive parts, which he plays with so striking a combination of rowdiness and charm that he has become something of a crusader on behalf of the less gentle aspects of life." The conservative "Photoplay," intended as a family magazine by editor James R. Quirk, kept its pages clean of Cagney and other Warners "toughs."

The springboard for such bitter reaction was initially *The Public Enemy* and later the many variations of Cagney themes throughout the Thirties, such as *Smart Money* and *Blonde Crazy*, a film that one periodical complained, "makes thievery rather dangerously attractive." *Blonde Crazy* (1931) was a tight, breezy little comedy about two con artists (Cagney and Joan Blondell) on a cross country spree. Today, this gutsy film is being gratefully rediscovered by feminists who are attracted by the equilibrium established between the two stars —Blondell at her stubborn finest, and Cagney stepping the keen line which divides laughter and serious purpose. Perhaps director Roy Del Ruth's most enduring work, *Blonde Crazy* boasts a richly funny script by the scenarists of *Public Enemy,* including an hilarious "fleece" scene with Warners regular Guy Kibbee. Important because it was Cagney's first real pairing with Blondell, *Blonde Crazy* also marks his first venture into movie comedy. He proves a sly clown, playing for laughs with the same indefinite quality that he applied to melodrama, extracting double meaning from the most meaningless of lines.

Very popular in the theatres, *Blonde Crazy* sparked the actor's first rebellion against Warners' management, the opening volley in a personal war which continued throughout his association with the studio. Unhappy with his "criminal" type-casting, angered at petty requirements of the standard Warners contract (such as personal appearances, sometimes for other performers' films) and emboldened by the success of his latest movie, Cagney balked publicly, demanding a higher salary. Like other top Warners stars were eventually to do—among them, Pat O'Brien, Bette Davis, George Raft and Humphrey Bogart —Cagney stalked off the Warners lot and returned to his native New York. Still a relatively unestablished star, Cagney's move astonished Warners executives. The actor was receiving only $450 weekly and he insisted on a raise. After three months of tense negotiations, during which it was rumoured in Hollywood that Cagney would never return to the screen, the actor signed an improved contract, offering $1000 weekly and the guarantee of periodic re-appraisal.

By any measure, Warners negotiated a good deal, because Cagney was to become their greatest asset in the Thirties, even as he continually increased his own salary to be widely reported as "one of the nation's highest paid persons" by the time he quit the studio in 1942. After 1934, none of his Warners releases grossed less than $1,000,000. (Certainly a major factor of the Cagney prosperity was Warners' own part monopoly of the market. Before federal anti-trust action forced dissolution in the early Fifties, Warners could count on half of its gross consolidated income and approximately half of the company's annual profits to come from the nearly 500 company-owned movie theatres, many of them located in large, metropolitan areas.) The phrase "Cagney vehicle" crept into the knowing critic's vocabulary, meaning a low-budget Cagney/Warners film designed for comfortable studio profit margins. "Tough guy" meant "business"—for the brothers Warner, that is.

Cagney returned to work in *Taxi!* (1932), directed by Roy Del Ruth, a "Cagney vehicle" in the best sense of the description, the story of a small band of taxi drivers, led by Matt Nolan (Cagney), who resist the hoodlum tactics of a massive taxi trust. Again scripted by the *Public Enemy* team, Kubec Glasmon and John Bright, *Taxi!* contains ringing, expressive dialogue and matching performances by a whole reliable ensemble of Warners regulars, including George E. Stone, Guy Kibbee, Matt McHugh, Polly Walters—and George Raft in an early screen appearance as a dancer in a public contest (who wins, incidentally, over Cagney and partner Loretta Young). The heart of the story, however, is the simmering romance between Cagney and his young, coolheaded co-star, Loretta Young—a romance which is nearly crumpled when Nolan becomes uncontrollably vengeful after a drunken racketeer murders his younger brother. She is nevertheless so determined to make a gentleman of the hothead, that she good-naturedly corrects his shortcomings in an elevator all the way en route to and even while standing in line at a marriage licence bureau.

Taxi! was followed by *The Crowd Roars*, also in 1932, probably director Howard Hawks's most obscure work, but undeservedly so. Based on an original story by Hawks (and Seton I. Miller), although the script was once again written by the *Public Enemy* dependables, Glasmon and Bright (plus Niven

With Eric Linden and Frank McHugh in THE CROWD ROARS

Busch), the film is an acute, sombre study of one top racing driver's compulsion to win. Joe Greer (Cagney) is the speedway hero: dapper and bold, he refuses to surrender his independence to romance with a loyal, devoted woman friend (Ann Dvorak in an elegant, moving role) and quarrels rabidly with his kid brother, an aspiring driver (Eric Linden), when the youngster himself falls in love. Angrily competitive during a crucial race, he causes the fireball death of a long-time buddy (Frank McHugh) and is so haunted with remorse that he becomes a haggard drifter until he is rescued from self-pity at the end by the forgiving ex-sweetheart. Overly long, paced rather conscientiously slow, *The Crowd Roars* was evidently a labour of love for ex-racing driver Hawks, who meticulously crafted the racing footage (including actual contests at Indianapolis, Ventura and Ascot, plus the participation of famous drivers such as Thirties Indianapolis 500 winner Billy Arnold) and documented the ugly emotions of the grandstand crowds. His affection for the subject matter was complemented by sensitive, unpretentious portrayals by the players: Ann Dvorak, Eric Linden, Guy Kibbee, Frank McHugh and Joan Blondell. Cagney handled his most melodramatic role since *Public Enemy* with considerable tact, even finesse. Sympathetic but never maudlin, his manner hinted at a certain plebeian nobility, a coarseness of character though hardly common.

Next in 1932 came another comedy, *Winner Take All*, directed by Roy Del Ruth, which begins on a bizarre note. Jimmy Kane (Cagney), a prize-fighter who is racked by physical exhaustion (alcohol? a terrific beating?) is introduced to a crowd at ringside. Kane is temporarily retiring to a rest home, the announcer reveals, and the scrappy pugilist needs some financial aid. "He always gave us more than our money's worth and we owe it to him," the announcer pleads. From the anonymous rows and rows of bleacher seats rains a blizzard of coins, tossed like unwanted refuse at Kane's nervous feet. Gaunt, pale and sickly, looking strangely forlorn, dodging the hail of money, Cagney stutters a halting appreciation but, unnerved, he cannot finish the words. "Folks," the loudspeaker voice interrupts, "What he is trying to say is, he thanks you."

From this unusual beginning develops an unfulfilled, awkward movie which shuttles back and forth in locale between Dr. W. Betts Rosario Ranch and Hot Springs in peaceful Arizona and the various, hectic habitués of the urban boxing world. As Kane, the poorly-educated battler who must choose his future and beloved from the two regions, Cagney offers his densest East Coast interpretation. His accent is thick, almost loutish, and his lines are salted with earthy jargon. "Spill it," he encourages Peggy (Marian Nixon) when she is sobbing inexplicably over cash problems. Then, when he secretly pays her bills, and she confronts him with happy, tear-filled eyes, he tells her, "Don't get sloppy." One scene in particular, in which he figures a plan to fight a "winner take all" match, all the while discussing something else, is particularly overwhelming. Cagney plays the entire exchange with his eyes abnormally widened, wildly scheming, his hands thrust deeply into his pockets, glancing absently away, talking in short, feverish spurts, chewing gum mechanically for the duration.

When *Winner Take All* switches to the bout scenes* and trades the severity of the Southwest for crude and familiar laughs at Kane's dullard efforts to climb the social ladder, the movie falters. Neither the wholesome female lead (Marian Nixon) nor the coy, showy society dame (Virginia Bruce) are talented enough to make the difference, and they are de-

---

* Cagney's sparring looks honest and impressive—he trained with ex-welterweight champion Harvey Perry, who also appears in the film; the actor did all of his own boxing, as he was to do later also for *The Irish In Us* and *City for Conquest*.

Above, publicity shot circa 1932. Below in training
with Harvey Perry, ex-welter weight champion

serted by the ordinary Wilson Mizner-Robert Lord scenario. The unevenness of the film is never admitted by Cagney, however, for he hurtles through the story like a juggernaut possessed, ending literally with a kick when he plants his toe in the rear of Joan Gibson (Virginia Bruce) after discovering that she played false with him; she was cheerily planning to escape on an ocean liner with another hapless lover. Reunited with his true-love Peggy, he cautions her in petulant tones to beware of his bandaged nose, gained in the boxing ring, while kissing: "It's full of firecrackers." One curious footnote: the citizen Kane of *Winner Take All* has a black assistant trainer named Rosebud (Clarence Muse).

By the close of 1932, Cagney was again uneasy with the terms of his contract, a significant point to record because, throughout his entire career, the actor's relationship with Warners greatly affected his yield, both in terms of project choices and how the actor would approach the individual works. It is clear that he was frequently an unwilling accessory to Warners' programmers. Even after his 1931 settlement, for example, he was dissatisfied with *Taxi!*, a feeling which sprang, some writers have suggested, from profound disagreements with the political resolution of the narrative. In his autobiography, "My First Hundred Years in Hollywood," producer Jack Warner describes a confrontation that occurred on the set of *Taxi!* when a frustrated Cagney refused in protest to shut a door properly during one phase of shooting. Perhaps the actor was again incensed by the minor clauses of the standard Warners contract which typically required stars to travel in grandiose publicity caravans to promote Warners films. In her autobiography, "The Lonely Life," actress Bette Davis describes one such galling experience, the Roosevelt Victory Caravan in 1932, sent cross country by the management to honour F.D.R. at his presidential inauguration. The "special gold-leafed Pullman train" stopped in major U.S. cities in transit, to promote Warners' films. Cagney was along for the ride. "The whole affair was fabulous," wrote Davis with manifest resentment, "Travelling in such luxury during a depression. We were afraid we might incite a revolution; but unlike the eighteenth century Frenchmen, Americans love their royalty and we were welcomed everywhere with open arms, although a few did stick their tongues out at us."

Shortly after finishing the popular *Winner Take All*, Cagney began work on a film entitled *Blessed Event*, but he never concluded the project. Still discontented with his salary, and still upset over his continuing "tough guy" roles, he quit the movie, and was replaced by actor Lee Tracy, ironically the same person who had substituted for him under reverse circumstances in 1926. This time, Cagney asked for a pay raise from $1600 weekly to $4000 weekly. Peak Warners paychecks at the time went to Ruth Chatterton and Dick Powell at $6,000 weekly. Edward G. Robinson, Douglas Fairbanks Jr. and Kay Francis received $4,000 weekly. Cagney told the press that he would "work in three more pictures without a cent of salary if, in return, the company would cancel the remainder of my five year contract." He also threatened to leave Hollywood forever and re-enter Columbia University to study medicine. Warners executives were dumbfounded by the obstinate actor who so fearlessly flouted the provisions of his contract, and they refused to budge from their bargaining position. The public began to choose sides in the feud. "We liked his swagger and his cocksureness," lamented one fan magazine in a premature obituary for the star, "and (especially in these depressed times) his willingness to scrap with the least possible encouragement. To see him no more. . . . would be a loss."

For six months, interrupting the bright ascendancy of his fledgling cinematic career, Cagney sat doggedly idle. Then, in September of 1932, arbitrator Frank Capra secured a revised contract of $1,750 weekly, a sum far removed from the original request, but also buttered with the promise of periodic readjustment. Cagney returned to Hollywood and Warners for a film with the ironic initial title of *Bad Boy*, later changed, still ironically, to *Hard to Handle* (1933). In Jack Warner's pithy words, the title "was appropriate for both the writer [erratic scenarist Wilson Mizner, who died during the shooting] and the actor." The studio obviously had a sense of humour about the situation—as well it could afford. Advertisements for the comeback movie declared "the Movies' Prodigal Son-of-a-Gun Returns" and " . . . All Is Forgiven!" "We sure have missed you," one display promotion read, "you rascal, you! We needed someone to put those hard-to-handle dames in their place . . ."

Though hardly a radical departure from past Cagney vehicles, *Hard to Handle*, directed by studio favourite Mervyn LeRoy (who was married to Harry Warner's daughter), was a slight, winsome story, funny and also sober. The film opens with a striking scene, rare for its subject matter in the cinema of the time, that cynically evokes the era of despondency: a dance marathon contest. Allen Jenkins is the histrionic master of ceremonies and a young, ever-slender Sterling Holloway is

With Ruth Donnelly in HARD TO HANDLE

a determined contestant. Cagney plays Lefty Merrill, an irrepressible swindler who plays on the widespread despair of people by organising the marathon event, and later by advertising a sham fortune supposedly hidden on the fairgrounds of a cheap carny. But Merrill is himself bamboozled when his partner in fraud sneaks off with the dance contest purse money, leaving the rather more honest cad to contend with the lynch emotions of the crowd. Worse, Lefty must explain the unwanted development to the exhausted contest winner, a young girl (Mary Brian) with whom he has incidentally fallen in love, despite the zealous objections of her mother (Ruth Donnelly). After following the girl from the West Coast to the East Coast and persuading her easily of his genuine love, Lefty masterminds a national craze for grapefruit—the link to *The Public Enemy* was simultaneously amusing and publicity-rich. The original script ending to the tale, which appears to have been exceptional, was highlighted by the accidental death of Lefty's child, caused somehow by the swindle, and a fierce tirade by the wiser Lefty against rapacious businessmen. Instead, the conclusion was focused less singularly on the gentler, comic side of Lefty's courtship. A monstrous hit, proving that Cagney's long absence had not adversely affected his formidable drawing power, *Hard to Handle* featured a peppery performance by underrated comedienne Ruth Donnelly; Cagney's own immensely energetic, affectionate characterisation; and smooth, unobtrusive direction by LeRoy. *Hard to Handle* is paid homage, nearly forty years later, when Mervyn LeRoy is introduced from the bleachers crowd at the marathon dance contest in *They Shoot Horses, Don't They?*

Cagney's next film, the imbalanced comedy-drama *Picture Snatcher* (1933), directed by Lloyd Bacon, was based on an actual incident in which a New York "Daily News" reporter photographed an execution. Cagney played reformed felon Danny Kean, an ingratiating, conniving mug who retires from the rackets in order to work for the "Graphic News," a sleazy tabloid. The movie photographer manages some startling scoops: first, he obtains an exclusive photo of a half-crazed fireman standing armed guard over the smouldering ruins of his own house (inside, the fireman's adored wife and her secret lover are discovered dead together in each other's arms); then, he straps a tiny camera to his leg in order to capture the death greeting of a female murderer condemned in the electric chair; finally, he talks his way into the hideout of ex-crime buddy turned cop killer, Jerry (Ralf Harolde), just in time to grab shots of the thug's bloody showdown with police. A rather unconventional photo-journalist, Kean accomplishes all of his daring assignments by semi-lawful stealth: lying, cheating and stealing in order to snatch his pictures, a form of behaviour that causes endless hostilities with his righteous girlfriend (Alice White) and her Irish cop dad (Robert Emmett O'Connor).

Like many gat and gag epics of the period, *Picture Snatcher* safely sidesteps the dilemma of how to mellow the plot for Hays Office approval by framing the story in the guise of a newspaper saga, thereby allowing all the standard guts and gore of pre-censorship days to be experienced by a criminal-like "legit" reporter. This was a common ploy after the first, great gangster cycle of the early Thirties, when outright lawlessness gave grudging way to gaudy newspaper yarns such as *Five Star Final* or *The Front Page*. But despite the changing times, and Cagney's own antipathy towards further "tough guy" roles (which must have subtracted from the brutishness of such films), *Picture Snatcher* remained only pseudo-reformist because Danny Kean was ultimately more gangster than not. "You're the lowest thing on the newspaper, a picture snatcher," his girl-friend tells him. "Stealing pictures from folks who are so down in the mouth they can't fight back—just a thug, doing the same thing you always did." Nevertheless, granting its *cliché* roots, the film is well-made: Bacon, with the aid of dialogue director William Keighley, speeds the narrative along; there are moments of authentic suspense, also authentic hu-

mour; Cagney is fleet and brazen if somewhat familiar here; and
Ralph Bellamy adds an amusing touch as Kean's boozing editor. This forgotten film is best remembered, perhaps, for its famous last words, the unofficial credo of journalism, uttered in
an ecstasy by Cagney: "Was you there, Charley?"

Next came another pseudo-reformist vehicle with considerably more punch, and some solid merit as well: *The Mayor*
of Hell (1933), cannily directed by Archie Mayo, owes much
to its intriguing script by Edward Chodorov, based on a story
by Islin Auster, based further on *Road to Life,* a 1931 Russian
film. Cagney, his usual snappy self, is virtually overshadowed
by the intricacies of the drama. The tale concerns Patsy Gargan (Cagney), a piddling hoodlum turned ward-heeler who accepts the supervision of a boys reformatory as patronage from
crooked politicos. When he arrives at the juvenile prison, he
is attracted by the institution's nurse (Madge Evans) and also by her visionary scheme to allow the young delinquents to
govern their own prison. Embracing the idea, Patsy fires the
cruel superintendent of the school, Mr. Thompson (played with
superbly mean, bureaucratic mediocrity by Dudley Digges), and
turns the reformatory over to the boys. All works out fine—
even the orneriest kid (young Frankie Darro in a sensational,
show-stealing role) is persuaded after he is elected reformatory
mayor—until Gargan reverts to his former identity, shoots a
rival gangster and crosses state lines to avoid arrest. Then, Mr.
Thompson returns in a fit of sadistic glory, re-instating the old,
harsh methods of administering the prison. He punishes a well-
liked youth by locking him in a small, freezing hut and the

Left, with Ralph Bellamy in PICTURE SNATCHER
Right, with Frankie Darro and Madge Evans in MAYOR OF HELL

lad, already subject to fearful spasms of coughing, dies. Aroused, the boys go on a rampage. They seize Mr. Thompson and put him on mock trial. When the terrified superintendent seeks to escape, he falls to his death from the roof of a burning barn, cheered on by the mob of juveniles. Patsy arrives too late to stop the killing but, in a shouting, stirring speech, he convinces the youths to halt the carnage before more harm to the ruling order is done.

Even today, certain of the sequences of *The Mayor of Hell* are incredibly exciting. The electrifying climax—in which the surly Mr. Thompson topples to his death with grisly bluntness onto the barbed-wire fence of a pigsty—is one of the most breathtaking scenes ever filmed at Warners. Like *Picture Snatcher*, however, *The Mayor of Hell* merely pretends reform. Despite a modest conclusion which pledged a return by the boys to legal means, the film was in spirit brutal, savage and anti-social, especially in the final mob scene. Still a gangster at core, if vacillating somewhat according to the indecisive whims of the script, Cagney contributed another stalwart performance, though he was dominated by a scenario which called for him to be absent at the critical stages of the story, in the mood-setting beginning and at the feverish end. Ever-enjoyable sidekick Allen Jenkins lent a helping hand that was offset almost entirely by the absence of lustre in leading lady Madge Evans as the nurse—but the real stars, the real heroes, were the alienated, embittered youth of *Mayor of Hell*, excellent actors all. Cagney's street manner essentiality to the film was illustrated negatively five years later, when dour, introspective Humphrey Bogart starred in the re-make, entitled *Crime School* (1938). Though the second version preserved in exact wording much of the original *Mayor of Hell* script, Bogart essayed a routine and dull characterisation, thus robbing the property of its inherent vitality that, without the backbone of an invigorating leading man such as Cagney, it had difficulty trying to maintain.

Footlight Parade (1933) followed—one of Cagney's finest early films. Excepting a few, quick dance steps in *Other Men's Women* and *Taxi!*, *Footlight Parade* was the ex-hoofer's auspicious movie debut as a singer-dancer—and he scored a resounding success. "One of the surprises is Jimmy Cagney," wrote a contemporary reviewer in "Film Pictorial." "Although he used to be in musicals in his stage days, he sings and dances here in a manner that makes one wonder why his talent in this direction has not been used before." As Chester Kent, the ingen-

With Frank McHugh in FOOTLIGHT PARADE

uous, hard-working producer who stages lavish theatrical prologues for movie theatres, the actor had his first major, law-
abiding, non-gangsterish role in the cinema. Faced with an in-
competent staff of assistants, threatened by looming, nigh-im-
possible deadlines for three new theatrical shows, and forced
to choose between two women (Joan Blondell and Claire Dodd)
dead set on marriage, Kent is saddled aboard a veritable mer-
ry-go-round of predicaments. In addition, the show biz tyro is
being cheated out of his rightful share of profits by wily co-
partners Gould (Guy Kibbee) and Frazer (Arthur Hohl), betrayed from within by a performer in the pay of a competitor,
and hustled by his ex-wife (Renee Whitney) for a jump in al-
imony.

Skilfully directed by Lloyd Bacon, who flashed that occasional expertise for which he could be relied upon, and Busby
Berkeley, the undisputed master of musical spectacle, the film
is a torrential flood of minor crises that barely keeps tempo
with the adrenalinised Cagney, who sputters orders, steps in
cadence and even trades punches in two-four time. Frank Mc-
Hugh as Francis, the whining choreographer who must mimic

a cat (he detests cats) for a new feline dance routine, is in his happy stride—he is a delightful bonus attraction of *Footlight Parade*. Joan Blondell as secretary Nan Prescott is crisp, fetching and thoroughly businesslike throughout. And the rest of the cast is almost without exception intoxicated with the tinsel atmosphere, including the effervescent Hugh Herbert as the "angel's" hired relative, Ruth Donnelly as mother protector of the male ingenue, and those croon-swoon, shuffle-off-to-Buffalo twins, Dick Powell and Ruby Keeler.

Cagney is simply prime. He surmounts all the contrived obstacles of plot almost without exertion, even as he simultaneously composes newfangled dance routines, offers pointers of technique while dashing from rehearsal hall to rehearsal hall, checks business details, keeps pulse with his various romances and dances a tantalising little, tugging the rest of the sometimes reluctant-seeming film along. He saves the eye-opener for the "Shanghai Lil" finale—just one of the three full production numbers at the end, staged by Busby Berkeley, which have rarely been matched for their pure, gaudy splendour—when, substituting at the last instant for the drunken lead dancer, he sweeps the entire programme into a grand conclusion with a glittering, controlled demonstration of song and dance. "He could learn whatever you gave him very quickly," Berkeley once said in admiring tribute. "You could count on him to be prepared. And expert mimic that he was, he could pick up on the most subtle inflections of movement. It made his work very exciting."

It has been argued, by some film critics, that Cagney in *Footlight Parade* represents then-President Franklin Delano Roosevelt—a cinema symbol to the nation of commanding leadership against crushing odds. Chester Kent, like F.D.R. who was faced with the massive Depression, has to confront spreading internal difficulties with qualities of positive, singlehanded guidance that might be appropriate for a national leader in difficult times. Since Warners had a well-known affinity for F.D.R.'s policies, the interpretation should not be casually dismissed—especially when *Footlight Parade* was such a divergence from normal Cagney fare. The change of pace was probably due as much to Cagney's own inclination, if not outright pressure, however, as to any particular national trend or studio bias, because the actor's increasing displeasure with "tough guy" roles was common knowledge, and after each of his protests or walkouts, the tone of his films changed, sometimes scarcely, sometimes drastically. This is the his-

toric lesson of Cagney's troubles with Warners: throughout
the Thirties—after the 1931 walkout, after the 1932 walkout, after the 1936 walkout and finally after the 1942 severance—Cagney's actions against Warners caused a noticeable, qualitative alteration in the kinds of films he was giv-
en to act in, a sure lessening after each walkout of what
might be called the "tough guy" factor, as Cagney fought
arduously to control the direction of his career. *Footlight Parade* is one example of the trend, but Warner Brothers, unea-
ger to forever bottle Cagney's box-office gold mine of gangster-
ishness, frequently followed the concession films with movies
that seemed a throwback in content and style. The struggling
actor never did obtain any measure of story control—only, much
later, perhaps when the desire had already died, story approval.

After *Footlight Parade*, for example: in 1933, a proposal by
writer Rosalind Keating Schaefer for a film called *Fingerman*
suggested a story about "a fellow, grown up in the slums of
New York (who) gets to running with a bad gang. He isn't
bad, just burning with resentment against the rotten breaks
life has handed him and his family." Early story treatments by
Warners studio writers Ben Markson and Lillie Hayward pic-
tured the "fellow" as an accomplished tap dancer, struggling
for breaks in the New York entertainment world, who accidentally gets mixed up with a gang of criminals. By late March,
1933, though, at least two months after the original story suggestion by Schaefer, Cagney had definitely been chosen by
Warners to play the lead role and the plotline of the drama
began to shift noticeably. A revised treatment by Markson and
Hayward, dated March 31, 1933, recommended re-shooting an
actual scene from *The Public Enemy*—the scene in which the
body of Tom Powers lunges into the camera—in *Fingerman*
to exploit Cagney's climbing popularity. "The use of an actually reproduced scene from *The Public Enemy*," they argued
in a private memo to Warners executives, "that is still in the
memory of everybody, might be a very novel and interesting
way of finishing the picture." The two scenarists asked for a
reaction to the proposal from producer Darryl Zanuck and, in
a pencil-scribbled reply (seen by this writer), Zanuck, or in-
coming producer Hal Wallis, disregarded the *Public Enemy* idea
and instead ordered the entire *Fingerman* script rewritten to
fit Cagney's studio-tailored image. "Develop tough, hard-boiled,
cocksure Cagney—knows it all," went the decree, "Gets start
in gangster craze—women like because of roughness—treats

everybody as a moll—he must start tough and rough."

By the time *Fingerman* came before the cameras as *Lady Killer* in late 1933, with director Roy Del Ruth at the helm, the changes, specifically to enhance Cagney's "tough guy" image, were severe. In the revised version, main character Dan Quigley (Cagney) is no longer a tap dancer; as the film begins, he is a theatre usher—in fact, Cagney doesn't dance a step in the entire movie. As the story evolves, the brash young usher becomes involved with a ruthless gang of con artists when he discovers their flourishing racket and muscles in. When one of the "pigeons" accidentally dies, Quigley escapes to Hollywood where he changes his name and becomes the newest he-man sensation in filmdom (partly on the strength of fan letters he ghosts himself)—an inside joke to members of the film colony because former criminals supposedly really did work in Hollywood at the time. And, significantly—considering the studio's edict that "women like because of roughness"—Quigley is transformed into a ruffianish "lady killer" in the final screen rendition of *Fingerman*, motivated by the prefabricated script to extraordinary violence towards gang moll Myra (poor Mae Clarke —the same victim of *The Public Enemy*'s excesses). A scene in which Cagney drags the actress by her hair the entire length of a room, then bodily tosses her out of his apartment suite, the whole sequence played unabashedly for laughs, is without exception the most violent scene in terms of treatment of women that Cagney has ever performed. An unsettling film with some inspired moments—the tongue-in-cheek satire of Hollywood movie-making, for example—*Lady Killer* ultimately fails through its episodic script and by the colourless support from Margaret Lindsay, as star Lois Underwood, and her underworld counterpart, the slightly-more-appealing Mae Clarke. Only Cagney rises above the material, almost salvaging the entirety, performing Hollywood cameos as an Indian and 18th century romeo, and thrashing his way courageously, unseriously, through the whole affair.

After *Lady Killer*, Cagney starred in *Jimmy the Gent* (1934), a frivolous, free-wheeling comedy. Though director Michael Curtiz, the hugely talented Hungarian-born film-maker, was rightly recognised by Warner Brothers as a major craftsman, he was handed this rather ordinary programmer to direct. In the early Thirties, no Warners director was given special consideration for projects by studio executives, except in-law Mervyn LeRoy—thus *Jimmy the Gent* is consciously more artistic, gratefully more stylish, than the average Warn-

With Allen Jenkins in JIMMY THE GENT

ers fare, thanks to Curtiz. Cagney plays Jimmy Corrigan, "Personal Contacts," a frenzied, impulsive business agent who happens to be in the racket of hunting up missing heirs to enormous fortunes—sometimes the lost relatives are "found" even when they are long dead. His closest rival in the dubious occupation is the gentlemanly Wallingham (Alan Dinehart) who is just as big a crook though he serves tea to his clients. A young, blonde-haired Bette Davis is Joan, once Corrigan's secretary, who now works for Wallingham, naively convinced of his honesty and chivalry. In this early role, she is too vigorously abrasive to be very likeable, and Cagney, who punches Allen Jenkins about in a poor imitation of slapstick, is likewise so forcibly brittle that he nearly whips the bantam storyline into brutal submission. Looking eerie with close-cropped hair and dark-shadowed eyes, Cagney offers a tense, jittery, racy performance. But *Jimmy the Gent* has some lighter features, namely Corrigan's never-ending, manic search for the proper social graces with which to impress his clients and Joan. "Ethics! Ethics! Who's got ethics?! Am I a gentleman or ain't I?" he screeches to helpmate Louie (Allen Jenkins) after being insulted by Joan, slapping his sorry friend around, and tossing a rock through his own front door window. "Sure, boss," the harassed Louie answers, "you been a sucker for ethics all your life." Though Jimmy is unwilling to halt certain of his less honourable, money-making practices, such as paying informers in Wallingham's employ, he does insist that all of his secretaries drink tea. In the blissful ending to this Bertram Milhauser-scripted tale, Jimmy unmasks Wallingham's skullduggery, is reconciled with Joan—and the destined lovers are married. "Ethics!" he laughs, hugging her as the screen fades, "I'm just crawling with ethics!"

Three other Cagney films were released in 1934: Lloyd Bacon's *He Was Her Man* with Joan Blondell; *Here Comes the Navy*, also directed by Bacon, with Pat O'Brien; and Ray Enright's *The St. Louis Kid*.

A grim, tender, unrequited love story which ends with Cagney's death by hired assassins, *He Was Her Man* is an obscure, unremembered film highlighted by the meticulous and exquisite romance between Rose Lawrence (Blondell) and Flicker Hayes (Cagney), she an ex-prostitute en route to a mail order marriage, and he a gangster on the lam from vengeful rivals. Their last film together is also, with *Blonde Crazy*, their best film together.

Here Comes the Navy, on the other hand, is a surprisingly sportive romp, a sea excursion with sailor Cagney replete with froggy pal Frank McHugh, hard-headed senior officer Pat O'Brien (in the pattern-setting first of their eight "you-hit-me, I'll-hit-you" films together), the inevitable rivalry over a woman (Gloria Stuart), and some ridiculous heroics besides. The actor's first film after the Legion of Decency code became official, *Here Comes the Navy* is a mild, entertaining slugfest, Cagney as rebellious as ever, so popular with audiences that it established the absolute model for two subsequent Cagney-O'Brien military films, *Devil Dogs of the Air* (1935) and *The Fighting 69th* (1940).

Less successful, and also less diverting, was *The St. Louis Kid*, also released in 1934, a weak comedy that became a weak drama midway through the story. Cagney played a combative, happy-go-lucky truck driver on the St. Louis to Chicago milk run; when downtrodden dairymen in the district call a milk strike and set up picket lines, driver Eddie Kennedy (Cagney) roars on by, a grinning, unconscionable scab. He swaps insults with his leading lady (pallid Patricia Ellis) before making her intimate acquaintance, then is lumbered with a murder accusation when a company goon kills a striking dairyman— at which point the story shifts clumsily from a promising investigation of strike politics to a standard fantasy about the criminal underworld. Ineptly fashioned by director Enright, and claiming only lovely sap Allen Jenkins as comic relief, *The St. Louis Kid* is surely one of Cagney's least notable pictures, distinguished only, in the words of "Time" magazine, because "it shows James Cagney receiving a cuff on the jaw from his leading lady instead of giving her one . . ."

Vying with *The St. Louis Kid* as a disappointment is *Devil Dogs of the Air* (1935), sparsely directed by Lloyd Bacon, the flying rendition of *Here Comes the Navy*, coproduced by Cosmopolitan Productions, the William Randolph Hearst Company that affiliated with Warners in the Thirties. A thinly-veiled military preparedness tract—the film came into its own with a Second World War (1941) re-release—*Devil Dogs of the Air* presents a flimsy re-write of the earlier Cagney-Pat O'Brien success: the story revolves around arrogant stunt flyer Tommy O'Toole's (Cagney) flirtations with a local waitress (Margaret Lindsay), who just happens to be the object of stone-faced affection from Lieutenant William Brannigan (O'Brien) of the Marine Flying Corps as well. But for some neat aerial photography, *Devil Dogs of the Air* is a near disaster, buoyed if not rescued by the chemistry of its stars—save Margaret Lindsay, who is insufferably cloying. As is customary, O'Brien is granite and Cagney is the chiseller. Best of all, Frank McHugh is skulking about with a wry smirk on his face. Like Allen Jenkins, McHugh has that essential idiot quality—a perverse, infectious irreverence for everything, even so exalted a project as *Devil Dogs of the Air*.

Cagney then starred in *G-Men* (1935), directed by gifted William Keighley, adapted by scenarist Seton I. Miller from contemporary headlines and the book "Public Enemy No. 1" by Gregory Rogers, a first-rate action film based loosely on the adventures of Chicago FBI agent Melvin Purvis, including a stormy scene modelled after the infamous John Dillinger shootout in rural Wisconsin. In a stunning conversion, "tough guy" Cagney played Brick Davis, an honest, responsible lawyer who joins the ranks of the special agents after an old college friend turned G-man is gunned down by merciless mobsters. Cagney is, of course, still "tough" in the film (he is a driving, bursting, impenetrable cop) but he is also awarded his most lawful role to date. "Hollywood's Most Famous Bad Man Joins the 'G-Men' and Halts the March of Crime," blared the studio advertisements. Many *cinéastes* have marked *G-Men* as a turning-point of Cagney's career, and also as a pivotal film in the history of the gangster movie—Cagney the ferocious mobster metamorphosed easily into a gang-busting lawman. True, but it is

With Robert Armstrong in G-MEN

important to recall that with *Footlight Parade*, a full two years earlier, the Cagney persona had already began to shed some vestiges of its criminality, just as much a result of Cagney's own judgment as either pressures from censors or business-motivated decisions by Warners officials.

G-Men was and still is a nimble, explosive movie. Keighley is an alert, purposeful director; his technique shines especially during the action sequences, such as the violent blood-letting at McKay's (William Harrigan) Wisconsin motel hideaway—so resourcefully staged and executed. Ann Dvorak is poignant as Brick Davis's old friend Jean Morgan, a "nice" girl trapped by her marriage to the Public Enemy, Brad Collins (Barton MacLane in his blankfaced, most sullen mood) Even some real members of the then recently-formed Federal Bureau of Investigation get into the act—credibly. The story is almost scuttled, sadly, by the presences of Margaret Lindsay, as the frigid, haughty romantic ideal, and Robert Armstrong, unusually and unnecessarily stodgy as Davis's FBI superior who almost rides an artificial current of enmity with Cagney into the ground. G-Men was enthusiastically received by fans and critics alike, despite its overtones of super-patriotism. Wrote one reviewer: "G-Men is James Cagney's best picture since *The Public Enemy*." One of his most durable if lesser movies, the film was re-released fifteen years later, on the FBI's twenty-fifth anniversary, with a special prologue enacted by actual federal agents to heighten interest in the story.

Only *The Irish in Us*, also released in 1935, shrewdly directed by Lloyd Bacon, could have followed such an earnest, solemn tale—the film is a lark, a meaningless, delightful, slap-happy comedy. Remembered Allen Jenkins: "The script was a weak sister and the director said, 'Boys, anything you can think up, put in.' It was an 18-day picture, a B picture frankly, and it made $2 million." The premise was humble: a close-knit Irish family composed of one pampering mother (Mary Gordon, of whom "Time" magazine wrote, her "brogue is so strong that, to the possible improvement of the picture, half her lines are virtually unintelligible") and three quarrelsome "boys" (Pat O'Brien as policeman Pat O'Hara; Frank McHugh as fireman Mike O'Hara; and Cagney as the ne'er do well Danny O'Hara who occasionally manages prize fighters) is disunited by a pretty girl (Olivia de Havilland, who decides torturously slow that she prefers Cagney to O'Brien) and an ever-glum, torpid boxer named Car-Barn McCarthy (Allen Jenkins) who comes up swinging every time he hears a bell, be it telephone or ringside. What happens? Danny O'Hara is naturally forced to substitute for Car-Barn during the "big match" at the end—he wins the fight, gets the girl and all finishes happily. The whole implausible saga is rendered so absent-mindedly, crammed with

With Frank McHugh, Mary Gordon, Olivia de Havilland and Pat O'Brien in
THE IRISH IN US

cheap Irish music and sentiment, that it succeeds in being gay, unelaborate, uninventive fun.

After *The Irish in Us*, Cagney was enlisted for one of the most lavish Warners productions of the Thirties, *A Midsummer Night's Dream* (1935), the long-awaited studio transfer to the screen of William Shakespeare's classic, directed jointly by European theatrical genius Max Reinhardt and Warners emigrant studio director, William Dieterle, who could translate for Reinhardt. The project boasted a truly all-star cast including Cagney, Joe E. Brown, Hugh Herbert, Frank McHugh, Mickey Rooney, Victor Jory, Olivia de Havilland, Dick Powell, Anita Louise and Arthur Treacher. Cagney played the rapscallion Bottom—his only role ever for Warners in which he did not officially portray an American (and one of the few in his entire career). It was also the closest to a highbrow subject that the actor who aspired beyond gangster films was ever to act in. Like the film itself (which received Academy Award nominations for Best Cinematography, Best Editing and Best Picture, but garnered scant critical praise), Cagney's performance earned few champions and instead widespread disapproval. Andre Sennwald of "The New York Times," for example, wrote "as Bottom, the lack-wit weaver who Puck maliciously endows with an ass's head, James Cagney is too dynamic an actor to play the torpid and obstinate dullard. While he is excellent in the scenes in the wood, in the 'Pyramus and Thisbe' masque he belabours the slapstick of his part beyond endurance."

Ever since its release, film critics have debated the merits of this strange attempt by Warners at "high culture," the only time the studio ever attempted an adaptation of Shakespeare. If *A Midsummer Night's Dream* is a failure, as many have contended, then it is at the very least a grand and ambitious failure—and Cagney is just superb, despite those who argue otherwise. The key to appreciating his bombastic performance is that he invented an unashamedly, wholehearted, Americanised Bottom; rather like colloquialising the Bard, Cagney tinted his portrayal with the slang characteristics, the vulgar tones, of a native son. When, for example, Bottom spits resolutely on his hands before reciting in the play-within-a-play, the gesture owes more to the habits of the twentieth century than the Shakespearean era. Cagney makes an exuberantly believable Bottom. And the rest of the cast is equally zany—especially wonderfully simple Joe E. Brown as Flute, goofy Hugh Herbert as Snout and young, taunting Mickey Rooney as the magical Puck. It is the technical side of the production which is so jarring.

With Joe E. Brown in A MIDSUMMER NIGHT'S DREAM

Though as individual aspects, the musical arrangements of Men-
delssohn's music by Erich Wolfgang Korngold, the art direction by Anton Grot, the costumes and make-up, and the dance
ensembles by Bronislava Nijinska and Nini Theilade were dazzling, they clashed injuriously with the contemporary-American
style of acting. The sombre, heavy-handed directorial manoeuvres of Reinhardt with his traditional, European interpretation
of Shakespeare, complete with mammoth, intricate settings and
production numbers, contradicted the natural neo-vaudevillian
technique of the players. Critics who wholly disregarded A Midsummer Night's Dream didn't realise that what might be extremely disrespectful Shakespeare was, in this case, mighty rev-
erent Warners.

In his autobiography, "Laughter is a Wonderful Thing," actor Joe E. Brown explains how the ranking members of the Warners stock company planned with clever malice aforethought to mould the Shakespearean characters along modern-day lines. "Some of us were certainly not Shakespearean actors," he wrote. "Besides myself from the circus and burlesque, there were Jimmy Cagney from the chorus and Hugh Herbert from burlesque. At the beginning we went into a huddle and decided to follow the classic traditions in which Herbert and I were brought up. I really believe Shakespeare would have liked the way we handled his low comedy and I'm sure the Minsky Brothers did. The Bard's words have been spoken better but never bigger or louder."

"Only one thing could have made me happier than actually playing in *A Midsummer Night's Dream*," Cagney told reporters, "And that is the knowledge that Shakespeare might have been aware of how carefully Reinhardt adhered to the spirit of his imagery. I honestly believe that the great playwright would have gotten an enormous kick out of seeing the *Dream* reborn in a new medium." Would Shakespeare have really approved? Would he have admired Cagney as much as his own master comedian, Will Kemp? The answers, of course, defy the imagination.

Frisco Kid, also released in 1935, returned Cagney to old form as Bat Morgan, a "dog eat dog," maverick Barbary Coast sailor who powerhouses his way to rule and riches among the less civilised denizens of San Francisco in the Gay Nineties. The aggressive seaman earns his initial reputation by killing the notorious, hook-armed Shanghai Duck (Fred Kohler) in a bar room brawl; then he joins forces with crooked political czar Big Jim Daley (Joseph King). In the end, their gambling, boozing mini-kingdom of vice is toppled by a gun-toting vigilante mob of enraged, upright citizens—but not before Morgan himself is swayed to more virtuous ends (and is trampled by a swarm of his own cronies for the bother) by local newspaper Managing Editor Jean Barrat (played by unwaveringly dull Margaret Lindsay). Dressed in a fancy wing collar, sparkling vest and brocaded waistcoat, his hair curled effeminately, Cagney submits a careful characterisation that balances between roughneck and gallant, taking neither extreme too sincerely. The film flags despite him: *Frisco Kid* seems a meandering stream of muddled thoughts, particularly when compared to Howard Hawks's *Barbary Coast*, released earlier the same year, a superior movie about the same era in San Francisco. Lloyd Bacon's account begins dynamically enough, with misty, atmospheric opening shots of the wharves and a murky, gloomy aura inspired by Morgan's near-shanghai, but it quickly dissipates into average romantic fiction. Forsaken by the script (written by Warren Duff and Seton I. Miller—becoming Cagney's most prolific scenarists), the movie banks on its several sure periodic highpoints instead—the scowling performance of villain Barton MacLane; the anguished scene in which Solly (George E. Stone), Morgan's dedicated friend, dies in Cagney's arms from a murderer's bullet; and the extravagant, unruly, burning, shooting, killing riot sequence at the finale.

The year tumbled to a finish with Howard Hawks's fine and underrated *Ceiling Zero*, a Cosmopolitan Production in association with Warners that involved the proficient ensemble of Cagney, Pat O'Brien, June Travis, Stuart Erwin, Isabel Jewell and Barton MacLane. Written by former naval aviator Frank Wead, based on his own popular Broadway play, *Ceiling Zero* was tragedy "packed with thrills," in the words of the London "Times," concerned with the courageous pilots who flew air mail missions during "ceiling zero" weather, when the fog curtain was so thick that it hung to the ground. A terse, gusty movie—with Cagney just splendid as the flamboyant flyer Dizzy Davis whose flirtations cause the air-crash death of a close comrade, and eventually his own death as well—*Ceiling Zero* was applauded by fans and critics alike. But Cagney himself was accepting few congratulations. Ever since his 1932

With Pat O'Brien in CEILING ZERO

walkout, the increasingly entrenched star had been searching for loopholes in his contract, still discouraged by his "tough guy" stereotype and still galled by a salary and work demands that he considered inappropriate to his talents. The release of *Ceiling Zero* constituted a technical violation of his contract which called for only four films per year. And, as Jack Warner later recalled, Cagney "was a tough opponent in the legal ring, and he was murder on technicalities."

In an unprecedented, daring move for the Hollywood domain, Cagney sued for breach of contract and once again departed from the Warners lot. He signed with Grand National Pictures—a "B" company which claimed Cagney as its only star—for a down payment of $100,000 cash and the essential stipulation that he could reject any story "that doesn't suit him." Besides citing the surplus of his films, the actor pointed to a California theatre which had listed Pat O'Brien's name above Cagney's on the marquee for *Ceiling Zero,* a billing order that also technically violated Cagney's contract. To the press, Cagney blasted Warners' producers for forcing him into films like *Devil Dogs of the Air* "which had no reason to be filmed under any circumstances." The star vowed never to return to the Warner studio. "I was sick of carrying a gun and said so," he later remembered.

Intentionally, riskily casting himself adrift from the Hollywood mainstream, Cagney stayed idle for a year while Grand National negotiated with the actor and sought the right property. Producers Samuel Goldwyn and David O. Selznick, among others, were interested in signing Cagney for their own projects but they were afraid of litigation by Warners and also of aiding an insubordinate performer. Instead, the Hollywood community of producers (including Goldwyn and Selznick) banded together to blackball the "tough guy." "Though rated among the top box-office draws of the time," the "New York Times" reported, "Cagney remained inactive for a year and it was generally believed in Hollywood that other studios were reluctant to hire him lest they be placed in the position of encouraging a 'rebellious actor.'" It was common knowledge in Hollywood, according to "The Times," that "other players, notably Bette Davis [who later sued Warners herself] are eyeing the company with interest and should the Cagney situation work out, it is possible that there will be considerable contract jumping."

Jack Warner was a determined taskmaster. An admiring portrait of the producer in the December, 1937, edition of "For-

tune" magazine included comment on the pending Cagney lawsuit and merrily blamed Cagney, the unwilling worker, as being the heretic of the situation. "In Dick Powell, O'Brien,
Blondell, Glenda Farrell, George Brent, Kay Francis and others," the "Fortune" writer opined, "Jack has assembled a sort
of permanent stock company who fall efficiently [note the business terminology] into each new role with an easy feeling that
they have seen it before and will get home for dinner.
But when he gets hold of a star with the authentic afflatus,
Jack is likely to have more than his share of trouble. He had
most with Cagney, who got sick of being typed as a girl-hitting
mick and of making five pictures a year instead of four. He expressed his dissatisfaction in such ways as growing a moustache, talking to Jack in obscene Yiddish and finally suing his
way out of his contract on a technical breach of the billing clause. Jack is still after him in the courts."

Hollywood exhausted all possible avenues to retrieve the in-
surgent actor. In his autobiographical "The Wind at My Back,"
actor-pal Pat O'Brien describes an occasion when Jack Warner tried to persuade him to personally convince Cagney to return. O'Brien, of course, refused—the loyal co-star of *Ceiling
Zero* had been himself suspended by Warners in the past for
refusing to play parts Cagney had rejected. In a snide remark,
typical of the reaction of the more conservative fan magazines
of the day, "Screenland" accused actress Ann Dvorak of "Doing a Cagney?" when she, too, left Warner Brothers over salary disagreements. The magazine gloated: "James Cagney, the
rebel who won screen fame so swiftly, is still, at this writing,
'resting.'" In her memoirs, Bette Davis described the widespread feelings of unrest in Hollywood in the mid-Thirties—
feelings inflamed by Cagney's third, decisive walkout—and she
attributed her own personal urge to desert Warners to Cagney's
influential action. "I was beginning to understand," she wrote,
"why Jimmy Cagney was on suspension for refusing to play
a certain part. Our contracts were outrageous and the security
I dreamed of on Broadway had become the safety of a prison.
I was being handed crumbs by the studio, financially as well
as artistically."

When Grand National finally scraped together enough funds
for full production and then selected, with Cagney, the actor's
debut independent features, the choices were significant. *Great
Guy*, Cagney's first independent for the new company, released
at the end of 1936, placed him squarely on the side of the law,
as zealous, good-natured meat inspector Johnny Cave. The ti-

With Mae Clarke and James Burke in GREAT GUY

tle of the film, especially significant considering Cagney's "tough
guy" reputation at Warners, perhaps derived, meaningfully, from
the last line of *G-Men* in which Jeff McCord (Robert Armstrong) grudgingly admits to his sister (Margaret Lindsay):
"Take care of him, sis, he's a great guy." Thus, in his newborn
autonomy, did Cagney associate himself with a film like *G-Men*
rather than the gangster-groundbreaking *The Public Enemy*. His
second (and final) Grand National film, released in 1937, was
a musical comedy, *Something to Sing About*, the story of bandleader Terry Rooney (Cagney), a quiet unassuming fellow who
travels to Hollywood and is "glamourised" for the movies
against his will. Though neither *Great Guy* nor *Something to
Sing About* were Cagney's maiden "great guy" or musical comedy roles (he accomplished both with *Footlight Parade* in 1933,
after his second studio walkout), the two Grand National films
distinctly mark a denial, a disavowal, an unsentimental goodbye to his Warners image. *Great Guy* (or *The Pluck of the
Irish*, as it was titled in England) and *Something to Sing About*
are seminal films in the history of the American cinema because
they testify, as no other Hollywood films of the period do,
to the individual sensibility of a major motion picture star estranged from the alienating workings of the movie system. Cagney sat in on all of the story conferences for the two films
and the result is explicit, thematic works.

At first it was rumoured in Hollywood that *Great Guy* would never be finished. Production problems, including the difficulty of persuading another studio to loan out a leading lady, ominously delayed the shooting schedule. When, after a suspenseful year-long hiatus, the film was finally released to the public, few critics were disappointed, if not outright impressed. Based on the "Johnny Cave" stories of "The Saturday Evening Post," *Great Guy* stars Cagney as the congenial crusader in the Bureau of Weights and Measures who singlehandedly battles a ring of crooks and grafters who are defrauding shoppers by cheating on grocery weights. Ably directed by John Blystone within the shoestring budget of Grand National's limited financial resources, the film is a lean, crackling work that contains unlaboured performances by a cluster of Irish actors, including gregarious James Burke, buoyant cop Edward J. McNamara, Edward Brophy, Ed Gargan and Mary Gordon. Cagney's co-star in the picture is Mae Clarke (though Joan Blondell was originally sought for the role—Warners refused to release her); thus is the grapefruit beneficiary of *The Public Enemy* repaid by Cagney for his impolite, historic gesture. She, too, gives a sweet, comic performance. The entire movie, wrote the reviewer for "The New York Times," "bears unmistakeable evidence of that Hollywood rarity, complete co-operation of the director and the story and casting departments."

True to its title, *Great Guy* assaults, disowns, reverses the principal conventions of a stock "tough guy" film—Johnny Cave is the antithesis of a character such as Tom Powers. In a meaningful switch, for example, Janet Henry (Mae Clarke) dominates the romantic relationship. She steers Johnny Cave. It is she, for instance, who decides where they will dine (in a simple cafeteria rather than, as Johnny Cave prefers, an elegant restaurant). It is she who then tells Johnny Cave just what and how much he should eat while they are shuffling through the cafeteria line. She wins every argument. Also, in *Great Guy*, a considered point is made by the script against the violence so prevalent in most, previous Cagney films. Himself hospitalised by roughnecks, Johnny Cave's supervisor specifically orders the intrepid inspector to make arrests and pursue his investigations without resorting to his fists—the accepted "tough guy" manner. The conscientious Cave abides by this advice until, challenged by a devious gas station attendant who purloins some useful evidence, he flashes a sudden, right-fisted punch. Then, gazing regretfully at his hand, he murmurs sorrowfully, "I promised . . ." Attempting to define his persona in

more compatible, personal, relevant terms, Cagney even inter-
jected quirks of his own into the story. In one scene, Johnny
Cave criticises girl-friend Janet's hat. Off-screen, the actor har-
boured an intense dislike for women's hats.

Cagney's performance is remarkably restrained, an immediate and dramatically discernible departure from his Warners
roles. Johnny Cave is a busy, vigilant fellow; he is talkative but
also ready and willing to listen; he is levelheaded and steady.
There is a short, powerful sequence in which Cavanaugh (Robert Bleckler), the villain of the piece, laughs into Johnny Cave's
face after having the deputy inspector falsely arrested and grilled
for a robbery he didn't commit. Silent, brooding, Cagney stands
before the interrogation, revealing only by his hot, dancing
eyes a comprehension of the set-up. Warners' Cagney would
have replied blindly with his fists. The wiser "great guy"
weathered the onslaught with abundant poise. In fact, Johnny
Cave yields to fisticuffs at length only once in the film, at the
finale when he locks astonished policeman Captain Pat Hanlon
(Edward J. McNamara) out of a room while he trounces the
top hooligan inside. Yet the scene is played for tongue-in-
cheek laughs. "Unlock this door or I'll break it in," Hanlon barks,
as his face gradually relaxes into a smile, then he lights a smoke,
"as soon as I finish this cigar."

Another of Great Guy's merits is a progressive political perspective that is in keeping with the best, most forward-looking
films of the Warners tradition. Like many films of the period,
Warners' own Bullets or Ballots, for example, released earlier
the same year, Great Guy is candid and uncompromising in
its revelation and condemnation of larcenous businessmen and
dishonest politicians. Even the local mayor of Great Guy is revealed as an ordinary thief. In one particular, central scene,
Johnny Cave, in pursuit of crooked grocery clerks, lectures a
roomful of agents, warning the crew (and the audience)
about criminal merchants and the big money stakes of price
fixing. And, he cautions the investigators further, bribes are an
everyday occurrence—so beware. Ironically, Great Guy stirred
complaints to the Hays Office, protests of a far dissimilar nature to the many provoked earlier by the underworld Cagney.
"The depiction of James Cagney as an honest, capable and competent employee in the department of weights and measures
in a great city," writes Raymond Moley in his authoritative "The Hays Office," "was the signal for vehement outcries
from retail grocers and gas-station owners who insisted that the
picture cast a reflection' on their honesty (curiously enough,

it never seems to have occurred to these protestors, as Breen pointed out, that the very existence of such departments as a department of weights and measures indicates the acknowledgement, by the community itself, that there is a need for the supervision of weights and measures in retail stores, including grocery stores and gas stations)."

Less consistent, less fulfilled than *Great Guy*, *Something to Sing About* (re-issued as *Battling Hoofer*), Cagney's second and final Grand National release in 1937, is nevertheless an enthralling film: the story, loaded again with precise meaning for Cagney followers, concerned the quest of New York bandleader Terry Rooney (Cagney) for Hollywood film stardom. Granted a movie contract, Rooney is informed by ebullient producer B. O. Regan (Gene Lockhart) that he will be the country's newest acting sensation—despite Rooney's pathetic insistence that he is really a singer-dancer at heart, and would like to so remain. Regardless, an absurd parade of make-up specialists, wardrobe experts and diction tutors begin to inspect and renovate the bandleader for imminent stardom. Already perturbed by his phony image-making, Rooney explodes when a pestering bit player annoys him during final shooting of his first film. He scrambles into a full-pitched brawl on the set, then stalks off the studio lot and sails on a honeymoon cruise with newlywed wife Rita Wyatt (Evelyn Daw). When Rooney returns, he discovers to his amazement that he is a true movie star, America's brand-new rage, for the shrewd director of his only film had kept the cameras rolling during the unrehearsed fracas: film fans are enamoured with the rip-roaring "tough guy" find. The trusting bandleader is coaxed into signing a lucrative movie contract with one catch—he must masquerade as a gay bachelor so as not to let down his fans and also to enhance his box-office value. A dilemma arises when gossip columnists float idle rumours of his supposed amorous entanglements with other starlets, and his jealous, heartbroken wife Rita withdraws to New against his will. Though neither *Great Guy* or *Something to* York. Resolved, sick of irresponsible press agents and nutty producers, Rooney also flees to home—he is reconciled with his wife and his former nightclub band just in time for a joyful musical finale. Like the actor who played him, Rooney is presumably permanently estranged from the dream factory called Hollywood.

Coming in the midst of his voluntary separation from Warner Brothers and the Hollywood establishment, *Something to Sing About* is a propitiously timed, categorical, even blunt, attack by Cagney on Hollywood, "show people" and the entire movie

In SOMETHING TO SING ABOUT

star syndrome. Producers especially (perhaps a deliberate swing at the brothers Warner) bear the animosity. Studio magnate B. O. Regan is, in the film, an empty-headed, deceitful blowhard who, in one main scene, conspires to award Rooney a catchpenny, sub-standard movie contract.

Directed without any verve by Victor Schertzinger, *Something to Sing About* is weakened by visibly inferior production values, including a mediocre off-camera crew of technical collaborators, surely due to Grand National's rapidly-sagging financial health. The settings are embarrassingly bare and the stage dressings are awfully simple. Of the cast, only affable William Frawley as chatterbug agent Hank Meyers, is particularly enjoyable, excepting Cagney, of course, who is inspired. As in *Great Guy*, the character he portrays is the antithesis of his previous roles: reserved, almost shy, placid though strong. Actually, he doesn't sing a single solo note in *Something to Sing About*— there is a gag at the beginning in which the words of a song are "stolen" every time he opens his mouth to warble. But he dances, though less magnificently than elsewhere, granting the formless choreography (one zippy routine aboard the ocean liner with a chorus of sailors almost seems improvised, badly). Yet, in the dances of *Something to Sing About,* there is an oblique reference, a psychic connection, to Cagney's future that parallels the allusion to *G-Men* in the title of *Great Guy*. In the opening musical extravaganza, "Something to Sing About," Terry Rooney prances down a flight of makeshift steps. It is the exact movement marshalled by George M. Cohan (Cagney) when he taps a descent from the White House stairs in *Yankee Doodle Dandy* (Johnny Boyle, the choreographer of his *Yankee Doodle Dandy* dances was a dancer in the chorus of *Something to Sing About*).

"*Something to Sing About,*" wrote Frank S. Nugent, "is an amusing piece, sardonic and frolicsome, and it slows down only when Mr. Cagney steps off stage. The best of the film is the satirising (obviously meat to Mr. Cagney who feels that way about the place) of the Hollywood star-building methods." Even more appreciative was the view of a British critic who wrote that the film "shows us an entirely new James Cagney, one we had never seen before, a band leader, a song and dance man, a film star who guys the Hollywood routine with all the flair of a born comedian and a born dancer who seems to out-do Fred Astaire at his own game. There is no one in Europe with such snap, speed and skill, who is at the same time capable of attuning all these gifts to the triumph of the social principle."

Grand National had at least one other Cagney work in progress, a promising subject entitled *Dynamite,* promoted in advance as a "dramatic tale of illegal oil traffic in Texas," when the "B" company surrendered its exclusive star. Plagued by the pressures of independent production, the inevitable, overbearing difficulties of financing, Cagney returned to Warners in 1938. In the interim, the court embroilments had been resolved in the actor's favour, the California judge ruling that Cagney had been worked beyond the limitations of his contract. And now the Warners studio lured the performer back with a pay boost to $150,000 per picture versus a percentage and the fundamental condition that only two films starring the actor would be released annually, plus some small leeway when it came to rejecting projects. In addition, Cagney's contract guaranteed the hire of his brother William as advisor and associate producer —at this stage of his career, William began to exert enormous influence over brother Jimmy's future film-making, both behind-the-scenes technically, and ultimately artistically. By any measure, the demise of the Grand National Pictures association was a tragic, fateful milestone in Cagney's career. If the relationship had survived (and so absolute was its "death" that the two Grand National features are still among Cagney's rarest-shown, most obscure films), the actor might well have been afforded the opportunity to flex his muscles, to expand, to experiment with a richer, varied, individualistic cinematic expression at this peak juncture of his artistry. But the Grand National venture was doomed from the start. The smaller organisation never had the same capacity for promotion and distribution that a company like Warners did. In 1937, his Grand National year, Cagney slipped from his customary spot on the theatre owner's list of top ten box-office draws. Soon after his return to Warners, he regained his stature in receipts.

The year 1938 was represented by two Cagney-O'Brien pairings: *Boy Meets Girl* and *Angels with Dirty Faces.* The former, a successful Broadway property bought by Warners to star Marion Davies, intended to be produced and directed for the screen by theatrical magnate George Abbott, was the actor's flimsiest comedic outing to date—a feeble comeback. Marion Davies was dropped from the project when she astutely complained about the deficient script, and Lloyd Bacon substituted as director. Even after the Bella and Sam Spewack scenario (based on their own stage hit) was re-written to accommodate Cagney and O'Brien, the exposition remained scarcely serviceable. Cagney and O'Brien played Robert Law and J. C. Benson, two wacky Hollywood screenwriters who concoct a scheme

With Dick Foran, Pat O'Brien, Ralph Bellamy and Marie Wilson in
BOY MEETS GIRL

to turn a cute little baby named "Happy" into a movie star;
"Happy" pictures become a revered national fad—the little tyke
even starring as the hero of shoot-'em-up westerns ("from the
story by Wm. Shakespeare—out of the plains and into your
heart")—and the two scenarists must contend with a doltish,
swellheaded screen romeo (Dick Foran) who is worried about
being upstaged by an infant. Well-received by critics when it
was first released, *Boy Meets Girl* wears badly with the passage
of time, and it pales as a satire on Hollywood beside Cagney's
own, biting *Something to Sing About*. The film is marred by
poor pacing, confused staging and an unceasing stream of jokes
and one-liners, many of them nonsensically unfunny. Again,
as in many Cagney films, the performances transcend the story.
Ralph Bellamy is the provincial, erratic producer C. Elliott Fri-
day. Frank McHugh is the very shifty shyster lawyer Rosetti.
Marie Wilson, as studio commissary waitress Susie, the touching, unworldly mother of "Happy," endows her thankless role
with a lovely, contagious, ethereal spirit. Cast purely as comics, without any gangster overtones or shading, but also without the benefit of enduringly comic dialogue, Cagney and
O'Brien are sorely taxed to be effectual, although they almost
make do, racing through the babble (playing multiple roles in
their own proposed screenplays) so hurriedly that there is faint

chance to reflect on the proceedings. Dressed in the Hollywood "uniform" of ascot, beret and trench coat, Cagney played one of his few non-limelight roles ever—undoubtedly, nonetheless, a part he himself lobbied for, as a new-image dividend of his fourth Warners contract. But Warner Brothers' lingering reluctance to showcase Cagney as anything but a profitable "tough guy" is illustrated by the film's treatment in England where, according to "Film Pictorial," *Boy Meets Girl* "was held up (until after the release of *Angels with Dirty Faces*) because Cagney is making a comeback after his quarrel with Warners and it was thought that English audiences would rather see him in one of his customary tough roles before they saw him in broad comedy."

Angels with Dirty Faces, also released in 1938, co-starring Pat O'Brien, Humphrey Bogart, Ann Sheridan and the Dead End Kids, is one of Cagney's most exceptional films. From the opening shot—a slow, steady pan from the newspaper headlines ("Harding Nominated for President") of a street-corner skimmer to the seedy, brimming tenements of New York City —to the closing, dazzling image—the writhing shadow of gangster Rocky Sullivan (Cagney) as he is led to the electric chair —director Michael Curtiz crafted a brittle, rousing entertainment. The Rowland Brown story (scripted by John Wexley and Warren Duff), originally purchased by Grand National but sold to Warner Brothers after Cagney left, bore structural resemblances to *The Public Enemy.* Cagney played Rock Sullivan, an infamous criminal whose dangerous exploits make him a hero to slum kids in his native neighbourhood. As a youth, Rocky had been chums with an equally spunky youngster who, escaping a run-in with police that sent Rocky to a boys reformatory, grew up to become the neighbourhood priest (Pat O'Brien). Now, still fast friends, Father Jerry Connelly begs Rocky to give up his life of crime. When Rocky is finally arrested for the murder of ex-partner James Frazier (Humphrey Bogart) and sentenced to death, Father Connelly persuades the soft-streaked hoodlum to feign cowardliness as he walks to the electric chair —to disillusion the idolising street gang of youths (the Dead End Kids). Cagney, in a performance that won him the New York Critics' prize as Best Actor and an Academy Award nomination, was galvanic, volcanic. The actor gave a physicalised, indefatigable, electrical show that also carried just the exact nuance of kind-hearted warmth. Alter ego O'Brien was sincere and paternal with an unmistaken touch of self-assured, rugged strength. As Laury Martin, Rocky's girl-friend, "Oomph" girl

With Billy Halop (left), Leo Gorcey (lower left), Bernard Punsley (right) and Gabriel Dell (far right) in ANGELS WITH DIRTY FACES. Below, with Humphrey Bogart and George Bancroft in the same film

Ann Sheridan makes her way nicely through an oblique role. The Dead End Kids, as almost always, are sumptuous—a wise-cracking, simpleton, angel-core gang of young toughs (Billy Halop, Bobby Jordan, Leo Gorcey, Bernard Punsley, Gabriel Dell and Huntz Hall). And Humphrey Bogart, as Rocky's double-crossing lawyer, in the first of his three screen appearances with Cagney, is adequately mean, sullen and glowering. The up-and-coming, new-generation "tough guy" lost his life in the film to the more experienced gangster Cagney, and eyed the original "Public Enemy" with the narrow gleam of a jealous lover.

"Cagney looked like a mushroom under a huge western hat," Bogart said of their next joint appearance, *The Oklahoma Kid* in 1939. "I was the heavy. I got shot and killed at the end." Cagney's first and only western for Warner Brothers, *The Oklahoma Kid* is a nonchalant, unserious horse opera about Jim Kincaid, "The Oklahoma Kid," the redoubtable, somehow-decent outlaw son of John Kincaid (Hugh Sothern), reform candidate for mayor of Tulsa, Oklahoma. The Kid must elude bounty hunters while he hunts for the leaders of a lynch mob that killed his father. He rounds up the desperadoes, dead or alive, is pardoned and even gets the inevitable girl (Rosemary Lane) before riding off into the sunset. Dressed in black, scowling as if he resented the familiarity of his role, Bogart plays slinky Whip McCord, the scoundrel who causes the hanging death of virtuous Kincaid Senior. Bogart wrestles with Cagney for a few unsuspenseful minutes at the end before succumbing to a bullet—his just deserts.

Dressed in white, the gunslinging Cagney makes a predictably winsome cowboy, especially when he interrupts the usual saloon chatter to sing a few bars of "I Don't Want to Play in Your Yard" with a nearby pianist's accompaniment, punctuating his melody with a few well-aimed pistol shots for the burly companions of Whip McCord who don't approve, or when he cradles an infant in his arms and sings "Rockaby Baby"— two versions, English and Spanish. The film is an exercise in exercise, with slender direction by Lloyd Bacon, James Wong Howe's handsome photography and a jaunty Max Steiner musical score. "There's something entirely disarming about the way he (Cagney) tackled horse opera," wrote Frank S. Nugent in "The New York Times," "not pretending a minute to be anything but New York's Jimmy Cagney, all dressed up for a dude ranch. He cheerfully pranks through every outrageous assignment his script writers and directors have given him." Wrote "Time" magazine: "Typical shot: Cagney—whose Bowery accent lends an admirably exotic touch to his impersonation of a bad-lands sharpshooter—blowing complacently through his pistol bar-rel when he shoots someone."

In 1939 also, Cagney only appeared in two films, William Keighley's *Each Dawn I Die* and Raoul Walsh's *The Roaring Twenties*, both sprawling, lusty neo-gangster epics. The more laconic *Each Dawn I Die*, which "Time" magazine summarised as "a fierce slugfest in handcuffs," co-starred the great infidel, George Raft (who danced beside Cagney in a minor role in *Taxi!*), who shared billing and also insured the cash flow of a box-office bonanza headlined by two of Warner's biggest stars. "Cagney Meets a Raft of Trouble," punned advertisements for the movie. The story was elementary: Frank Ross (Cagney), a muck-raking journalist with idealistic faith in the machinery of justice, is framed into a prison sentence for manslaughter by a crooked district attorney whom he has discovered in the act of fraud. Unable to obtain a pardon, disillusioned, envenomed, Ross becomes friendly with hardened lifer Hood Stacey (Raft) and decides to help the convict escape in return for a pledge from Stacey to search out the thug who can finger the assail-ants who drenched him with alcohol and then rammed his car into an innocent pedestrian. Once on the outside, Stacey learns that the key mobster has just been sent to the very prison he escaped. Loyal to his vow, Stacey strolls back through the front gates (after taking a taxi cab to the prison walls) and then joins a suicidal jail breakout—coercing a confession from the hood, within earshot of the warden, before perishing in a volley of gunfire.

Raft has that rare mix of talent and composure, a face, a look, a style that automatically clamours for heed, a sure sense of himself that is conveyed without apology. The stillfaced, scratchy-voiced actor is one of the neglected virtuosos of the gangster film era, and *Each Dawn I Die* demonstrates the dig-nity of his contribution. Such are his steely, untrusting eyes that he can play an entire scene without lines, depending on-ly on the slight flicker of his visage to communicate his inner feeling. Frank Ross's *fiancée* (Jane Bryan) implores Stacey for his help in onè scene, for example, telling the fugitive that the newspaperman has gone to "The Hole" for punishment rather than reveal the details of their escape plan. "You're a slum kid who never had a chance," she says, "But so is Frank. He hates crooked cops and rotten politicians as much as you do. The on-ly difference is you chose crime—the easy way. He's spent his life fighting." Stacey remains silent; coolly, calmly smoking a cig-

With George Raft in EACH DAWN I DIE

arette in that pointed, informative way of his, Raft betrays the gangster's compassion first by a slow slackening of his countenance. He is sublimely paired in *Each Dawn I Die* with the gymnastic, demonstrative Cagney who gives a convulsive performance—particularly in the frightening scenes in which, unnerved by prison life, stir-crazy from solitary confinement, he breaks down into a screaming, sobbing paroxysm. Their friendship (a friendship paralleled in real-life by an acquaintanceship that went back to their Broadway hoofing days together) is so believably developed, sometimes in spite of the wandering story-line, that even so awkward an instance as the maudlin coda to the film is almost plausible. As Ross is leaving the prison, exonerated, the warden (George Bancroft) hands him a photograph left by Stacey before he died in the breakout fusillade. The inscription? "To Ross: I found a square guy." A crisp, vehement film, directed by Keighley with an eye for velocity and action —consider, for example, the precisely-timed, fast-moving, spellbinding, murderous shootout between prison guards and desperate cons at the climax—*Each Dawn I Die* is ultimately a film that belongs to its stars, Raft and Cagney. The unerring Cagney performance had none of the blurry, comic margins of his earlier, ambiguous films, such as *Blonde Crazy* or *Lady Killer*,

and little of the self-kidding of later films like *St. Louis Kid*
and *Frisco Kid*. His matured persona was still hard-as-nails,
still palpably soft besides, but no longer innately comical—now
sober, almost more realistic.

Cagney bade farewell to the Thirties and also, for ten years,
to the gangster film, in *The Roaring Twenties* (1939), a gran-
diloquent parable about bootlegging in the Twenties. Bogart co-
starred—his third and last appearance with Cagney. The film
simultaneously capped Cagney's prolific mobster career of the
Thirties and prefaced Bogart's emergence as the principal
"tough guy" of the Forties. Based on an original story by Mark
Hellinger (adapted into a screenplay by Jerry Wald, Richard
Macaulay and Robert Rossen), the movie begins with a nostalgic prologue by Hellinger, a spoken narration against a background of news clips and simulated history that explains the
writer-producer's fond recollections of the era, "a memory of
the past" (thus, as with *Angels With Dirty Faces*, *Oklahoma
Kid* and *Each Dawn I Die*, a premise is established at the outset for rationalising Cagney's "criminal" behaviour—therefore in
keeping with his post-1936 image). The story unravels in flashback: three soldiers in a First World War foxhole cross paths
after the war. Cagney plays former garage mechanic Eddie Bartlett, a run-of-the-mill guy who turns to bootlegging liquor
after the war when he can't find an honest job, teaming with
old trench cronies George Hally (Humphrey Bogart), a sadistic ex-rival rum-runner, and lawyer Lloyd Hart (Jeffrey Lynn).
When Bartlett falls in love with a young singer (Priscilla Lane)
who, in turn, falls in love with Hart and eventually marries the
lawyer, the kingpin's mini-empire of booze begins to disinte-
grate. Broke, dejected, Bartlett becomes a taxi-cab driver. One
day, years later, his passenger is the singer, now happily married. She tells him that Hally, still a vice lord, has threatened
to kill her husband, now a local D.A.—and she begs Bartlett's
help. On New Year's Eve, the tired, drunk ex-underworld chief
goes to Hally's luxurious suite to plead for his mercy. There,
he shoots Hally and is himself shot, dying after a spinning,
bloody, carnage-strewn shootout with Hally's henchmen. "The
Roaring Twenties was still a frightening image in the mind of
the public," Bogart said of the film, "and to do these gangster
shows in the Thirties was still close enough to make people realise the stark realism was part of an era that really has existed
in our time."

Majestically directed by Raoul Walsh, who perhaps better
than any director grasped the noble scope, the full, tragic di-

mensions of the Cagney persona, *The Roaring Twenties* is a vast and compacted dream song, a passion play of American shortcomings, dominated, indeed defined, by its titan perform-ances—not the least of which are the secondary support, es-pecially homespun Frank McHugh as Bartlett's loyal pal Dan-ny Green, and Gladys George as jaded, celestial nightclubber Panama Smith, also Bartlett's devoted friend. But *The Roaring Twenties* is foremost an opportunity to inspect Bogart and Cag-ney at odds, the two chief cinema gangsters of all film history squaring off in death-urging rivalry. "Mr. Cagney, of the bull-calf brow, is as always a superb and witty actor," wrote Graham Greene. "Mr. Bogart is, of course, magnificent." As the two mobsters vie for control of the liquor rackets so too do the two actors vie for dramatic focus and acting honours. Though both expire before the finis, Bogart really defers to the more intricate, profound Cagney portrait—a judgment endorsed particularly by the last sequence in which a lush, wasted Bartlett visits Hally to implore the favour. Cagney plays a vital, tear-jerking scene, while Bogart can only manage those cowering, quivering traits of a diehard movie villain. Some of that potency is due to the role itself—Bartlett is intrinsically a more vivid character than Hally—but much is also owed to Cagney's embroidery. He performed with a manic force that physically subdued the less volatile, stern, detached Bogart. The cinema moment has rarely been equalled in which Bartlett—stunned and wounded in a gunfire exchange with Hally's min-ions—stumbles onto the city sidewalks at the film's climax, gasp-ing for breath. Bent, contorted, Cagney runs a twisting, falter-ing zig-zag in retreat, nearly straightens with a final shove of might, then falls, crumples, sprawled dead and motionless on the great steps of a church. Panama Smith runs to the body and stands abjectly posed as an anonymous cop races over. "Who was he?" the officer wonders. Without pause, she tear-fully answers, "He used to be a big shot."

William Keighley was the thrifty director of Cagney's two 1940 releases: *The Fighting 69th*, a prevaricating account of the exploits of Manhattan's famed First World War "fighting Irish" regiment; and *Torrid Zone*, an exuberant comedy about a Latin American revolutionary's see-saw struggle over an Unit-ed States-owned banana plantation. Cagney-O'Brien features both, *The Fighting 69th* particularly was a poorly moulded im-itation of *Here Comes the Navy*, like *Devil Dogs of the Air* lacking the loose energy of the original. The film described the story of swaggering coward Jerry Plunkett (Cagney), a soldier

In THE FIGHTING 69TH

whose refusal to follow orders eventually causes the deaths of army comrades. Finally, the penitent Plunkett is persuaded to perform heroic deeds at the film's climax by troop chaplain Father Duffy (Pat O'Brien). A middling war film, "with all its obvious theatrics, hokum and unoriginality," in the words of the "New York Times," *The Fighting 69th* is to be recommended only for the sturdy bunch of Warners players: George Brent, Jeffrey Lynn, Alan Hale, Frank McHugh, Dick Foran, Henry O'Neill, Sammy Cohen, George Reeves, a pious Pat O'Brien and an ignominious Cagney. Aside from big-budgeted battle panoramas, Warners also advanced money for a large-scale promotion campaign for the film, including a widely-publicised meeting in New York City between Cagney, O'Brien, the real Father Duffy and surviving members of the squadron. Five thousand fans welcomed the two movie stars at New York's Grand Central Station; concurrently, the film was a smash box-office success.

Torrid Zone, based on an original screenplay by Richard Macaulay and Jerry Wald, photographed through a sometimes steamy lens by James Wong Howe, is less troubled by artifice because the film is whole-heartedly, unashamedly, rapturously synthetic. Shot in forty-one production days by the mercurial Keighley on a seaport, banana grove and tropical jungle built on Warner Brothers' thirty-acre annex, *Torrid Zone* bulges with preposterous notions. A few: George Tobias as an easy come, easy go, accented, sombreroed bandit revolutionary; Ann Sheridan as a sultry torch singer hitchhiking her card shark way through the hinterlands; O'Brien as the cigar-puffing, imperious, white-suited (with black tie) head of the local banana plantation; and Cagney as a gun-slinging, horse-riding fruitcrop trouble-shooter with just the suggestion of a cavalier moustache. They somehow lace into one of the Forties' silliest comedies. "There is a punch line a minute," wrote one ecstatic reviewer, "some of them so close to the borderline that they must have necessitated the use of the Hays office censorial slide rule . . . As the foreman, Mr. Cagney again shows that he has more tightly muscled energy as an actor than half the Hollywood leads put together; Mr. O'Brien is scowling, loud-mouthed and credible, and there should be special mention of Andy Devine's dimwitted Number One Boy and George Tobias as the loveable revolutionist who is nearly shot a week ahead of schedule to forestall an untimely demise by hunger strike. But if the males are two-fisted, Miss Sheridan meets them blow for blow, line for line."

Cagney's first release in busy (three films) 1941, *City for Conquest*, directed by Anatole Litvak (and associate produced by William Cagney in the first of five consecutive Cagney picture assignments), is also the actor's most puzzling achievement. Despite mixed reviews and soul searching post-production analysis by the director and star, the film is notwithstanding a pungent, zestful, stirring if flawed work, less a realistic *exposé* of the boxing world like such a film as *The Harder They Fall* (1956) than a religious fantasy about metropolitan morality—seen through Hollywood's rose-coloured camera sights. Cagney plays Danny Kenny, a New Yorker who is versatile enough with his fists to be a professional boxer. Nevertheless, Kenny is content with being a workaday truck driver until his ambitious girl-friend (Ann Sheridan), herself travelling the theatre circuit as a glory-bound dancer, convinces him to enter the boxing ring. He is an unremitting winner as a fighter—till his opponent during a championship fight splashes a burning chemical compound into his eyes and then grinds it in with windmill gloves, blinding the battler for life. Of *City for Conquest*, Litvak later told "Films and Filming": "Only once in my life did I ever have any difficulty and this was with Jimmy Cagney . . . He couldn't quite adjust to the part and I came to an impasse with him. And that's the only time in my whole career that I had any troubles with any actor." Cagney revealed his own misgivings about the film to Hollywood columnist Hedda Hopper. "I was born nervous," he told her in the Fifties. "Won't even go to previews of my own pictures. The last one I ever saw was *City for Conquest*. When it was over, I sat there, thinking, 'Was that what it was about?' It didn't add up to the hours and days of work that had gone into it. It was all right, but it didn't represent the effort we'd all made. Now I figure when I've finished a picture I've done as well as I can, so let it go."

All the more mysterious, then, that *City for Conquest* is seemingly such a heartfelt film, exhibiting one of Cagney's most humane performances. While the film is surely the most maudlin of Cagney's entire career, the scenario (by John Wexley and Robert Rossen) aspires to a certain, ill-defined, gritty, urban naturalism also. Thus is Cagney most assuredly in his element—cast, as in *The Public Enemy,* as one of the faceless millions with a message for the uncaring world. So when the director implies that Cagney disagreed with him about how to interpret the character of Danny Kenny, and when Litvak infers further that Cagney resolutely clung to his conception (therefore it is Cagney's Kenny more than Litvak's, that is in the film as released), it is quite transparent that Cagney's Kenny belongs to the true meaning of the story—an instinctively moral, optimistic, uphill-scrapper, American role, as real and sincerely heartbreaking as any of his better-known characterisations. On the contrary, it is director Litvak who sporadically violates the true spirit of *City for Conquest* by inserting antinaturalistic, gimmicky cinematic ploys to emphasise certain key facets of the melodrama. In this ruinous category can be placed Litvak's dreadful-obvious superimposition of Cagney's smiling figure during the triumphant Carnegie Hall concert of brother Eddie (Arthur Kennedy); and his adoption of *Wonderful Town* narrator Frank Craven as the omnipresent, omnipotent old-timer of *City for Conquest* (Craven's part is edited to drastic, cryptic proportions in the television version of the film). European in style (like Max Reinhardt's *A Midsummer Night's Dream*), sluggish in explication, Litvak's traditional, elocutionary mode of storytelling rubbed injuriously against Cagney's swift, native demeanour.

But Cagney served *City for Conquest* well. He invests his characterisation with a schmaltzy fibre and kindly temperament that undercuts the incredibility of the plot. The film concludes with a perfect, gorgeously sentimental passage. The blinded

With Arthur Kennedy (left) and Frank McHugh in CITY FOR CONQUEST

Kenny is reduced to streetcorner newspaper-selling and he is listening, with one cocked ear, a broad and happy smile on his face, to his younger brother's radio concert, the "City for Conquest" symphony being played at Carnegie Hall and dedicated to him. Then, with the other ever-watchful ear, he hears the faint, nearing footsteps of sweetheart Peggy Nash—she, too, is down on her luck, jobless and haunted by the injury to Kenny she indirectly caused. With blurred vision and understandably misty eyes, still smiling, he extends his hand. "I knew you'd come by this corner someday," he says. "You'll always be my girl, Peggy." The tentative last shot brings to mind the Chaplin of other circumstances in *City Lights*. The lustrous cast includes Donald Crisp, George Tobias, Arthur Kennedy, Frank McHugh as Kenny's worshipful tag-along, Anthony Quinn as the smooth, satanic dancer who nearly steals Peggy away and Ann Sheridan as the engaging, destructively-aspiring girl-friend Peggy. Future director Elia Kazan, in one of his only two film roles, fills a tiny but marvellous part as "Googi," Kenny's boyhood chum who has grown up to become a suave gangster—"Googi" dies by sneak bullet at midway, managing to gasp surprisedly before he folds, "Gee, I never figured on that." So acute, so penetrating are the players that *City for Con-*

With Frank McHugh (left) and Elia Kazan in CITY FOR CONQUEST

quest is salvaged beyond its flirtation with bathos and, even more surprisingly, rescued above its otherwise irredeemable, idealist philosophy that the poor masses are happy being poor and, further, that Carnegie Hall is just around the corner from every blinded boxer's brother.

Based on James Hagan's play "One Sunday Afternoon," which was already filmed once in 1933 with Gary Cooper, *The Strawberry Blonde*, Cagney's next release in 1941, was a resonant diversion—a gentle, rolling, bittersweet, turn-of-the-century romantic comedy with all the essential elements of an ideal matinee entertainment. Directed by Raoul Walsh, again with his taste for expansive atmosphere, wittily adapted to a New York City locale by scenarists Julius J. and Philip G. Epstein, and photographed by the sanitary James Wong Howe, the film is a fond, semi-musical impression of life in lower Manhattan gone by, with all the various, innocent attractions of a dream-like 1910: suffragettes, horseshoe pitching in the backyard, moonlight rendezvous in the city park and the elusive "strawberry blonde." Cagney plays Biff Grimes, a dentist who learns his craft by correspondence, a tough, young plug who "don't take nothin' from nobody" 'cause "that's the kind of hairpin I am." As the story opens, he has just been released from prison for (undisclosed) "crimes." The phone rings one Sunday afternoon; it is a prominent city alderman who would like to have his tooth pulled. Biff is about to refuse, seeing as how it is Sunday, when he hears the name—Hugo Barnstead. Why yes, he quickly replies, with a malicious glint in his eyes, come right over, Hugo . . .

Flashback: like everyone else in his neighbourhood, as a youth Biff Grimes was starry-eyed over the "strawberry blonde," dainty Virginia Brush (Rita Hayworth); but, on a blind date arranged by conniving pal Hugo Barnstead (Jack Carson), Biff gets stuck with Virginia's plain-jane friend Amy Lind (Olivia de Havilland), a uniformed nurse and "free thinker" who smokes cigarettes (rather badly) and has some "independent" ideas about men. They don't exactly "hit it off." "There's something about the country air," sighs Amy. "I like city air," Biff harrumphs in reply.

On their next double date, Biff is more fortunate. He ends up with Virginia and they "do" the town: an expensive proposition for the neophyte dentist who must even pay a band conductor to play "The Strawberry Blonde" for Virginia's benefit. Nevertheless, the elated Biff believes he has captured Virginia's heart—until he learns from Amy, several nights later, that Virginia has eloped with Hugo. Indignant but undaunted, somewhat on the immediate rebound, he asks Amy to be his steady, and she accepts—he also discovers, incidentally, that she is not much of a "free thinker" after all, only a sweet, ordinary girl who is insecure about romance. In time, they are married and one day Biff encounters Virginia, now Mrs. Hugo Barnstead, who invites the couple to dinner at their resplendent mansion, where she also persuades the ever-bloated Hugo to offer Biff a job as vice-president of the Barnstead contracting firm. Against his own better thinking, Biff accepts and is then bewildered by an executive position in which he does nothing all day but sign papers he needn't read. However, when company graft and dangerous building falsifications (which cause the death of Biff's own father, a company foreman) are discovered, Biff gets all the "credit." Hugo blames the luckless vice-president and Biff goes to jail while the devoted Amy waits behind. In prison, he finally receives his diploma in dentistry.

The present, again: a free man, philosophically ready to begin a new life, Biff happens on the chance to pull one of Hugo's aching teeth. He struggles with the possibility of gassing Hugo to death but then Hugo and the still-attached "strawberry blonde" arrive—bickering, quarrelling, spitting insults at each other. As a minimal revenge, Biff decides only to extract Hu-

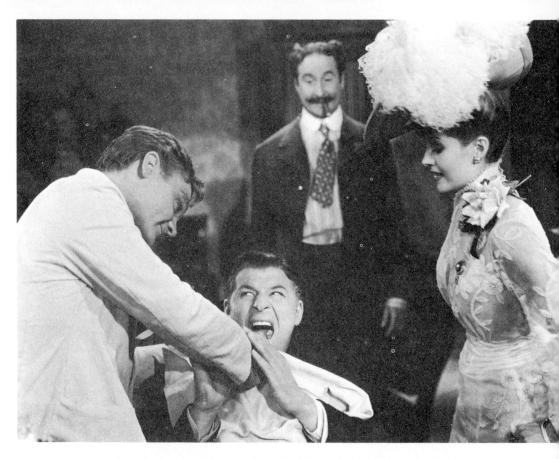

With Jack Carson, George Tobias (background) and Rita Hayworth in THE
STRAWBERRY BLONDE. Below, with Olivia de Havilland in the same film

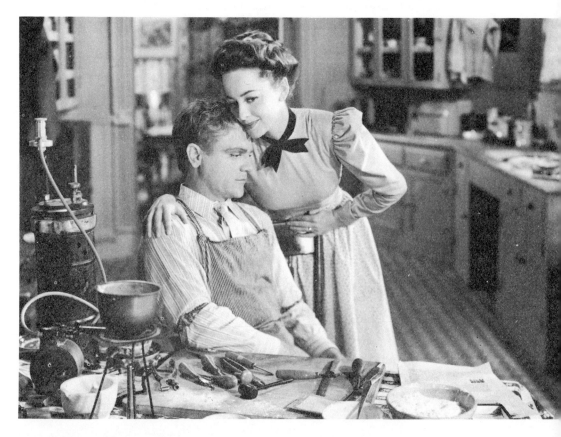

go's tooth without pain-killer. Why? "I just realised," says the pugnacious dentist, "I'm a happy man and he is not."

Flooded with honest sentiment, *The Strawberry Blonde* is a tender comedy which, in the hands of Walsh, becomes an informal probe of the tragedy of a man who never quite forgets the fantasy gal who got away. The film is chock-laden with wonderfully delicate moments—for example, the painful death in the hospital of Biff's beloved-rapscallion father (Alan Hale). Or the unsophisticated love scenes between Amy and Biff, described in three distinct stages—adversary, sweetheart and wife. And *The Strawberry Blonde* is also salted with frequent, seeming-spontaneous bursts of delectable mood—as when Biff garners his first buss from the "strawberry blonde," then turns ecstatically, vaults into a handspring and kisses a nearby horse. Cagney gives an individual, effortless performance; and he is well-mated with blithe Olivia de Havilland who proves that she is a far more adept comedienne than normally presumed. Rita Hayworth, of course, gives the appropriately ravishing, appropriately shallow portrait of a love goddess in hoopskirts; Jack Carson, one of the screen's foremost hollow men, blusters his way through an exquisitely insufferable role. And Alan Hale (as lecherous Old Man Grimes) and George Tobias (as stoic Nick Pappalas) are around to extend clever support.

Less amusing, also less heart-warming, was Cagney's second comedy and third film of 1941, *The Bride Came C.O.D.*, also scripted by the brothers Epstein but directed by active William Keighley. While *The Strawberry Blonde* is infectiously easy-going, *The Bride Came C.O.D.* is distressingly high-strung, strained and tense—the result of a scenario and direction that exaggerated farce, slapstick and the truculence of its two major stars, "bitch" Bette Davis and "tough guy" Cagney. The hypothesis was promising: a Texas oil tycoon (Eugene Pallette) pledges charter flyer Steve Collins (Cagney) ten dollars per pound for the air freight delivery to Amarillo, Texas, of his daughter (Bette Davis)—unmarried, for the spoiled heiress is about to wed obnoxious bandleader Allen Brice (Jack Carson). Abducted on the eve of an elopement that was to have been broadcast world-wide by a resourceful radio promoter (Stuart Erwin), the heiress finds herself falling loathingly in love with her unexpected pilot—after she forces their plane to crash into the desert. All the while, police and reporters are searching frantically for clues to the ruthless "kidnapping." The company of performers were deft and daft, including chubby, gravel-voiced Eugene Pallette as the oil magnate ("I don't mind

With Bette Davis in THE BRIDE CAME C.O.D.

having a fortune-hunter in the family, but I don't want a pi-ano-player"), Jack Carson, William Frawley, George Tobias and Stuart Erwin. But Bette Davis is so bristly (recalling *Jimmy the Gent*) and Cagney so likewise rigid that the film experien-ces a mortal wound from its combative stars from which it nev-er quite recovers. Wrote Bette Davis in her autobiography: "It was called a comedy. It had been decided that my work as a tragedian should be temporarily halted for a change of pace. Jimmy, who had made the gangster artistic—Jimmy, who was one of the fine actors on mine or any lot—Jimmy, with whom I'd always wanted to work in something fine, spent most of his time in the picture removing cactus quills from my behind. This was supposedly hilarious. We romped about the desert and I kept falling into cactus. We both reached bottom with this one."

Worse yet was *Captains of the Clouds* (1942), ostensibly a tragedy, actually a catastrophe, starring Cagney as Brian Mac-lean, a cocksure American northwoods bush pilot in Canada who joins the Royal Canadian Air Force in time for the Second World War. Directed by Michael Curtiz, redeemed only by some praiseworthy Technicolor aerial photography and back-woods scenic vistas, *Captains of the Clouds* is a blunt military preparedness doctrine *à la Here Comes the Navy, Devil Dogs of the Air* and *The Fighting 69th* without partner Pat O'Brien.

The tale was hampered by, among other things, a split story-line: the first half of the drama takes place in the wilds where adventuresome pilot MacLean filches flying jobs from competitors; the second half shifts awkwardly and implausibly to the runways of the Air Corps for some flying heroics. Cagney seemed familiar, even threadbare, though he "is much better than his thankless role," in the words of "Time" magazine. So redundant was the role that Cagney actually died (as in *Ceiling Zero* and *The Fighting 69th*) via the proverbial sacrificial-suicidal plunge—annihilating himself deliberately in a kamikaze air dive during a sky battle with Nazi raiders. Neither trusty secondary performers Alan Hale and George Tobias—nor 1,000 genuine RAF Cadets who are awarded their wings by First World War flying ace and Air Marshal William Avery (Billy) Bishop in a cameo sequence—bolster the movie sufficiently. Advertisements for *Captains of the Clouds* called the film "the Leader of All His Hits" and "So Full of Spectacle and Glory It Had to Be in Technicolor." Critics, however, generally berated the patriotic pseudo-spectacular; audiences, meanwhile, still flocked to the theatres to see Cagney.

But the actor dearly needed an artistic hit to revive his sagging critical reputation. In 1942, with war clouds on the American horizon, Cagney happened upon his greatest subject, his greatest theme and, incidentally, his greatest attainment: *Yankee Doodle Dandy*, the musical biography of patriotic song-and-dance man George M. Cohan. Still a unique film, one of Hollywood's all-time best, an unchallenged monument to Cagney's full-blown talents, *Yankee Doodle Dandy* not only climaxed his early Warners career but also commended the actor (with *Public Enemy* and the later *White Heat*) to cinema posterity. As George M. Cohan, the toast of Broadway and the nation, Cagney created his most enduring, fully-realised characterisation. He staggered fans and critics who regarded him as hardly more than a crude cinema gangster by demonstrating conclusively, as he had only insinuated earlier in *Footlight Parade* and *Something to Sing About*, that he was a masterful, consummate song and dance artist besides. The film bears lasting testimony to Cagney's acting intelligence. He begins the story as youthful, over-weening George M. Cohan, advances to flamboyant middle-age and ends as an old, restless codger who dances down the White House steps with more up-and-go than a juvenile delinquent. He was the plenary showman: Cagney sang with a proud, clipped, sonorous, staccato voice; he danced with a turbulent fury that belied the lithe, graceful moves of better-known dancers; he acted with a power and restraint that was bruising.

The film traces the career of entertainer Cohan, from his early, lean vaudeville years to his multiple Broadway triumphs, closing (and opening—the story actually unfolds in flashback) with a sequence in which the ageing performer is honoured with a congressional medal by the President of the United States (Roosevelt-lookalike Captain Jack Young). Though Cohan himself oversaw the birth of the production, and chose Cagney as his personal favourite for the role, *Yankee Doodle Dandy* is actually a slack, liberal version of the true account of Cohan's life. Against the wishes of Warners' executives, and without Cohan's prior consent, Cagney fought to amend certain of the less cinematic developments of Cohan's personal history. The story goes that the three Cagneys involved in the project—James, associate producer William and co-star sister Jeanne—threatened to quit the film unless they could tinker with the proposed scenario. Some of their alterations accommodated Hollywood nicely and some of them accommodated Cagney. For example, Cohan abhored love scenes. "This taboo on love scenes didn't bother me," Cagney later wrote, "For the way I do a love scene it's never a necking party. To me, a panting and grappling love scene is embarrassing when I see it on the screen. So when I sang the song 'Mary' to the girl who played Cohan's wife, I just told her the lyric, as she played the melody. I poured coffee, put sugar into it, stirred it and handed it to her. Then I sat down, drank the coffee and she sang the lyric back to me. The way we did it, it was an effective love scene—without any lashings of goo." The script also designated the name of Cohan's wife as "Mary"; Cohan, at the time, was married to his second wife whose name wasn't Mary, one of the reasons why Warners officials worried that Cohan, who had insisted on final approval of the movie, might not be enthusiastic. An anxious private screening was arranged for Mr. and Mrs. Cohan. Soon afterwards, Cagney received a brief, congratulatory telegram: "Dear Jim, How's my double? Thanks for a wonderful job. Sincerely, George M. Cohan."

Directed buoyantly and with boundless love for his adopted country by Michael Curtiz, with star-spangled photography by James Wong Howe, and including all of Cohan's best-known tunes, the completed two hour-plus movie is utterly captivating and wholly dynamic, defined as much by its intimate sequences—as, for example, the sweet-tempered scene in which Cohan persuades an "angel" (S. Z. Sakall) to finance his as-yet-

With S. Z. Sakall and Richard Whorf (right) in YANKEE DOODLE DANDY.
Below, with Jeanne Cagney (left), Rosemary De Camp and Walter Huston in
the same film

unwritten musical in collaboration with a partner he's never met (Richard Whorf as Sam Harris)—as by its beaming musical extravaganzas—particularly "Give My Regards to Broadway" and "Yankee Doodle Boy," so exuberant that at one point Cagney scales the proscenium arch. Curiously, even in such a celebrated impersonation, Cagney doesn't entirely abandon his "tough guy" image. In the early sequences of the film, he plays an uncivil, swell-headed, youthful George M. Cohan; thus does the image of "The Public Enemy" carry over to so distant a reverberation. Though Cagney had never personally seen Cohan on the stage, he recreated his own spitfire portrait of the famous theatre artist from friends' suggestions and his own ornamentation—adding idiosyncrasies of gesture, speech and performance. His characterisation was lofty and fever-driven as if, by his assaultive song-and-dance form, he was vengefully dispelling his gangster past. The other players were also marvellous: bucolic Joan Leslie made a surprisingly darling Mary, Cohan's wife. The versatile and brilliant Walter Huston played Cohan senior; Rosemary DeCamp, Cohan's mother; and sister Jeanne Cagney was sister Josie Cohan. (Evidently, casting sister Jeanne was originally the director's idea. Curtiz spotted Jeanne, then working in summer stock and Broadway, when she visited brother James on the set of *Captains of the Clouds,* and said, in his inimitable dialect, "Cheanne, you should be Chosie!") Visually as well as thematically, *Yankee Doodle Dandy* has still never been rivalled for its brazen avowal of sheer, unadulterated, old-fashioned patriotism. It is one of the most fully, truly American films ever produced—a movie which salutes the most avid constituents of the native consciousness: the flag, the family and the American ethic of up-the-ladder success.

Incidentally, perhaps not entirely accidentally, *Yankee Doodle Dandy* bears fascinating parallels to Cagney's own life. Like Cohan, Cagney began his career in vaudeville and, after years of struggling, rose to the pinnacle of his profession—for Cohan, Broadway and theatre; for Cagney, Hollywood and films. Also like Cohan, Cagney surrounded himself with members of his own family after his success. At one point, James had brothers William and Ed plus sister Jeanne on the Cagney Productions payroll. And, like the fictional Cohan of *Yankee Doodle Dandy,* Cagney married early in life to a show business woman who "retired" after their marriage while he went on to bigger achievements. The conclusion of *Yankee Doodle Dandy,* meanwhile, is strangely prophetic. When "modern-day" kids tell the elderly Cohan at his farm retreat that they

YANKEE DOODLE DANDY

have never heard of the famous performer, the scene predicts Cagney's own retirement into near-oblivion in the Sixties, and his own embrace with farming at the end of his career.

Yankee Doodle Dandy, still the actor's favourite film, opened to near-unanimous applause and widespread critical acclaim at a special New York City *première* in which seats were sold at prices ranging from $25 to $25,000 cash—the estimated $5,750,000 proceeds were then donated by Warners to the U.S. Treasury Department. New York reviewers practically swooned. "*Yankee Doodle Dandy,* the story of George M. Cohan, actor, songwriter, author and producer, is as perfectly timed for 1942 as *Sergeant York* was for 1941," wrote Archer Winsten of "The New York Post." "The latter came to a nation moving reluctantly into war, matched its objections with a famous conscientious objector of the last war, and solved his and our problems in a magnificent real life display of heroism. The former, now showing at the Hollywood Theatre, comes as our soldiers and sailors depart to fight on the seven seas and five continents. What could be more timely than to have recalled for us the career of America's lustiest flag-waver, the author of 'Over There'?" Wrote Howard Barnes of "The New York Herald Tribune": "The magic of *Yankee Doodle Dandy* is conjured up by the consummate Cagney portrayal. He even looks like Cohan at times and he has the great man's routines down cold. The point is that he adds his own individual reflections to the part, as should certainly be done in any dramatic impersonation of a celebrated figure. He has given many memorable and varied screen performances in the past, but this is nothing short of a brilliant tour-de-force of make-believe."

The film was nominated for eight Academy Awards: Best Picture, Supporting Actor (Huston), Original Story (Robert Buckner), Director (Curtiz), Editing (George Amy), Sound (Nathan Levinson), Musical Scoring (Heinz Roemheld and Ray Heindorf) and Actor (Cagney). Praise for Cagney was crowned by his second New York Critics prize for Best Acting and his first Academy Award as Best Actor. "Sensible people who attended the Academy dinner say Hollywood reached a new high in sappiness that night," reported a contemporary magazine. "Actresses wept unconvincingly and pushed other actresses around when those other actresses, also weeping unconvincingly, tried to hog the stage. It was a night of speeches in which some of the biggest people in motion pictures behaved as though they were bereft of their senses . . . only two speakers seemed to return a sense of balance. One was Irving Berlin and the other was James Cagney." When Gary Cooper tore open the envelope, the ovation was thunderous. Cagney's acceptance speech was brief. "I've always maintained," he said, "that in this business you are only as good as the other fellow thinks you are. It's nice to know that you people thought I did a good job. And don't forget that it was a good part, too. Thank you very much." The next day, according to contemporary accounts, Cagney placed the Oscar statuette on brother Bill's desk, to acknowledge his closest advisor's aid.

But, for Cagney, *Yankee Doodle Dandy* was the short-lived, bogus Emancipation Proclamation. Still impatient with Warners' roles, the bright exception of *Yankee Doodle Dandy* notwithstanding, and still itching to niggle with independent production, to control his own career, financially and artistically, he took advantage of the film's boom popularity (and a deceased contractual bind to Warners) to quit Warner Brothers once again. He announced the formation of his own Cagney Productions to be distributed through United Artists. Brother Bill signed on as company president; brother Ed hired on as company business manager; brother James, of course, was the company star. An embittered Jack Warner warned prophetically: "He'll find out that he needs me as much as I need him." Wrote one contemporary periodical: "One of the first orders received by Chuck Daggett, Cagney Productions' clever press agent, was to 'kill' the socko Cagney. Jimmy wanted the chance to appear as an artist." Financial support for the new movie production outfit came from the Bankers Trust Company of New York and Security First National of Los Angeles.

In an illuminating interview, shortly after the great divide, William Cagney traced the infamous Cagney/Warners schism straight back to *The Public Enemy* and the over inflated "tough guy" image that the actor was so wary of. "After that (*Sinner's Holiday*, 1930, Cagney's first screen role), some unimportant parts and what happens? Jimmy gets the lead in *Public Enemy*," Bill Cagney told "The New York Times." "You see how it works out. Suddenly, Jimmy clicks as a strictly 'dese, dem and dose' guy. A tough mug, so tough that every gangster in the country was nuts about him. They'd look at him up there on the screen and say to themselves, 'There's the guy who's tops in my business.' If they weren't too scared, they'd try to shake hands with him whenever they happened to see him in person. Jimmy was made but that wasn't all. He was typed—typed as exactly the kind of guy our mother had tried to push us farthest away from. So for ten years, Jimmy makes five pictures a year

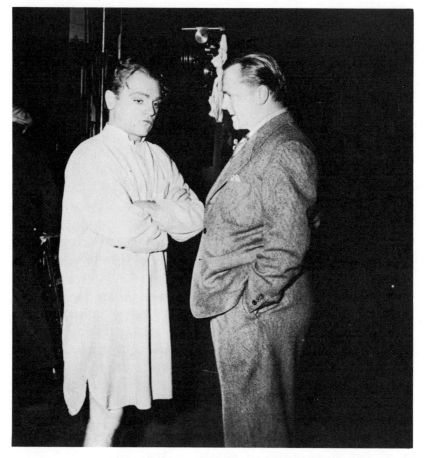

With Bill Cagney (on the set of JOHNNY COME LATELY)

and all the same Warner Brothers formula—Jimmy is a heel
for eight reels, then clean him up in the ninth. You didn't like
it, you argue, you're suspended, you get a reputation as a difficult actor—so usually you give in."

Thus did one of the most creative actor/studio alliances in
the history of Hollywood end. A close study of the actor's thir-
ty-seven Warner Brothers (and two Grand National) films produced during this early period reveals a tradition infinitely more
appealing and intriguing than the close-shaven, time-worn image
in which Cagney reaches across the breakfast table, half grapefruit in hand, and lets Mae Clarke "have it." The powerful,
profound Cagney persona was sometimes developed in spite
of, as much as because of, the tempestuous Cagney/Warners
collaboration. The conflict between studio and actor often mysteriously improved Cagney's films; other times it diminished their
quality. But with a bullet in his gut or a song in his heart, in-
eluctably, certain Cagneyesque characteristics stayed constant.

3

'Tribute to a Bad Man'

Independence, Backlash and Retirement:
from *Johnny Come Lately* to *One, Two, Three*

*"For a fellow who started film life as a mobster, Cagney
has come a long, laborious way. In his latest picture, United
Artists'* The Time of Your Life, *the movie adaptation of
William Saroyan's Pulitzer Prize play, Cagney is seen as a
whimsical and benevolent philosopher who dispenses help
and counsel to everyone who comes within his kindly orbit.
In other words, the man who started as the 'Public Enemy'
has emerged after a 17-year film evolution in the role of a
public benefactor. But it was a long, hard pull. After his
triumph as the ruthless hood in* Public Enemy, *his producers
rushed Cagney into a succession of tough guy roles. In movie
after movie he was shown, gun in hand, butt in mouth,
'rubbing out' rats or cops with monotonous regularity. Inevitably, a twin reaction set in. Public opinion rebelled
against movies which 'glorified gangsters.' And James Cagney objected to playing gangster parts. After prolonged
feuding with his producers, Cagney won his point. But even
to this day, a considerable section of the movie-going public
still thinks of Cagney primarily as a cinematic gangster."*
CAGNEY PRODUCTIONS PRESS RELEASE

What is most readily apparent about Cagney's post-1942 work
is the surprising extent to which producers tried to capitalise
on his Warners legacy, reducing his roles (but not always his
performances), in many instances, to flat, cartoon representa-
tions of earlier Cagney portrayals.

In his Fifties films, audiences could expect to encounter
(and did) familiar, battleworn qualities of the Cagney persona
in film after film after film. The pioneer Cagney-Warners films
of the Thirties became the models for the older, mature Cagney. *White Heat*, for example, parodies *The Public Enemy*. The
fresh, young hoodlum of *Public Enemy* becomes, with the passage of time, the eerie and brutal killer of *White Heat*. Simi-

larly, Roy Del Ruth's *West Point Story* is sewn together on a collection of "inside" Cagney jokes (such as the scene in which a West Point chorus boy wears a placard labelling himself a "Strawberry Blonde") quoted from past Cagney-Warners films. *One, Two, Three* is likewise constructed entirely on Cagney-based humour. Even the wall clock is a decorated Uncle Sam figurine in miniature that chimes "Yankee Doodle Dandy" on the hour. In *Starlift* (1951), Cagney plays himself in a cameo as a celebrity; in *Seven Little Foys* (1955) he plays himself playing George M. Cohan.

Cagney played Cagney, yielding to the public relations definition of the image, to a greater and different extent in the Fifties than he had ever been accused of doing by critics in the Thirties. The perennial dilemma of middle-aged movie stars in America haunted him. No longer was he ripe for romance pictures, the Hollywood staple, though he was still frequently and absurdly cast opposite rising ingenues. No longer could he be any sort of a "mama's boy." He was limited on the outside by the perimeters of Hollywood tradition and on the inside by his growing reluctance to agitate for better, out-of-the-ordinary roles.

He was affected by the principle of image-rebound: that an actor in the twilight of his career suffers from the reverberations of an image accumulated over the years. The prime of any film actor's career (especially in the Thirties when stars were usually show business lifers and not simply overnight sensations) is taken up by a relentless pressure—artistic as well as financial—to introduce an original screen character (personality), to develop that character and to cultivate a mass following, thereby achieving genuine and permanent star status. The route to such success is, by nature, slow, measured in years gone by, and the unfortunate by-product of the journey is a backlash. The performer becomes bound to his own past. Theoretically, though success should enable a performer to expand the depth and variety of his characterisations, time narrows the scope and star status actually prompts an opposite effect. Filmmakers, audiences and eventually the performer himself come to know, appreciate and exploit only the long-operative image. The uncommon bids for deviation are customarily met with bewilderment on the part of audiences. What happened to Chaplin and his fans with the misunderstood *Monsieur Verdoux* also happened to Cagney when he produced *Johnny Come Lately*: image-rebound. In the Fifties, Cagney was defined by his past. His parts were confined generally to mirror-reflection roles, trimmed to their common and recognisable essence. Only Cagney Productions, his short-lived independent company, attempted resolutely to offer Cagney roles of a greater and richer variety.

All the more remarkable then, that Cagney's post-1942 films still often exude such a high degree of professional integrity, due to Cagney's basic honesty as a performer, and his thankful ability to support or sustain the most improbable storyline. Some of his post-*Yankee Doodle Dandy* work is even superior to much of his Thirties Warners fare. And two of his independent films, *Johnny Come Lately* and *The Time of Your Life*, are among his best films, for only as an independent did Cagney ever approach the realisation of his own, individual artistic vision.

Johnny Come Lately, the first Cagney Productions film and Cagney's first screen appearance after *Yankee Doodle Dandy*, was (and is) the most complete and exhilarating exposition of the Cagney "alter ego" on film. In the movie, described by brother Bill for the "Saturday Evening Post" as "a simple tale of human hearts" (and reportedly chosen by the Cagney brothers only after 400 scripts had been examined), Cagney offers a characterisation which could not be more spectacularly opposite from his gangster image; it is his most accomplished reversal, drawing background for its legitimacy not only from the earlier independent films, *Great Guy* and *Something to Sing About*, which feature crusading and lovable good guys, but also from Cagney's omnipresent other side, the inbred charm and goodness, here displayed in their purest form. *Johnny Come Lately* is the most personal cinematic accomplishment of his career.

The little-seen *Johnny Come Lately* side of Cagney's screen persona is Chaplinesque as well as Cagneyesque. The Tom Richards (Cagney) of *Johnny Come Lately* is, like Chaplin, literally a tramp, a hobo without means of subsistence, a kindly and courageous person who mysteriously hops a train to an unknown destination after he has entered a small town and stirred a great, grass roots uprising. The tramp connection is unmistakable, almost as if Cagney had intended the analogy and modelled his role after Chaplin (just as, in *City for Conquest*, the ending is too similar to *City Lights* to be entirely unconscious).

In fact, liberties were taken with the background story, "It Takes All Kinds" by Louis Bromfield (originally titled "You Get What You Give" and later retitled "McLeod's Folly"), which indicate a calculated effort to mould the leading character, Tom Richards, into a Chaplinesque personality. In the novelette, the character's name is Tom Richardson, age 29, from Boston, Massachusetts, living in New York City, a "cold and stiff" fellow who is "writing a series of articles on how badly the wandering honest fellow out of work is treated." In the Cagney film, all of this restrictive information is dropped: the character's name becomes Tom Richards, his age becomes unknown (and thus ageless), his background becomes unknown (and thus mysterious), and his personality becomes pure samaritan.

The Tom Richards of Cagney's *Johnny Come Lately* is a worldly, sensitive, charming, and heroic tramp. Like Chaplin, Cagney disappears into the distance at the end of the film, a nameless wanderer aboard a freight train, making his lone way, like Charlie, down the road of life. These Chaplinesque qualities have been commandeered by Cagney to fit his own conception.

It is apparent from the first moments that *Johnny Come Lately* is an extraordinary and special film. The camera, guided by director William K. Howard, drifts peacefully along the streets of a small town, pausing to catch the conversation of several hoboes and stopping to observe the slow waking movements of the populace. The rest of the film is as leisurely as the beginning: it is nearly two full hours before the entire tale unfolds, several minutes before the lovely newspaper publisher Vinnie McLeod (Grace George) is introduced, and a part-reel before Cagney as tramp newspaperman Richards is presented as he sits beneath a town statue, absorbed in a volume of Dickens. *Johnny Come Lately* is not as vigorous and fast-paced as so many of Cagney's other films (save *The Time of Your Life*). It is instead a calm and nostalgic evocation of a make-believe rural (not urban) past, seen here through rose-coloured glasses, and given loving treatment by Cagney Productions.

The story concerns a campaign by elderly, crusading newspaperwoman Vinnie McLeod, a smart, beatific lady who cares for tramps who are passing through her home town, and who enlists the aid of Richards in her journalistic battle against town corruption. *Johnny Come Lately*'s greatest asset is undeniably veteran stage actress Grace George, who was persuaded by Cagney to take her only film role ever as Vinnie McLeod. She is simply elegant, radiating a beauty and dignity which is as uncommon in Hollywood as in real life. Quiet, smiling, plodding on despite the death of her husband, threats by her

With Grace George in JOHNNY COME LATELY

competitor and the reluctant pawning, piece by piece, of her estate, she is the embattled picture of honour and noble resistance. The elderly editor wraps her treasured houseware in plain paper so that her friends and neighbours will not know what she is selling—and also so that she can pretend to herself that she is not relinquishing her beloved family relics. She defends Richards in court, rescuing him from a vagrancy sentence, and then explains her actions by telling him that it was "because you were reading Dickens." Her logic is as impeccable as her virtue; she is a grey but luminous presence throughout the film.

She is aided by one of the most delightful troupes of supporting players ever. Hattie McDaniel is Aida, the cook of the McLeod household, with a smile as broad as her bulk and a sultry, Germanic glare that complements her name. She fairly rumbles through her part with the authority of a hard-to-dislike bulldozer, flirting with Cagney to certify her sexuality and stubbornly refusing at one point to even prepare a "decent" meal until McLeod and Richards will include her in their business affairs. Still another middle-aged woman, Marjorie Main as saloon madam Gashouse Mary, is the cockeyed third partner of the triumvirate. Bejewelled, feathered, decked out in fancy dance hall satins, she is a raucous cynic who will not join the town-cleaning crusade until her old friend Vinnie is nearly killed by a nocturnal assassin. Earthy and loud, she is looked down on by the local high society crowd but she nevertheless insists, "I run a straight place."

Even the minor roles in *Johnny Come Lately* are filled by a cast of eccentrics, all perfectly small-town types who dispatch their roles with flourish and enchantment. Among the company are Edward McNamara as the crooked politico (a man who sings melodious nonsense rhymes to himself while

With Marjorie Main in JOHNNY COME LATELY

passing the time), Robert Barrat as timid legislator Bill Swain (who was once engaged to Gashouse Mary; they broke up when he insisted on pouring catsup over everything), Margaret Hamilton and George Cleveland as the Fergusons, life-long employees of the McLeod paper (he, ever-drunk and bumbling; she, complaining and old-maidenish), and even a little pet mouse "who comes around every lunchtime for his food." A quaint, witty and pacific scenario by John Van Druten ("Nothing ever gets changed around here," reports one player. "That's the charm of the place"), and a lilting score by Leigh Harline round out the notable technical contributions to the production.

Cagney himself delivered his most individual performance. Like the real-life actor—who off-screen, is an avid amateur poet and a skilled artist—Tom Richards is a poet and an artist. *Johnny Come Lately* is the only film in which these most private Cagney concerns are publicly demonstrated. A fellow bum quotes a thoughtful verse entitled "Open Road to Freedom" and then tells Cagney as they ride along the countryside in an open box car that some fellow named Tom Richards wrote it. Cagney only smiles. For McLeod's paper, Richards sketches bold caricatures in swift, confident strokes; his clever cartoons stimulate a sharp upsurge in the local circulation. The vagrant journalist is discovered initially as he sits against a city square park statue laughing to himself as he peruses Dickens' *Pickwick Papers*. In his hand a pencil is poised to underline memorable passages. Later, he is nearly jailed by the town magistrate when he refuses to be adjudged transient; the tramp explains calmly that he prefers travel to work.

Of Richards' past, nothing is known. It is hinted that he once was involved in an unhappy love affair, and lost. He implies that he was once a crusading journalist full-time ("I tried it once myself," he says). He seems barely interested in the obvious romantic possibilities between himself and young Jane (Marjorie Lord), Vinnie McLeod's niece. Instead, he lavishes attention on Grace George, Hattie McDaniel and Marjorie Main, playing long and elaborate "love scenes" with each in turn, flirting softly with the three women who (in spite of the contrary Hollywood tradition) are all closer to Cagney's real age than the ingenue.

Cagney resorts to violence only twice, and briefly. The first instance he tosses a chair through a window in sudden anger when Vinnie McLeod's life is threatened by a stooge in the pay of W. W. Dougherty, the town boss. The second time is a gentlemanly square-off between Richards and Pete (Bill Henry), son of Dougherty. Thus, in *Johnny Come Lately*, the Cagney persona underwent its most drastic revision, as Cagney Productions steered the actor's career along his own preferred course. Sweet, gentle, quixotic, magical—these were the qualities of Tom Richards. They were the same characteristics long considered the "charming" side of Tom Powers, Cagney in *The Public Enemy*. Cagney (and many critics) had been waiting over 12 years for the one self to completely overwhelm the other; *Johnny Come Lately* fulfilled the expectations.

Resembling a Frank Capra film, but perhaps even more optimistic, idealistic and visionary, *Johnny Come Lately* espouses the same brand of populist politics as a film like Capra's *It's A Wonderful Life* (1946). The difference is that Capra's problems are never really resolved at the conclusion of his films (the banker of *It's A Wonderful Life* is free to continue his crooked, financial deals) while the small-town citizens of *Johnny Come Lately* oust newspaper magnate Dougherty permanently, and all is therefore well. This is the hopeful message of *Johnny Come Lately*: that the problems of the world can be solved by teamwork and goodness. *Johnny Come Lately* was Cagney's last and most assured hurrah as a full-blown reformist and humanist. Cagney ultimately changed and so did his films. The movies which followed *Johnny Come Lately* become increasingly sceptical, progressively cynical, and, ultimately, reactionary.

Johnny Come Lately was a dismal failure, financially (it bombed at the box-office) and even critically; and it was two full years before Cagney Productions could recover sufficiently to mount a second film, *Blood on the Sun*. Released in the midst of the Second World War, *Johnny Come Lately* was already an anachronism in 1943, a year which was deluged from January to December by war films. The whimsy of *Johnny Come Lately*, so untimely and so atypically Cagney, offended critics who expected more conventional, hard-hitting films from the new production firm.

Wrote John T. McManus in "P.M.": "*Johnny Come Lately* is almost the kind of business that might result if Jimmy Cagney, the immortal Hollywood movie star, had returned to play the lead in the annual production of his old high school's Masque and Film Club. *Johnny Come Lately* is so palpably amateurish in production and direction, so hopelessly stagey, uneven and teamless in performance and so utterly pointless that it is bound to cause raised eyebrows wherever it is shown."

"To put it bluntly," echoed Archer Winston in the "New York Post," "it is an old-fashioned story told in a very old-fashioned manner. Please, Mr. Cagney for the benefit of the public, yourself and Warners go back where you made pictures like *Yankee Doodle Dandy*."

The few reviewers who recognised the high merit of *Johnny Come Lately* raved about the film in terms starkly unlike those accorded the production by most contemporary critics. "Grace George," eloquently wrote the critic for "Time," "seems effortlessly to have learned what so many transplanted Broadway actors ache over—how to project her touching elegance in a medium new to her. James Cagney, who in his time had to plant fists or a grapefruit on young ladies' faces and shoes on young ladies' behinds, here develops his tenderest relationship with middle-aged ladies (the Misses George, Main and Hattie McDaniel), and each of them is worth a dozen average love scenes . . . These pleasures would have been all but impossible to manufacture in any of the large studios, for they are given their warmth and life by the pleasure that the Cagneys' large cast and the whole production outfit obviously took in doing a job as they wanted to do it. Bit players who have tried creditably for years to walk in shoes that pinched them show themselves in this picture as the very competent actors they always were: there has seldom been as good a cinematic gallery of U.S. small-town types."

After *Johnny Come Lately, Blood on the Sun* (1945), his next independent work, is an outright disappointment. Directed by Frank Lloyd (for whom Cagney had once appeared as an "extra" in M-G-M's *Mutiny on the Bounty*, 1935, during a Warners walkout), the film is a distressingly obvious attempt to cash in on anti-Japanese sentiment during the Second World War. An abrupt change-of-pace from *Johnny Come Lately* (the box office lesson was apparently well-learned) and the most ordinary of all the Cagney Productions' films, *Blood on the Sun* is a blunt manipulation of Cagney's "tough guy" image.

The story, with Cagney as an American newspaper editor in Tokyo in the Twenties battling a secret Tanaka plot by Japanese militarists to conquer China, is studded with moments which are unbearably hackneyed and unbelievably lacklustre. Tanaka, for example, is called "an Oriental Hitler" in case the then-current analogy would escape dullards. In the popular politics of the day, the film is staunchly anti-Japanese and avowedly pro-Chinese. The Japanese are nicknamed "monkeys" by Nick Condon (Cagney)—one of them is portrayed

With Jack Halloran in BLOOD ON THE SUN

with absolute amateurishness by Jack Halloran, an ex-Los Angeles cop turned actor who gave Cagney judo lessons for the
film. In his first scene, Halloran squeezes his hand nervously,
just within the camera frame. Another of the Japanese is in
the unlikely hands of Robert Armstrong, Cagney's old friend.
In Oriental make-up, bald and monocled, Armstrong is hope-
less as Colonel Tojo, the conniving Japanese militarist. Sylvia
Sidney, returning to the screen in *Blood on the Sun* after an
absence from Hollywood, is equally ludicrous as the Mata Hari-
ish half-Japanese, half-Chinese (she is working for a "free China") double spy who mysteriously slips in and out of the shadows.

The script is ruinous. Sidney says to Cagney, "You've had
me off balance ever since you came in." And Cagney tells her,
as the Japanese Secret Police storm through the doors of their
hideout: "You'd better hurry, darling. This neighbourhood is
getting rundown." Cagney is saddled with one of his most hope-
less parts as Nick Condon, the newsman who risks his life to
save the China Republic. The risk never seems too dangerous,
however, for Condon, a masterful Judo expert, seems capable
of felling countless Japanese villains with one foul blow. At the
end, when Condon taunts the slow-witted Oshima (Halloran)
into duelling with him as an equal at Judo, the newsman's triumph is inevitable. What transpires is several minutes of sheer

groans and thuds, as Halloran and Cagney battle it out in a raw and exciting struggle. The fight is authentic, because Cagney trained long and hard for his judo scenes. But Condon wins, of course, by resorting to his fists (the American way) and escapes, eluding several dozen Japanese police along the way. The brief judo recess is unfortunately not enough to rescue the entire movie.

Blood on the Sun is the least independent-minded of all the Cagney Productions movies, and an unforgivably mediocre film besides. It nevertheless has links to *Johnny Come Lately* and, specifically, to Cagney, that are interesting. The major characters of both films, for example, are crusading newspapermen in search of justice (much like Frank Ross in *Each Dawn I Die*). And both crusaders (remembering the usual optimism of Cagney Productions) are successful. The later, more universally-oriented *Blood on the Sun*, concludes when Condon, wounded and surrounded by hostile Japanese, stumbles into the court of the U.S. Embassy, to safety. "The United States doesn't settle for a deal," Cagney shouts as he is led inside. "Forgive your enemies, but first get even." The message is considerably cruder, less idealistic, than *Johnny Come Lately* but for Cagney it was the coming direction. Lukewarm in all respects, *Blood on the Sun* prompted a response in kind from critics and audiences.

The relative failure of his first two independent films prompted Cagney to sign with 20th Century-Fox for a role in *13 Rue Madeleine,* directed by Henry Hathaway. His contract stipulated eight weeks of work for $300,000 for his role as Bob Sharkey, leader of the wartime O.S.S. (a part Rex Harrison reportedly declined). "James Cagney was a marvellous actor," Henry Hathaway has said, "but then he formed his own company and nobody could get him any more except for pictures with his own company. When you cast a picture you get the kind of a man—fast-talking, aggressive, strong—who could run this spy school in *13 Rue Madeleine.*"

"Fast-talking, aggressive, strong"—it was a return to Warners form for Cagney. Described by one character as "this wonderful tough guy from Minnesota," Sharkey is a methodical spy who gives his life behind enemy lines during the Second World War in a desperate mission to gather intelligence information and kill an infiltrating German double agent. The film is rendered in mock-documentary style, modelled after producer Louis de Rochemont's *March of Time* series and his previous documentary-fiction success, *The House on 92nd Street* (1945).

In 13 RUE MADELEINE

Slickly assembled and competently acted by an efficient cast
(including Annabella, Richard Conte, Frank Latimore, Sam Jaffe and Blanche Yurka), *13 Rue Madeleine* is a solid film though
unimportant to Cagney's career, except for a few particulars.
It is notable, firstly, for an ending which is strangely prophetic. Captured by the Germans, Sharkey is blown to smither-
eens by his own forces when the allies order the demolition of
13 Rue Madeleine, the address of the German spy headquarters in France; the allies fear that Sharkey may be tortured into revealing important war secrets. Battered and bruised, the
walls of the building crumbling around him, Sharkey laughs
hysterically, maniacally, gleeful that his enemies are going to
their deaths with him, happy that he has withstood the torture.
The scene predicts Cody Jarrett's likewise eruptive death in
White Heat.   It seems relevant that here Cagney is martyred
without needing to go through the process of reform, the *Fighting 69th* kind of death. Certainly it is because he is a "wonderful tough guy" and *13 Rue Madeleine* is a curiously transitional film in that it begins to introduce the socially-accept-
able Cagney. Though he was to die without undergoing reform
in *White Heat, Kiss Tomorrow Goodbye* and *A Lion is in the
Streets,* he died in all those post-WWII films as a gangster.
13 Rue Madeleine clears the path for later "wonderful tough guy"
films of the Fifties, films in which the Cagney character did

not, would not have to, die. Most importantly, the funds from *13 Rue Madeleine* afforded Cagney the opportunity to make *The Time of Your Life,* his swan song as a happy-go-lucky charmer.

It was again two entire years before Cagney Productions could release another film but it was well worth the wait for *The Time of Your Life* (1948), blood relative to *Johnny Come Lately.* Playwright William Saroyan turned down lucrative offers for the film right to his play from several major studios; then he leased the rights to his famous property to Cagney Productions for seven years. The odd terms of the agreement is the main reason why *The Time of Your Life* is the rarest of all Cagney films, unavailable for television showing or rental in the United States today (only two known copies exist —in the Cagney Productions vault and in the Library of Congress). Yet it is also, with *Johnny Come Lately,* the most wistful and imaginative, the most beautiful of Cagney's films. It is not only, like *Johnny Come Lately,* blankly opposed to the heretofore public image of Cagney as a knuckles-in-the-face rowdy, but it is an independent Cagney Production in the most complete (family) sense: James Cagney starred, William Cagney produced, Jeanne Cagney co-starred and Edward Cagney served as Assistant Production Manager.

As in *Johnny Come Lately,* the major strength of *The Time of Your Life* lies in its assortment of outlandish cast members. The Saroyan play is about a bizarre collection of people who frequent a San Francisco waterfront bar and scenarist Nathaniel Curtis faithfully adapted the drama. William Bendix is Nick, the bartender and owner, who is in love with his occupation but forever grumbling about the weird ways of his customers. Wayne Morris is little-boy naïve as Tom, the sidekick; and Jeanne Cagney is melancholy ex-hooker Kitty Duval. Broderick Crawford and Ward Bond enter briefly to swap arguments and sip beer. James Barton is crusty and magnificent as Kit Carson, the great pretender of the West who spins tales even he doesn't believe. Paul Draper is Harry, the mercurial dancer, and James Lydon is the ingenuous Dudley, a young gallant who cannot reach his girl-friend on the phone. Blick, the seedy, cruel villain of the piece, is played with brute force by an obscure actor named Tom Powers (shades of *Public Enemy* and a curious irony).

Like Tom Richards in *Johnny Come Lately,* Joe (Cagney) is a mysterious person. He sits about Nick's saloon drinking bottle after bottle of expensive champagne and listening to turn-of-the-century records. He is an amateur philosopher; he buys children's toys on a whim, bets large sums of money on chance horses and impulsively chews huge wads of gum. Cagney's characterisation is absolutely removed from any reference to his Warners past, save the finale. Joe is cheerful, inquisitive and marvellously fanciful, more profound and intellectual than the Warners Cagney. He is always deep in thought, and always good-natured.

The difference between the Cagney of *The Time of Your Life* and the Warners Cagney is further stressed by physical staging. Joe never moves from his seat at the table in front of the bar. He is asked to dance twice, but both times he refuses, explaining that he cannot dance. "I don't even like to walk," he adds. The Warners Cagney was virtually defined by his physicality. More than other performers, Cagney constantly found his entire body within the camera frame, attesting to the fascination of directors for the movement and action of his body. *The Time of Your Life* discounts this heritage and Cagney spends the entire movie seated. Instead of his arms and legs, Cagney uses his face—voice and eyes—to accomplish his role.

Only once does Joe in *The Time of Your Life* establish his physical presence and that is at the conclusion of the film, in which Saroyan's original finish is abandoned in lieu of a Cagney Productions substitute. In the play, Blick is shot and killed off-stage by Kit Carson. This ending was actually filmed but discarded after audience previews. Instead, in the Cagney Productions version, Blick is thrashed by Joe in an extended brawl. He pounds Blick with windmill fists until the thug collapses in an unconscious heap on the floor. When Blick revives, Nick throws the bully out of the saloon, and Joe and Kit Carson return to drinking and swapping stories, as the film fades out. Though the altered climax gave Cagney an excuse to use his fists (all of his non-gangster films, even his independent productions, still contain the mandatory fight scene —evidencing his reluctance to completely disinherit his violent image), it was also really less violent than Saroyan's conclusion. In the Cagney version of *The Time of Your Life,* no-one is killed. All ends happily. In line with the independent policy begun by Cagney with *Great Guy,* the film is a self-contained world in which the problems are resolved by righteous campaign.

"Early one morning two or three weeks ago," wrote Saroyan in a letter to Cagney Productions, "I stood in line at the

With Jeanne Cagney and Wayne Morris in THE TIME OF YOUR LIFE

United Artist Theater and bought a ticket to the first showing of *The Time of Your Life* in San Francisco. I did this because as you know, I wrote the play and wanted to find out as quickly as possible if my kind of writing could be made to mean anything at all in a movie. The people came into the theatre and sat down and finally the lights dimmed and the movie started. It wasn't more than three minutes until I had forgotten that I had written the play. I was too busy enjoying it to care who wrote it. Before I knew it the film was over, and as far as I was able to tell everybody in the theatre was sorry it was over. That bar was just naturally a very good place to visit. All by way of telling you I think you have made one of the most original and entertaining movies I have seen. Furthermore, I have no intention of pretending that it's my fault that you have made such a film, for I think the truth of the matter is this: that you and your associates have expertly edited and translated into the medium of the motion picture a most difficult and almost unmanageable body of material. I send you congratulations, profound thanks and all good wishes."

Saroyan's enthusiasm was not shared by most critics and, at the box-office, *The Time of Your Life* plunged to failure, perhaps because audiences, again as with Cagney's other independent projects, had difficulty adjusting their view of him. There were some defenders, including the always perceptive and astute James Agee who wrote a complimentary appraisal of the production in "Time" magazine: "Those who made the picture have given it something very sure. It's obvious that they love the play and their work in it, and their affection and enjoyment are highly contagious."

Since *Yankee Doodle Dandy,* Cagney had sought in vain for a smash hit property. The Forties was his leanest period of activity. Only four Cagney films, three of them independents, were produced and released within a seven-year stretch, from 1942 to 1949. Cagney Productions badly needed an economic booster.

Mediocre box office, poor distribution and even lawsuit difficulties (with the Sam Goldwyn Studio—Cagney Productions reneged on a space rental contract—the suit was settled out of court) combined to pressure Cagney into a bargaining position. The actor signed a distribution-production deal with Warners and an agreement to return to profitable gangsterism in the climactic *White Heat.* The films which opened and closed the Forties for Cagney could not be more unalike. *Yankee Doodle Dandy,* a rousing musical, had granted an avenue to independent production and personal themes. But the avenue was detoured and at the end of the roadway was *White Heat,* still the most savage gangster film ever produced. For Cagney, it was a comeback, the logical retreat for the ageing star. Yet it was also a re-birth. *White Heat* began Cagney's career anew, in much the same way as *Public Enemy* had crystallised his future nearly twenty years earlier. As the earlier gangster film had introduced the young Cagney, replete with characteristics and mannerisms destined to become familiar to Thirties audiences, so did *White Heat* present the older Cagney, in updated form, with a style suited to the changed Cagney and the changed times.

The most significant difference between Tom Powers and Cody Jarrett, between the Thirties "tough guy" and the Fifties "tough guy," between the young Cagney and the mature Cagney, was the near abolition of the sympathetic qualities of the Cagney persona. Cody Jarrett was not irresistible or green or engaging like Tom Powers. Jarrett was wild and neurotic and murderous. Tom Powers could flirt teasingly with

In WHITE HEAT

young women or laugh with easygoing abandon. Cody was intense and cold and unrelaxed. Any moment, he could be triggered into a dangerous outburst. Paunchy (for the first time) and greying, Cagney had changed physically, too. The change meant that Cody was no longer a romantic commodity and it soured his relationship also with friends and relatives—his mob, his wife and his mother.

Like Cody, his Ma Jarrett is a twisted and insane person, without compassion. She is as vicious as Cody. And Cagney's legendary background—the consideration always prominent in the script that the Cagney persona was either from a broken home or a poverty-stricken childhood—is missing in *White Heat*. Cody is described as simply deranged, just mad. *White Heat* is the official goodbye from Warners to the social consciousness gangster films of the Thirties and Forties. For Cagney it was a brusque and permanent severance with a portion of his image, with a segment of his past. What remained was a variation of the "tough guy"—tougher and less complex—and this new revised Cagney persona became Cagney's Fifties trademark.

White Heat is, regardless, along with *Yankee Doodle Dandy*, Cagney's best film, boasting a singular compound of compatible elements, technical and artistic, which unload a mind-boggling sting: Raoul Walsh's surging direction; the frightening, original story by Virginia Kellogg (and screenplay by Ivan Goff and Ben Roberts); terrifyingly cold-blooded performances from Virginia Mayo, Margaret Wycherly, Steve Cochran and Edmond O'Brien.

Cody Jarrett is Cagney's consummate gangster portrayal. "You got a good memory for names," the pot-bellied thug warns a train engineer at the beginning of the film, as he and his gang are holding up the train. He calmly points his gun at the man and shoots, blasting him to the floor of the cab, but as the engineer falls, he jars a lever which releases steam from the side of the train: it is the first appearance of the motif of white heat. A luckless member of the mob is seared by the blinding hot spray; several days later, Cody abandons the dying man in a mountain retreat after instructing a confederate to shoot the suffering gang member and "put him out of his misery." These berserk incidents begin a long series of increasingly violent happenings that do not end until Cody kills himself in the finale. Throughout (during a prison interim and a daring plan to rob a California oil company), Cody suffers from severe, recurring headaches which threaten to push him into lunacy, and eventually do. "It's like having a red hot buzz saw inside my head," he tells Ma Jarrett, who lovingly massages his neck to relieve his pain—until she is murdered by a bullet in the back and replaced in her task by Hank Fallon, Cody's only friend, a surrogate mother, an insidious Pat O'Brien figure (played by Edmond O'Brien).

Cody is crazy and unpredictable. He is a mama's boy ("Where Ma goes, Cody goes," explains an FBI agent) who clings to his mother with the zeal of a fanatic and the faith of a child. Cagney is the only actor who could have merged these disparate elements—the violence, sickness and maternal dependence—into a believable whole. He did it by sheer energy and vitality and presence. It is his casualness which is so disarming, as in the scene when Cody chews a hot dog absent-mindedly while he shoots a stooge through a car trunk. It is also his steep, wild-man pose that is so thrilling, as in the memorable, compelling sequence in which Cody, in prison, learns of his Ma's death. Stricken, screaming, garbling indistinguish-

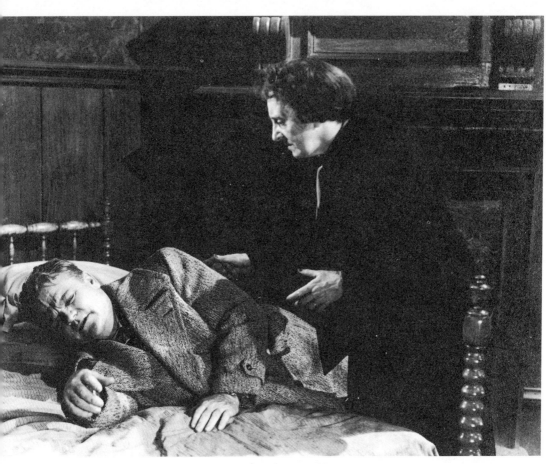

With Margaret Wycherly (above) and Edmond O'Brien (below)
in WHITE HEAT

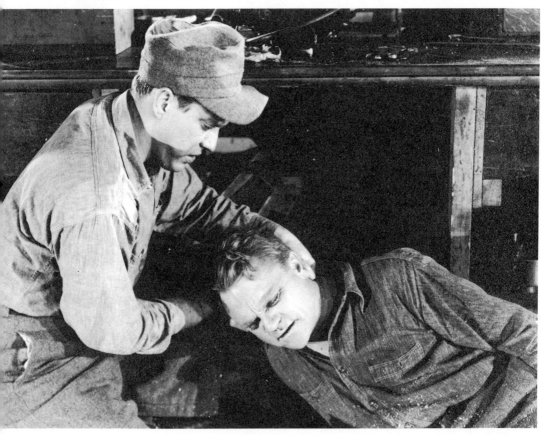

able words, Cagney staggers to his feet and blindly swings his fists at guards who try to subdue him; his moans virtually echo off the walls of the huge prison commissary as he is led away, howling at the top of his lungs.

The brilliant and stunning climax has Cagney laughing and wailing simultaneously atop a huge oil tanker as police swarm around him like waiting buzzards. The laugh belongs slightly to the Thirties Cagney, the charmer, in an odd way. Out of place and out of time, it is a properly perverse final proof that Cody has at last teetered over the brink. Fallon spies Cody through a telescope lens and shoots him with a long range rifle. Cody laughs. Fallon shoots again. Cody laughs again, louder. Fallon shoots once more. Cody stumbles to his knees, still laughing, and then stands straight and unafraid. He aims his own pistol at the gas tank beneath his feet and shoots. There is a terrific, uproarious explosion, and, as the flames surround and envelop him, his voice is heard audibly above the din: "Made it, Ma! Top of the world!" And, strangely, he is still laughing. It is not simply death but a defiant suicide. Cody Jarrett's farewell is also (with few exceptions) a farewell to the Thirties Cagney.

White Heat raised a critical storm. Noted critics worried aloud whether Cagney's performance was socially injurious because it was so raunchy and, seemingly, sympathetic. Even Bosley Crowther in the "New York Times" admitted, after praising the production, that "*White Heat* is also a cruelly vicious film and its impact upon the emotions of the unstable or impressionable is incalculable. That is an observation which might be borne in mind by those who would exercise caution in supporting such matter on the screen." "Cue" magazine agreed: "In *White Heat*, you are subjected to an unending procession of what is probably the most gruesome aggregation of brutalities ever presented upon the motion picture screen under the guise of entertainment."*

West Point Story followed *White Heat*, also for Warner Brothers in 1950, reuniting Cagney with director Roy Del Ruth for the first time since *Lady Killer* in 1933. It was a musical comedy and rough re-make of Warners' *Flirtation Walk* (friend Pat O'Brien played in the feeble 1934 original directed by Frank Borzage with Ruby Keeler and Dick Powell). The Brothers evi-

---

* "If it has a pernicious social influence," countered Kenneth Tynan later in his famous essay, "that is probably Cagney's fault, and there is no space here to balance the old scales between art and morality. For myself, I do not mind walking the Edgware Road in peril as long as there is a Cagney picture at the Marble Arch."

dently hoped to ape Cagney's blockbusters *Yankee Doodle Dandy* and *Footlight Parade* in the same loose manner as *White Heat* aped *Public Enemy* and achieve equally triumphant results. Alas, Roy Del Ruth was no Michael Curtiz, lead character El-win Bixby was no George M. Cohan and *West Point Story* was no *Yankee Doodle Dandy*.

Bixby (Cagney), an out-of-work Broadway musical director, reluctantly agrees to stage the annual West Point variety show, as the film begins. The crafty impresario is also scouting the talents of cadet Tom Fletcher (Gordon MacRae), who could be a Broadway star, according to Bixby, if the young cadet can be persuaded to resign from the Academy. "The measure of Mr. Cagney's impact upon the whole tenuous show," wrote Bosley Crowther in a typical review for the film, "is patently indicated when he is not on the screen. For then the thing sags in woeful fashion, the romance becomes absurd and the patri-otic chest-thumping becomes so much chorus-boy parade."

Cagney is joined in *West Point Story* by a dim cast includ-ing Virginia Mayo (Warners intended a re-run of the *White Heat* team's success), Gene Nelson, Alan Hale Jr., Doris Day and Gordon MacRae. Continuing in the *White Heat* vein, Cag-ney gives a raging, blistering performance, virtually pounding, single-handedly, the West Point show into shape. At one point he throws a *White Heat*-like fit when the cadets cannot man-age to march in unison. He stamps his feet, yells, jumps up

With Virginia Mayo in WEST POINT STORY

and down in a frenzy and kicks a nearby piano. Then he demonstrates the proper method of dance, bounding and stepping
barbarously. He is good and rambunctious, so good that the
rest of the story can be gratefully ignored. Though Virginia
Mayo is obviously too young to be his sweetheart and though
Cagney is painfully too old to masquerade inside a bulging
West Point uniform, *West Point Story* almost (but not quite)
overcomes its weaknesses through Cagney's grand burst of vitality.

West Point Story is the first in the line of Cagney vehicles
of the Fifties, films tailored to the older Cagney, but it is not
without its exact references to Cagney's filmic past. As in Del
Ruth's own *Lady Killer,* the running gag of *West Point Story*
is the Cagneyesque right-fisted punch. Bixby, ever hot temered, slugs his producer whenever he settles a contract; and the
impresario, shades of General Patton, is even thrown out of
West Point because he slugs a cadet. Other citations are even
more specific. Eve Dillon (Virginia Mayo), Bixby's secretary,
complains to West Point personnel that Bixby's grudge against
the Army began "when he asked for a size eight shoe and they
gave him a twelve. And he hasn't been the same since" (a scene
which occurs nearly verbatim twice, in *Here Comes the Navy*
and *The Fighting 69th*); and Bixby dances the "Brooklyn" number finale as a last-minute substitute after he accidentally k.o.'s
the lead dancer (an exact parallel to the ending of *Footlight
Parade*).

By the terms of his *White Heat* contract, the actor's cherished Cagney Productions was kept alive by a clause that guaranteed at least two additional films to be co-produced in association with Warners. The first of these two productions was
an adaptation, in 1951, of a seamy novel by Horace McCoy
entitled *Kiss Tomorrow Goodbye*.

Today the film enjoys an immense underground reputation
among gangster film fanatics, and also a devoted following
among *film noir* enthusiasts who swear by its violent lunacy.
For example, Paul Schrader, in his widely-circulated notes on
"The Film Noir" for a recent retrospective at the Los Angeles
County Museum of Art, cites *Kiss Tomorrow Goodbye* as the
sickly legitimate follow-up to *White Heat*—a movie, like *Kiss
Tomorrow Goodbye*, in Schrader's opinion, that orgiastically celebrates a psychotic Cagney as *noir* hero. Well-known critic Raymond Durgnat reserves a special comment for the film in his
respected "The Family Tree of Film Noir," published in August, 1970 in the British "Cinema." Classifying *Kiss Tomorrow*

Goodbye under "Crime as Social Criticism," sub-headed under the cryptic "Prohibition-type Gangsterism" category, Durgnat calls the film "quiet but astonishing," and compares it to George Stevens's *A Place in the Sun*, also released in 1951 (both films employed the same scenarist, Harry Brown). "Post war gangster films," argues Durgnat, "are curiously devoid of all social criticism, except the post-war appeal to conscience, apart from its devious but effective reintroduction in *Bonnie and Clyde*." Both Schrader and Durgnat, in concert with the current, popular thought among *film noir* devotees, contend that *Kiss Tomorrow Goodbye* fulfils the basic criterion for excellent *film noir*: dark, pessimistic, corrupt and relentlessly cynical (Durgnat's description).

Yet *Kiss Tomorrow Goodbye* is the most misunderstood and misinterpreted film Cagney ever produced. Consider the history of his independent film-making—a history of reaction to the actor's much-touted image. Steadfastly, throughout his career, Cagney maintained an opposition to the overindulgent, super-violent excesses of his Warners-honed screen persona. He responded to his bulging image as America's cinema "Public Enemy" first by newspaper and magazine interviews in which he consistently attacked the redundancy and social unworthiness of his roles, then by a series of celebrated walkouts in the Thirties, and finally by his high-minded independent productions. *Kiss Tomorrow Goodbye* can only be appreciated in this personal context. The grimy property that was originally Horace McCoy's was transformed into a James Cagney adaptation. "*Film noir*" is a hindsight analysis. Nothing could be further from the actual circumstances, style, intent and content of the production.

Actually, *Kiss Tomorrow Goodbye* is Cagney Productions' retort to the genuine article—*White Heat*. While *White Heat* is a violent, uncompromising movie that brilliantly exploits every dirty angle of criminal degeneracy, *Kiss Tomorrow Goodbye* is really an ethical, moral, socially principled work that trickily reverses the major premises of *White Heat* into an *exposé* and condemnation of unbridled gangsterism. The major figures of both films are homicidal paranoiacs and the main situation of both stories concerns a jailbreak and then a "big job." There the similarities end, for Cagney is the hero (however unconventional—nevertheless, the sympathy-tinged protagonist) of *White Heat* and the villain of *Kiss Tomorrow Goodbye*. After *White Heat*, Cagney complained to a reporter, "It's what the people want me to do. Someday, though, I'd like to make just one picture kids could go see." Early in the next decade, William Cagney telephoned director Gordon Douglas to offer him a finalised script that brother Jimmy "believed" in. If his mobster fame, given new life by *White Heat*, precluded children's films, then at the very least Cagney Productions could put the underworld Cagney to the service of a positive theme— and that is the very obvious purpose of the celluloid *Kiss Tomorrow Goodbye*.

The story (never very inventive but accomplished with great flair in the Horace McCoy literary rendition) concerns Ralph Cotter (Cagney), self-proclaimed big-shot hoodlum who engineers a bloody prison jailbreak and then masterminds a daring blackmail and robbery scheme involving the local constabulary. The film opens with a scene that is uncharacteristic of *film noir*—a plain, honest, straightforward courtroom sequence in which all of the Cotter cohorts are revealed to be on trial. The aroused district attorney delivers a round of accusing oratory into the camera, indicting several of the sour-faced persons seated on courtroom benches before the judge. The narrative then proceeds in flashback. Meaningfully, that sequence does not occur in the Horace McCoy novel; according to director Gordon Douglas, the trial prologue was in the original script which the Cagney brothers offered him—not a last-minute addition to mollify potential censors, as some cineastes have guessed. The scene is there in the film, certainly, because it offers a concrete, wilful antidote to other beginnings, especially that of *White Heat* (to which the later film must be seen principally as a reply) which opens with Cody Jarrett's ferocious, bestial, wholly insidious train robbery. There is less ambiguity, indeed little theatricality, about the introduction of *Kiss Tomorrow Goodbye*. Cagney Productions determines from the start that Ralph Cotter is a despicable no-good and that anyone connected with his way of life deserves little compassion; the film proceeds on that assumption. The prosecutor adjudges Cotter and his kind to be legally and morally bankrupt, and those prefacing remarks encompass the rest of the film.

Then comes the headlong rush of violent deeds—the camera doesn't shrink from recording Cotter's barbarism. The camera records grimly as Cotter betrays and murders his sidekick during the hairsbreadth jail escape; the camera records grimly as Cotter whips sweetheart Holiday (Barbara Payton) with a bundled bathroom towel (the only scene, according to Douglas, which was toned down to avoid possible censorship). Thus the distinction between the violence in *White Heat* and the violence in *Kiss Tomorrow Goodbye*—and one of the main reasons why the latter film doesn't qualify as truly subversive *film noir*—is that Ralph Cotter has been clearly and explicitly pronounced a villain, by due process, at the start. There is surely no effort to glorify his criminality.

There is also a crucial parallel of contrasts to the finales of both *White Heat* and *Kiss Tomorrow Goodbye*. *White Heat* concludes with that explosive suicide in which the laughing, shouting Cody Jarrett destroys himself rather than submit to capture by the cops. Nobody wins. The climax of *Kiss Tomorrow Goodbye* is less equivocal. Shot down in a jealous rage by his unrequited lover, Cotter dies, twisting and groaning on the floor of a shabby apartment, the triple victim of justice, retribution and a fair revenge. Coda: the courtroom scene is re-introduced and the final witness of the case is put on the stand. Lest there be any doubt, the last testimony is given by Cotter's brother, once described by the dead thug as "one of the few honest men left in the world." And the crowning irony is that Cotter's brother is played in *Kiss Tomorrow Goodbye* by William Cagney, brother of James, former actor and long-time co-conspirator in the fight to reform Cagney's film career. The district attorney spins a phonograph record of the local cops taking payola, and Cotter's brother (back to camera) nods his head perfunctorily to confirm that it is Ralph Cotter's voice also on the recording. The evidence is sealed, Ralph Cotter is damned in his grave and the string of accomplices in Cotter's crimes are punished—a verdict delivered long before in the courtroom "frame" of the movie. Righteousness triumphs. Seen from this perspective, *Kiss Tomorrow Goodbye* emerges not as a grisly and graphic masterpiece of *film noir* but instead as a movie which is really very conventional in many ways, striking mainly as a revelation of Cagney's personal temperament at the time.

The further discrepancies between Horace McCoy's dark, brooding *magnum opus* and the Cagney-ised cinema revision illustrate the undeniable tenor of the film. Cagney Productions (probably with the advice of the actor himself, who was noted for sitting in on story conferences) cleansed the novel of its most exaggerated aberrations. In the book, for example, the narrator is Ralph Cotter—in the first-person "I," he describes and defends his matter-of-fact deeds, thus assuming an empathetic, almost sympathetic, character. In comparison, the film is detailed from an objective viewpoint, with scant fondness for Cotter and a cool, dispassionate prologue that attaints him from the word go. Also in the book, Holiday, the hoodlum's moll, is a hell-raiser, "full of vinegar," a rough, scrappy woman with a background of criminal involvement; behind Cotter's back, she shares bed with confederate Jinx, the cop Reece, prison guard Cobbett and Mason, the untrustworthy garage attendant. Thus she is explained as a depraved and unsympathetic figure, deserving (supposedly) all the mistreatment she receives at the hands of Cotter. In the film, contrarily, Holiday has the innocent demeanour of a high school cheerleader. So, when Cotter cheats on her with socialite Margaret Dobson (Helena Carter), or swats her in the famous towel-lashing scene, it is he who is manoeuvered by the script into the pose of absolute villain.

Simply the manner in which the towel sequence is handled can explain the deceptive method of the film *Kiss Tomorrow Goodbye*. In the Horace McCoy novel, the incident recurs several times—happening in each instance nonchalantly, undramatically, practically offhand. "I picked a hand towel off the wall rack," explains Ralph Cotter indifferently in the book, "and very carefully folded it into a wide strap and soaked it under the running water and then wrung it out and turned and slapped her across the face with it." The incident is executed therefore very casually, without embellishment or glamourisation —the ordinariness of evil that is at the very heart of any definition of *film noir*. In the film version, however, the scene occurs only once: quickly, cruelly, gruesomely—for shock value.

Ralph Cotter's character also undergoes an interesting metamorphosis, a veritable streamlining, in the painful transplant from literature to cinema. In McCoy's book, the raunchy gunman is a complex and mysterious person, a Phi Beta Kappa university graduate with a John Dillinger hang-up, a native-born southerner who used to play in an orchestra, a fancy dancer whose brother is Rev. Stephen C. Apperson, "the biggest minister in the United States." As he himself explains in the book, "I didn't grow up in the slums with a drunk for a father and a whore for a mother and come into crime that way. I hate society too, but I don't hate it because it mistreated me and warped my soul. Every other criminal I know—who's engaged in violent crime—is a two-bit coward who blames his career on society. I need no apologist or crusader to finally hold my lifeless body up to the world and shout for them to come and observe what they have wrought. Do you know one of the first things I'm going to do when I get some money? I'm going to have Cartier make me a little gold thing for my wrist, you know, that identification thing the army guys wear, on a solid, gold chain and do you know what I'm going to have inscribed on it? Just this: 'Use me not as a preachment in your literature or your movies. This I have wrought, I and I alone.'" McCoy's Cotter is a guilt-ridden psychopath who secretly murdered his grandmother when but a child.

In the film, this background, this aura and ultimately any vestige of the human element is stripped away from the character of Cotter—leaving only a simplistic, black-and-white, cartoon representation of Hollywood "bad." Cagney's Cotter never elucidates his past, never hints at his motivations and never describes any of the intriguing experiences that are so central to the Cotter of McCoy's invention. This neglect doesn't make the cinema Cotter a mystifying character (because there is no clue that anything about the cheap hood is either subtle or fascinating) but rather a one-dimensional, cardboard personality. In the middle of the movie, for instance, Cotter launches into a brief, inexplicable theoretical analysis of sorts, saying, "I've always thought that the fourth dimension was neither philosophical nor mathematical, but purely intuitional." The comment—straight from the Phi Beta Kappa killer of McCoy's fiction—is strangely awkward, eerily out-of-character in the movie because Cagney Productions, in its unwavering enthusiasm to paint Cotter a wicked colour, didn't bother the film script with the ruffian's academic history. The dehumanisation, romanticisation, and Cagneyisation of Cotter can also be discovered in the brief scene in which he shares a speeding car with Margaret Dobson, a bold, young flirt who nudges the vehicle above a dangerous 100 m.p.h. In McCoy's book, Cotter is scared, downright petrified by her audacity, and he screams, "Goddam it, this is too fast!" In the film, Cagney's Cotter calls the woman's bluff, slamming his foot viciously down on the acceleration pedal until it is she who screams for him to stop.

Even visually, *Kiss Tomorrow Goodbye* boasts few of the optics normally associated with a *film noir* style: long takes, indirect lighting, shadows or moving camera etc. The film has that flat, pinched, hurried look—of ordinary, unembroidered, "B" shooting—due, no doubt, to the fact that the film was produced on a "very short schedule," probably twenty-eight days, according to director Douglas. Harassed by the pace, and also by a scenario that was racked by weak continuity, Douglas submitted a direction that was the essence of spotty, commonplace technique.

Nevertheless, though it is a far more incomplete and dis-

With Barton MacLane, Steve Brodie and Ward Bond in KISS TOMORROW
GOODBYE

torted work than usually suspected, *Kiss Tomorrow Goodbye* is
a compelling, if flawed, document. Though much of the dialogue is far-fetched, cursory and banal—such as Inspector Web-
er's (Ward Bond) dour physical threat to Cotter, followed
by a lame "I'm going to hate myself in the morning for doing
this"—and though principal character Cotter remains an undeveloped, uninteresting enigma, the cast includes certain competent old friends who salvage the undertaking. Ward Bond
essays a swarthy, snarling portrait of a cop on the take; Matt
McHugh (brother of Cagney buddy Frank) and William Frawley fill bit roles; and ageing, grumpy Barton MacLane is a subordinate detective. The rest of the troupe, particularly angel-
faced Barbara Payton, are unfortunately pedestrian. Only Cagney is omnipresent sustenance to the film, despite the carica-
ture nature of his role. Middle-aged, greying, stocky, the actor hurtles through a movie with more obstacles than lesser performers could survive. He erupts notably in a breakfast scene,
which grotesquely mocks the more famous breakfast scene of
The Public Enemy, when Holiday provokes him by her bickering to a fast boil. "No cream?" he yells, and tosses a cream
pitcher at her. "How about some sugar?" he adds, and flings a

↑ Not true! She tosses this at him!

sugar bowl. Then, all of a sudden, without explanation, in one of those frequent, inexplicable turns of the erratic *Kiss To- morrow Goodbye* film plot, the two lovers fall into each other's arms, laughing and kissing wildly. Still later, at the climax, blind-jealous Holiday shoots the gangster to death. "You can kiss to- morrow goodbye," she warns him as he begs her mercy. Fatal- ly wounded, Cagney twists and dives in a perverse parody of the classic gangster's one-last-gasp demise. Like so much of the rest of *Kiss Tomorrow Goodbye*, it is eye-catching spasm with- out passion. The petty bum rated the momentous bullet all along, the brothers Cagney thematically insist, and, but for a softened mean streak and lunatic rage, the fellow really bore little resemblance to Horace McCoy's genuine miscreant after all.

Gordon Douglas also directed Cagney's next feature, a Warner Brothers production, *Come Fill the Cup* (1951), remem- bered by the director as "one of Jimmy's best pictures." Not ex- actly, but *Come Fill the Cup* (scripted by Ivan Goff and Ben Roberts) is that rarity, a male sob story—like *The Lost Week- end* (1945), about the pitfalls of alcoholism. Cagney plays Lew Marsh, a hard-drinking reporter who beats the liquor lure and becomes a crime-busting newspaper editor, also a guar- dian angel to a bevy of reformed journalist-lushes, including the publisher's egocentric pianist-nephew (Gig Young). The nearly two-hour film is really two stories. The first tale is of drink, given an unexpectedly fluid gloss by director Doug- las (who introduces and seals the movie with sly, blinking im- ages of electric neon alcohol signs); the second story is late to bloom, a gangster-revenge yarn that begins after the mob-ar- ranged highway death of Marsh's reformed alcoholic bud- dy (played with magnanimous goodwill by James Gleason) well into the last reel. Both currents flow improbably together in the final, climactic moments of the piece when the thug chieftain (Sheldon Leonard), on a murder mission, has Marsh and the publisher's nephew at the mercy of his gunbarrel and asks sarcastically, "What is this—an AA meeting?" Then, he orders the two ex-souses to down slugs of bourbon—to disguise as suicides their impending homicides. Gripping the shot glass with a look of irony (after having spent the entire drama avoid- ing a fatal sip), Marsh hoists the cup for a toast, splashes the liquid suddenly into the hoodlum's eyes and, in the ensuing tumult, conquers the crime czar and, evidently, his thirst. Ser- ious-minded and solid, if unexceptional, *Come Fill the Cup* in- cludes an able cast: especially Gig Young as the headstrong juvenile drinker who received an Academy Award nomination for Best Supporting Actor for his demanding role (under his real name, Byron Barr, Young appeared in a small role in *Captains of the Clouds* with Cagney in 1942).

Cagney's part was actually fashioned after the life of a friend, Jim Richardson, City Editor of the "Los Angeles Examiner"; the story was penned by another friend, Harlan Ware. The actor consulted Richardson for his characterisation as an alcoholic, incorporating some of the incidental mannerisms of habitual drinkers, including "this thing of the walk." Cagney discovered "this is what happens to alcoholics—they lose muscle tone, and in order to keep their legs working they've got to keep them practically stiff; and that was one of the things I learnt for the part. What emerges from Cagney's scrupulous study is a brooding, earnest, fine-edged portrait of a middle-aged joe haunted by alcohol, scared by the rustle of "angel feathers" he hears every time he is dead-drunk, and perpetually on the edge of surrender to another stupor. Particularly effective and disturbing are two raffish sequences: in the beginning of the story, Marsh sails on a huge drinking spree—groggy with drink, unshaven and pale, virtually unconscious, he stumbles into the path of a careening car; also telling is the scene in which Marsh learns of the fatal "accident" of his friend —his eyes tighten and he begins to sob. Then he shuffles over

With Gig Young in COME FILL THE CUP

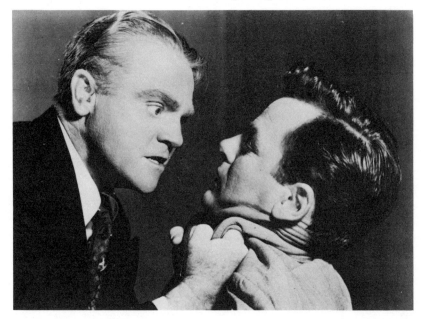

to Boyd Copeland (Gig Young), whose apparent carelessness caused the killing, and he erupts—flashing like lightning bolts quick wrist slaps back and forth across Copeland's astonished face, choking back a half-laugh, half-cry sound and sputtering a train of enraged recriminations. That edge of imminent disintegration—of teetering collapse—was the pervasive quality of Cagney's impersonation in *Come Fill the Cup.*

Cagney's other 1951 release was his last collaboration with Roy Del Ruth. *Starlift,* a celebrity-studded musical, was a pathetic shadow of Cagney's Thirties Del Ruth films. Cagney played himself in a brief, cameo appearance (an extreme example of Cagney's Fifties tendency to cater to his own image) amongst a bevy of stars which included Doris Day, Gordon MacRae, Virginia Mayo, Gene Nelson, Ruth Roman and Gary Cooper. Cagney's bit predictably called on him to utter a few "tough guy" phrases during a visit by film stars to Travis Air Force Base.

The film, a pale love story, encountered some topical objections from certain reviewers. "*Starlift* was Hollywood's ill-starred project of ferrying troupes of movie performers to Travis Air Force Base, north of San Francisco, to entertain replacements bound for Korea and wounded veterans on their way back to U.S. hospitals," wrote "Time" magazine, "But *Starlift* is guilty of its worst breach of good taste when it takes a low bow for Hollywood's patriotic gesture, makes the project seem exclusively Warner's, includes in its cast some stars who never troubled to fly to Travis Air Force Base. And the $1,000,000 *Starlift* is entertaining U.S. theaters just a month after Hollywood's Operation Starlift shut down, after running out of the $5,000 that Hollywood chipped in for its expenses."

Failure followed failure: *What Price Glory?*, directed by John Ford for 20th Century-Fox in 1952, proved to be one of Cagney's worst films and also one of Ford's least distinguished. Ford himself had once directed a stage version of the Maxwell Anderson-Laurence Stallings play with Pat O'Brien but his remake of Raoul Walsh's superb 1926 silent version (which starred Victor MacLaglen, Edmund Lowe and Dolores Del Rio) was strangely uneven. The updated screenplay was an exercise in rant, a squeamish piece of writing that lacked the sensibility of the original. Perhaps the misinterpretation was aggravated by the fact that the film was originally intended (and so announced) as a musical version of the pacifist play to be entitled "Charmaine," written by eventual scenarists Henry and Phoebe Ephron. Several songs lasted into the final screen ver-

With Dan Dailey in WHAT PRICE GLORY?

sion but *What Price Glory?* emerged as a comedy without humour but with music.

The film exaggerates Cagney's histrionic toughness (the direction suggested by *White Heat* and *West Point Story*) to blowhard excess. As a too-chubby Captain Flagg, Cagney squares off against Dan Dailey as Sergeant Quirt and they screech and browbeat their way through the script, resulting in a lot of noise which signifies nothing. The original antiwar message of *What Price Glory?* (which could have been relevant to the Korean War) was forfeited in the translation from the Twenties to the Fifties. Ford spent his eye on harsh and craggy, supposedly farcical dialogue. But the humour was strained. "The total result is deplorable," wrote the "New York Post's" Archer Winston, "which is shocking when you see the name of John Ford as director." "James Cagney and Dan Dailey," agreed Alton C. Cook of the "New York World-Telegram and Sun," "have lowered their acting standards in keeping with the spirit of the vehicle."

A Lion Is in the Streets (1953) is the final (but for an amorphous corporate association with 1961's *The Gallant Hours*) independent Cagney Production film, truly a Cagney family collaboration again, with James as star, William as producer, Jeanne in the supporting cast and Edward as story editor. Purchased by Cagney Productions on a ten-year lease in the Forties, the Adria Locke Langley best-seller was postponed for production until the Fifties. By then, *All The King's Men* (1949) had been produced as a successful motion picture, an Academy Award winner, and *A Lion Is in the Streets* suffered by comparison: both properties concern the story of a Huey Long-ish southern politico. *A Lion Is in the Streets* is at once the shoddiest and possibly most promising of the Cagney independents, rich in potential but short in actual achievement. Cagney plays Hank Martin, a brassy, self-taught swamp peddler-lawyer who bluffs his way into a reputation as a defender of sharecroppers' rights, and subsequently becomes a front-running gubernatorial candidate. Exposed by his friends and even his own wife as a fraud, he is assassinated at the finale, a victim of a bullet launched by one of the people he cheated in his Machiavellian rise to power.

As with *Kiss Tomorrow Goodbye*, the continuity of *A Lion Is in the Streets* is annoyingly sketchy. In the first scene, Hank Martin meets Verity Wade (Barbara Hale) and in the second scene he marries her. The courtship is undeveloped; the wedding is abrupt. Later, the peddler carries on an affair with a seductive backwoods girl named Flamingo (Anne Francis); his love scenes with the young firebrand inexplicably and immediately follow scenes in which he explicitly rejects her advances. The weak continuity can perhaps be ascribed to the inexperience of story editor Edward Cagney; too, the film reportedly endured heavy pre-production editing due to interference from lawyers for the Huey Long estate.

In A LION IS IN THE STREETS

Raoul Walsh's direction is also erratic, sometimes sharp and sometimes bleak, moving from a ravishing opening sequence which features Cagney dancing a merry, childish prance amidst a monsoon-like rain, mooning at nearby Barbara Hale and singing "Oh, I met the girl I love, the girl I am going to marry", to an anticlimactic, sensationalistic clash with wild alligators in the wetlands. Only Harry Stradling's beautiful colour photography is uniform throughout.

The cast—Barbara Hale, Anne Francis, John McIntire, Jeanne Cagney, Frank McHugh, and Lon Chaney Jr.—never seems very assured, and often looks plainly awkward. Cagney loads his characterisation with enough flavour to support the film on his considerable shoulders but even he slips. He slides from acting-school Southern dialect ("That would be plummmb fascinating") to pure New Yorkese, in and out, forgetfully.

But A Lion Is in the Streets, if inferior to other Cagney independents, continues the thematic policy of Cagney Productions. The villain of A Lion Is in the Streets is exposed and halted by the people, and death avenges his misdeeds. Evidence of the changes in Cagney Productions' philosophy since Johnny Come Lately—what might best be described as a hardening of the humanistic arteries—can best be understood by the means which are employed to "solve" the villainy of A Lion Is in the Streets: the gun, not the peaceful persuasion of earlier independents. Further proof of the changes wrought by the passage of time are to be found in the casting. Old friend Frank McHugh, in his last appearance with Cagney, plays the "heavy," and sister Jeanne Cagney is the appointed assassin who shoots her actor-brother down cold in the last scene. Dying (perhaps wondering how the family dynasty had arrived at such ends), Cagney's Martin eyes his murderess disbelievingly and mounts his odd-and-ends wagon for a fantasy getaway. "I told you I'd lead you to glory!" he sputters to the surrounding crowd before plunging to the ground. "You told on me, Sweetface," he gasps to his wife before he dies. Then, a meaningful postscript: the Lincoln Memorial is flashed on the screen and Lincoln's famous words are paraded before the viewer—"You can fool some of the people some of the time, etc . . ." The last words of Cagney Productions are Lincoln's.*

* A Lion Is In the Streets was, unhappily, the last Cagney-initiated project completed by Cagney Productions. Stray Lamb, based on the Thorne Smith novel, was long planned by the studio, with Cagney intended as the bearded Russet Man, but the film was eventually abandoned. Two cavalry pictures—Only the Valiant and Bugles in the Afternoon—were sold to Warners and produced for that studio. Tentative plans for Port Royal, with Cagney as a swashbuckling pirate, never materialised.

. The brief saga of Cagney Productions is the story of aborted projects and box-office flops and—even more—of thwarted artistry and muffled genius. The promise of *Great Guy* and *Johnny Come Lately* was muted in *Kiss Tomorrow Goodbye* and *A Lion Is in the Streets*. The big-hearted reformers of the former films became the miscreants, respectfully qualified by strong anti-crime themes, of the latter films. The humanist instincts of the Warners era faded as time slipped by. The independent Cagney productions were the only bulwark against a tide which ultimately swept Cagney through the Fifties on the remnants of his Thirties image.

Cagney did not appear in any films which were released in 1954; so, when four popular Cagney movies flooded the market in 1955, critics spoke reverently of a comeback. "Comeback, hell," snorted Cagney. "I've never been away." Of the four films, a western, *Run for Cover*, is the most thoughtful; and, according to director Nicholas Ray, the film contains a character who is the closest Cagney ever came to playing himself as he is in real life.

Possibly so. *Run for Cover* is surely one of the few Fifties films in which Cagney is humane, and also one of the few in which he does not abuse his female co-star (Viveca Lindfors). Matt Dow (Cagney), the principal character of Cagney's first western since *The Oklahoma Kid*, is a man who is wary of strangers but he is also a patient, considerate and genial fellow. He is tender and protective towards his wife, Helga Swenson (Lindfors), and fatherly towards young Davey Bishop (John Derek). However, Ray's expectations for *Run for Cover* (and for the character of Matt Dow) fall far short of realisation. The film is really just an average cowboy yarn—adequate but hardly superior entertainment fare—which buckles under the weight of philosophical (and epic) pretensions.

The story begins when Matt Dow (Cagney) is released from jail after several years of imprisonment for a crime he did not commit; he travels West and meets Davey Bishop, an orphan youth who is cared for by the people of a small town. The two men are wrongly accused of masterminding a local train robbery and they are assaulted by a posse; Davey is wounded in the leg and crippled. Grief-stricken, Dow remains in the town to nurse Davey and eventually agrees to become the town sheriff. Bishop is hired on as his deputy. But Davey is treacherous—bitter about his injury. He secretly conspires with a band of robbers who are planning a bank robbery. When the robbery occurs, none of the townspeople will ride

With Viveca Lindfors in RUN FOR COVER

with Dow to capture the bandits, and so the sheriff sets out alone with Davey. However, the youth reveals himself as a confederate of the robbers, ambushes the sheriff, and escapes. Wounded but bulldogged, Dow catches up to Bishop and the head bandit just as the two comrades are dividing their loot; both men simultaneously lunge for their guns; Dow shoots Bishop but the conscience-ridden lad has aimed his gun at the other bandit, killing him. The wounded Bishop dies in Dow's arms.

Run for Cover is constructed on familiar Fifties motifs, both an argument against and a victim of McCarthy era paranoia and Cold War fears. For example, the strangers in Run for Cover are all untrustworthy; suspicion is the watchword. Dow nearly shoots Bishop at their first encounter when noise of the youth's approach startles him. And, another concession to the climate of the times, the principal characters of the film are all bogus—not what they appear to be. Bishop for instance, is exposed as a Judas and a thief; Dow is discovered to be an ex-con. As in High Noon, the "masterpiece" of the Fifties era of distrust (and Run for Cover even has a recurrent theme song patterned after High Noon), the townspeople will not assist their sheriff when he is forced to chase the mysterious bank-robbers alone at the finale. Dow must shepherd the flock and capture the criminals solo, thus setting the example of leadership. Ray's not-so-unusual twist is that traitor Davey

Bishop is mistakenly shot and killed by Dow at the climax, iron-ically just as the boy is ready to side with Dow and rebuff his past. The tragic irony, evidently a commentary on the excesses of the Fifties, is nevertheless inadequate as a resolution of the drama, which is so founded on the opposite assumptions of McCarthyism.

Cagney is the moral centrepiece of the tale, haranguing the townspeople for their shortcomings ("What kind of a man are you," he asks accusingly of the town sheriff, "to hang a man without a trial?") and sermonising vaguely to Davey about life ("There's a lot of people in this world who had a rougher time of it than you . . . the only difference is they don't run for cover"). Dramatically, the most moving moment of his per-formance occurs at the finale when, realising that he has killed a repentant Bishop, Cagney weeps openly and poignantly be-fore the camera. It is an emotional instant in a film which is otherwise self-conscious, irreparably damaged by high-sounding and well-intentioned if vacuous dialogue, a poorly-developed ploy of romance and the badly-developed symbolism of univer-sal distrust.

Undercut by these failings, *Run for Cover* is memorable primarily for its clean, handsome photography (by Daniel Fapp); and for reuniting Cagney and Grant Withers (who ap-peared together in *Sinner's Holiday* and *Other Men's Women*), who plays the brigand chief. When Withers storms into the midst of church services to announce that his gang is staging a hold-up, Sheriff Cagney stands apart from the congregation and confronts him. They are old buddies. They served time to-gether in prison. Cagney and Withers eye each other neigh-bourly, like old cronies; in another era, Cagney would have played the Withers role in the confrontation. It is a sardonic and double-edged moment.

"We've always seen Cagney as the tough little squirt who's throwing a grapefruit in a girl's face or taking on somebody twice his size and kicking hell out of him," Ray has said. "But Jimmy has not only a great serenity, such as I've not seen in an actor, outside of Walter Huston at times, he has a great love of the earth, and of his fellow man, an understanding of lone-liness. I wanted to try and use all that. The vehicle itself wasn't strong enough for it and we didn't have the time to, be as in-ventive as we would have liked."

M-G-M's *Love Me or Leave Me*, directed by Charles Vidor, is Cagney's minor Fifties masterpiece, a compassionate gang-ster film in the great tradition of *Public Enemy* which allows

Cagney his deserved last ovation as a pseudo-Warners style criminal. "It was grown up and I was there at the time," said Cagney, "so I did it." *Love Me or Leave Me* is the story of singer Ruth Etting and her marriage of convenience to Chicago laundry racketeer Martin "The Gimp" Snyder. Cagney played "the Gimp," a character based on the real-life Martin Snyder, who strong-arms Etting (Doris Day) to show business fame and traps her into a tragic, loveless marriage.

Like the real "Gimp," Cagney's "Gimp" was physically deformed: club-footed and bent. Cagney walked with a twisted, ugly limp, spoke with a vainglorious sarcasm and accented his face-slapping, punching, slugging facade with nervous knuckle-cracking and tense outbursts. Despite his bestiality, the man is lonely, frustrated and desperate, according to Cagney's interpretation. "Now look here, you stupid little broad," he screams at Etting in the film, "do you know who I am? Do you think I let dames talk that way to me?" It is the "Gimp's" way of romance; the only method he knows is attack.

The racketeer loses Ruth finally and shoots her lover-accompanist Johnny Alderman (Cameron Mitchell) at the end of *Love Me or Leave Me;* he wounds Alderman and lands himself in jail. Released on bail, he visits his own newly-opened nightclub where Ruth is performing for the evening, to pay her "debt" to the "Gimp." Surrounded by reporters, advised by friends to let her continue singing, angry with himself and fighting back tears, he admits only, "Got to give her credit. The girl can sing. . . . About that I never was wrong." It is a sorrow-laden moment but the façade is quickly returned as the "Gimp" lunges into a brash posture and the scene fades.

Love Me or Leave Me is one of Cagney's finest films of his later period, overshadowed but not far surpassed by *White Heat,* and the "Gimp" is one of his most lasting and complex characterisations. The script, hard and realistic and true-to-fact and ultimately unhappy, is among the most authentic yet still entertaining biographies Hollywood has ever produced. Vidor's direction adheres to the serious spirit of the tale but includes some funny, ironic bits (a sign in Etting's dressing room, for instance, announces that "the management will not tolerate rough stuff or fighting in this dressing room"). And, oddly, Doris Day (in her third film with Cagney) is revealed as Cagney's best-matched female co-star of the decade, offering a bread and butter performance that belies her present-day reputation. She is a surprisingly vibrant singer and she performs a robust Ruth Etting imitation with songs such as "You Made Me Love You,"

With Doris Day in LOVE ME OR LEAVE ME

"Ten Cents a Dance" and "I'll Never Stop Loving You," but she is at her peak during her several free-wheeling battles with the "Gimp." The gangster dashes a vase to the floor during one especially-heated argument and she, with that vital grasp of the Cagney persona, waves away the hysterics disinterested-ly—saying, "Don't go into dramatics."

They were mutual admirers—Cagney and Doris Day—and their acting rapport was slightly reminiscent of the Thirties Cagney and Blondell. "He's the most professional actor I've ever known," she told interviewers. "He was always 'real.' I simply forgot we were making a picture. His eyes would actually fill up when we were working on a tender scene. And you never needed drops to make your eyes shine when Jimmy was on the set."

Cagney received his third Academy Award nomination for Best Actor in *Love Me or Leave Me* and the film itself received five other nominations, although it won only for Daniel Fuchs in the Best Original Story category. Regardless, the critics raved. "Dazzling performances," said "Look" magazine. "Brilliant," wrote the "Christian Science Monitor." "Cagney," said William K. Zinsser in the "New York Herald Tribune," "has created a fascinating portrait of the Gimp. In every mannerism—heavy limp, coarse speech, taunting sarcasm, flashes of rage—he moulds an obnoxious character who tramples over everybody in his lust for power. It's a high tribute to Cagney that he makes this twisted man steadily interesting for two hours."

Love Me or Leave Me was followed by two additional Cagney films in 1955: *Mister Roberts,* more image calisthenics, and *The Seven Little Foys,* the George M. Cohan rendition of *West Point Story.* "I did it for a lark," Cagney said of his role as the Captain in *Mister Roberts,* "And it was one of the easiest pictures I ever made. Everyone else had to jump and holler all the time. I just pulled my cap over my eyes, walked on deck, barked a command or two, and then went home."

Mister Roberts was destined to become a hit movie shortly after it became a best-selling book in 1946 and a smash Broadway play in 1948. The property was transferred to the screen by John Ford and Mervyn LeRoy (LeRoy took over from Ford midway when Ford became ill, and once estimated that 90 per cent of the completed film is his) and the film received three Academy Award nominations, including Best Picture. Cagney was "simply great," said "Variety." "Cue" called his performance "a gem of choleric characterisation." The "New York Herald Tribune" said it was "another remarkable portrait."

But *Mister Roberts* is an innocuous diversion. Directors Ford

With Henry Fonda in MISTER ROBERTS

and LeRoy would have been wise to shave thirty minutes off the two hours-plus running time. Over-long, with a synthetic, sentimental plot about a near-mutiny aboard a Navy vessel, caused by a proto-fascist commander but stop-gapped by a humane underling-officer, the film claims, primarily, effortless comedic performances by Henry Fonda, Jack Lemmon, William Powell and a whole crew of likeable sailors. And Cagney himself played the cranky Captain with an ease which betrayed his familiarity with the role, so accustomed was he by this point in his career to playing a petty tyrant, *à la West Point Story*. (The parallel might be made between *Mister Roberts* and Bogart's more complex petty-insane ship captain tyrant in *The Caine Mutiny*, released in 1954.) The same might also be said of *Seven Little Foys*, another *déjà vu* role, in which Cagney makes a brief reappearance as George M. Cohan, dancing a tabletop routine at a Friars Club dinner with buddy vaudevillian Eddie Foy (Bob Hope). The short soft-shoe con-

With James (Jimmy) Cagney Jr., Bob Hope, Mrs. "Billie" Cagney and Kathleen Cagney on the set of THE SEVEN LITTLE FOYS

test (danced to Cohan's "Mary") is the high point of Hope's otherwise too-typical picture: the role is, like *Starlift* (and many of his other Fifties films), Cagney as Cagney, tip-top, but not innovative. Cagney himself must have realised this when he told a reporter, "You couldn't call *Seven Little Foys* a whole picture. I just played a characterisation—the George M. Cohan role—as a favour to Bob Hope." The film might be considered a payment for the cameo by Eddie Foy Jr. in *Yankee Doodle Dandy*.

Cagney worked in *Seven Little Foys* without contract as a favour to Hope, his friend, and as an excuse to lose weight during dancing rehearsals. "When I'm taking off lard for a hoofing picture," Cagney said, "and the piano is thumping, I usually wear a sweat shirt. Over that I pull on a rubberised silk thing. On my head I wear a kind of beret teamed up with the sleeves of another sweat shirt that I wrap around my neck. I can work up quite a sweat that way and the blubber pours off me." Hope rehearsed strenuously with Cagney for their tiny bit. "The man is a horse," he told reporters, "a workhorse. Here he was doing this thing free and working like a demon. Why he danced ten pounds of suet right off me. And I'll bet he lost a good fifteen pounds himself."

When Spencer Tracy was "fired" by M-G-M in 1956 during

In TRIBUTE TO A BAD MAN

the filming of *Tribute to a Bad Man* (Tracy actually forced his own discharge because of disagreements over the script and location shooting, voluntarily ending 25 years of association with M-G-M), he was replaced by friend Cagney. The story and title nevertheless suit Cagney well. *Tribute to a Bad Man* is perhaps a suitable metaphor for Cagney's entire career, which took on the form of a grudging salute to an ageing, surly but likeable "tough," in this case one Jeremy Rodock, the horse rancher and pioneer who is so overly-protective of his holdings that he customarily hangs rustlers.

"I was a boy when I entered Mr. Rodock's valley, but when I left, I wasn't a boy any more," narrates young cowboy Steve Miller (Don Dubbins) at the beginning of the film. Miller joins Rodock's ranch as a hired hand but falls in love with Jocasta (Irene Papas), Rodock's mistress. The elder westerner is a merciless pioneer: when his cattle stock is rustled, Rodock gets "hanging fever" and sets out on horseback in a murderous frenzy ("Sorry, I've got to go," he tells Jo. "You come as close to me to meaning everything as anything but I've got to go"), seeking revenge. Begged by Jocasta and Steve to "go easy" on one band of robbers, Rodock instead forces the thieves to tread barefoot over miles of hot, dusty and rocky terrain.

As is to be expected with Cagney, however, Rodock has his decent aspects. In peaceful moments, he puffs contentedly on a pipe, tinkers with a piano, sings a few robust, off-key notes and lavishes attention on Jocasta, ultimately yielding her without a fight to young Steven when it seems that that is what she wants. She rides away in a buckboard with the young cowboy, but is torn with regret: she decides to return. Happy and forgiving, the "bad man" asks her to marry him as the film ends.

The moral of Jeremy Rodock's behaviour in *Tribute to a Bad Man* is the lesson of the Cagney persona: he is bad and good. Love him for the good and disregard the bad.

Irene Papas, in her first American film, is a graceful Jocasta and Don Dubbins, a colourless youngster, plays the tinhorn. The Robert Wise direction, Miklos Rozsa music and Robert Surtees photography give technical lustre to an otherwise weak film. "Anyway you look at it," wrote the "New York Times," "the old master, James Cagney, really is at home in *Tribute to a Bad Man*. He's got 'hanging fever' and his word is law. The eyes narrow, the nose wrinkles, the mouth twists arrogantly, the fore-finger coolly grips the trigger and the voice, oozing venom, says, 'Do-o-on't move.' And nobody moves."

With Don Dubbins in THESE WILDER YEARS

Dubbins, one of Cagney's favourite young actors, co-starred also in *These Wilder Years* (originally titled *Somewhere I'll Find Him*), with Barbara Stanwyck, directed by Roy Rowland for M-G-M in 1956. The film suffers an undeservedly bad reputation nowadays; though the story is maudlin, often-tedious soap opera fabric, the performances are staunch and the intent is noble enough. The drama follows the search of wealthy steel tycoon Steve Bradford (Cagney) who, middle-aged and regretful, visits an adoption home called "The Haven" (motto: "anybody's child is everybody's child") to find the illegitimate son he fathered in his youth. There, he meets Ann Dempster, administrator of the home, who refuses to accept Bradford's reasoning for the late interest in his offspring—"I got older and I got lonely"—and goes to court rather than bend her personal code of ethics and locate the youth. The resolute industrialist ultimately loses the judicial decision, but encounters his long-lost sibling, now happily and contentedly settled with his foster parents, in a local bowling alley. Placated, wiser, Bradford decides instead to adopt a young woman (Betty Lou Keim) who herself has just given birth to an illegitimate child, thus becoming a father and grandfather in one fell swoop; as the film concludes, he has patched up his quarrels with Miss Dempster also, and there is certain hint that they may wed in the future.

Besides Barbara Stanwyck—who contributed her usual fiery, fetching performance—the cast included a dignified Walter Pidgeon, as Bradford's lawyer, newcomer Betty Lou Keim, as the doe-eyed unwed mother, Don Dubbins again, and the blustery Edward Andrews. Cagney was the absolute executive: businesslike, unfeeling, polite and obstinate throughout, rendering a portrayal that was so steady and accurate that it smartly bolstered the drooping script (sample: "Don't cry about tomorrow. Wait until it's yesterday"). Roy Rowland's direction was admittedly without style, somewhat plodding, but also meticulous and unaffected; the music (by Jeff Alexander) was appropriately syrupy, although on a tolerable scale. Most critics were nonetheless negative. "The intent of this drama is lofty enough, as one can see, and Mr. Cagney and Miss Stanwyck go at it with becoming restraint and goodwill," wrote Bosley Crowther. "But the story is hackneyed and slushy and Roy Rowland's direction is so slow and pictorially uninteresting that the picture is mawkish and dull."

Almost another "comeback": *Man of a Thousand Faces*, directed by Joseph Pevney for Universal-International in 1957, might have been an extraordinary film, but the production is irreparably scarred. Its major asset is Cagney, as silent-film star Lon Chaney, who essays a superior performance under the almost unbearable weight of dreadful scripting and threadbare direction. The film's similarity to *Yankee Doodle Dandy* gives it a redeeming *déjà vu* tone, especially in the scenes which focus on Chaney's vaudeville years. There is a small but splendid moment, for example, early in the picture when Cagney, made up in blackface, dances a pantomime tap with a broom and a shadow that is worthy of Cagney at his peak, and also of Cagney's Cohan in *Yankee Doodle Dandy*.

Because mimicry is his special *forte*, Cagney impersonates Chaney superbly, combining a striking physical similarity to the master of disguises with an unmistakable empathy for Chaney's troubled background as the son of deaf parents. (Pevney says that Cagney did the project partly because "he empathised with the problems of the deaf and he felt close to Chaney's vaudeville background"). The actor uses the hand-gesture deaf language, which he learned for the production, several times in the film in an entirely easy and natural manner. Especially heart-rending is the climax when Chaney, near death and unable to talk, must ironically revert to the silent speech of his parents.

Man of a Thousand Faces is filled with brief glimpses of

With Rickie Sorenson (above) and Jim Backus (below) in MAN OF A
THOUSAND FACES

genuine sparkle: Cagney, as "old Lady Murgatroyd," in wig, granny glasses and shawl, sewing his fingers together comically to amuse his son, young Creighton Chaney (later in real life, Lon Chaney Jr.); Cagney, his body knotted in crippled contortions, crawling, imploring the help of a faith-healer and then straightening up, cured, *à la* Chaney in *The Miracle Man;* Cagney, hairy and animalistic, crying out in pain as he is tortured for being *The Hunchback of Notre Dame.*

Whenever Pevney's camera strays from Cagney's deft impersonations, though, the story melts into tawdry melodrama. For example, Chaney takes his wife-to-be (Dorothy Malone) home to meet his family, without telling her of his parents' deafness, and the *fiancée* predictably runs from the dinner table to hide upstairs from the accusing silence of the family meal. She is pregnant and tells Chaney amidst a torrent of tears that she does not want to have their child for fear the baby will be deaf. "Clara, I want that baby," he tells her softly. "I don't!" she replies (the musical soundtrack thumps a melodramatic bom-ba-bom), "but I'll have it!" (bom-ba-bom again).

Man of a Thousand Faces is basically true to the facts and frustrations of Chaney's life, and the tragedy of his early death, but the film stretches credulity at certain personal (in this case, melodramatic) climactic events in Chaney's career: the attempted suicide of his first wife, the chance reunion with girl-friend Hazel Bennett (Jane Greer) and the ghostly reappearance of his first wife, plus the subsequent effort to hide son Creighton Chaney from her sight. The cast is, excepting Cagney, uniformly obtuse, especially Roger Smith, a Cagney protegé in the first of their two films together and Jeanne Cagney, in her last appearance with her brother, appropriately playing Chaney's sister.

Short Cut to Hell, produced in 1957, is the puzzler of Cagney's career, a low-budget re-make of *This Gun for Hire* without any redeeming qualities. It was the only film Cagney ever directed, made for Paramount and friend-producer A. C. Lyles, but his directorial debut was so inauspicious that even so faithful a follower as "The New York Times" politely declined to review the film. The "New York Daily News" nevertheless saw some "crisp flashes" of the old Cagney and "Time" said the novice director "manages to beauty-spot a few of the bare places with some characteristic Cagney touches."

The film tried to capitalise on Cagney's fame in a short, unique prologue. Seated in a director's chair with his name grandiosely emblazoned on the back, Cagney turns to face the

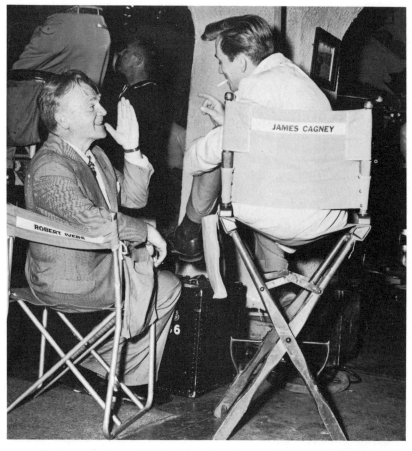

Above, conferring with Robert Ivers on the set of SHORT CUT TO HELL.
Below, a scene from the film with Ivers and Georgann Johnson

camera. He explains that *Short Cut to Hell* is his first directing endeavour. He explains further that he is "thrilled" to introduce two "exciting" young actors—Robert Ivers (as Kyle) and Georgann Johnson (as Glory Hamilton)—and that said, he turns his back, and the film begins.

But *Short Cut to Hell* is humdrum, downright trite and just plain routine. Cagney's contribution is difficult to unravel but it is certain that his one fling at direction was an unqualified disaster. Most of the story's impact belongs to the original Graham Greene novel, as reworked into a screenplay for the first version by W. R. Burnett, author of "Little Caesar." The weirdly sympathetic killer, with his affection for cats; the sweet young girl oddly attracted to the killer; and the rich bigwig who has been cheating on building specifications—all are basically inventions of scenarist Burnett.

Very little about *Short Cut to Hell* is distinctly Cagneyesque. Robert Ivers and Georgann Johnson are both monotonic actors; there is nothing in their flat performances to suggest Cagney's energising influence. The murder of the two Engineering Department employees, the "climax" escape sequence, Kyle's death scene—all are executed in a strangely indistinctive fashion that could just as well mean that no one or anyone was giving orders behind the camera.

At the beginning of the film, Kyle viciously manhandles a young girl named Daisy (Yvette Vickers), bouncing her sadistically out of his apartment: it is the first and only hint of any kind of Cagney touch, of any connection with a fierce, hard-boiled gangster tradition that might be considered Cagneyesque. Why did Cagney fail so utterly as a director? The most immediate reason must be his inexperience and his apparent directorial indifference to the project, outside of doing a favour for a friend. The vital Cagney persona was simply more at home in front of a camera, communicating directly, than behind a camera, forced to rely on technical and mechanical means of explanation. Perhaps, if he had been younger, the result would be different. As it is, the film must be described as a half-hearted experiment from the actor who, in his own words, would try anything once.

Never Steal Anything Small, for Universal-International in 1958, is the prototypical late-career Cagney film, a "tough guy" musical which is implicitly related to the whole Cagney canon. The film opens with an announcement which not only functions to introduce the story but signals through its carefully-chosen rhetoric Cagney's participation in the project. It also sets the somewhat conservative political tenor (drastically different from the films of the Warners Cagney) of the piece: "This picture is sympathetically dedicated to labour and its problems in coping with a new and merry type of *public enemy . . . the charming, well-dressed gentleman who cons his way* to a union throne and never needs to blow a safe again."

Cagney plays Jake MacIllaney, a hoodlum stevedore who steals from company coffers and rigs elections to become the president of the United Stevedores workers' union. Even more vehemently anti-labour than the *St. Louis Kid,* the film would have shocked Thirties critics who supposed Cagney to be leftist politically. The film is nevertheless studded with oblique, self-serving references to the younger Cagney: a bright song-and-dance number with Cara Williams called "I'm Sorry, I Want a Ferrari" has the performer strutting on a treadmill *à la Yankee Doodle Dandy;* the new "public enemy" couches his romantic language in classic Cagney vocabulary ("I lose round

With Shirley Jones in NEVER STEAL ANYTHING SMALL

one," he tells Shirley Jones good-naturedly after she repulses his propositions, "but it's going to be a long fight, a long one." She tells him: "You know, considering you're a crook and a horror, you're really very nice company").

Never Steal Anything Small is Cagney's fifth and farewell film appearance as a singer-dancer. In Hollywood, where virtually no male is permitted to make a living as a singer-dancer (Fred Astaire and Gene Kelly are the too-rare exceptions) the loss may be taken for granted but it is still a cause for mourning to consider what Cagney's "other self" might have been. *Never Steal Anything Small* cannot help but be disappointing under the circumstances. Cagney is awarded only one complete song, and the song is a highpoint: the number is so ridiculous (coming from nowhere in the middle of this semi-serious story about labour troubles) that Cagney and Cara Williams saunter through their paces and toss away the lyrics, almost tongue-in-cheek.

The rest of the tunes (by Allie Wrubel and Maxwell Anderson) are as forgettable; the story, based on the play "Devil's Hornpipe" by Maxwell Anderson and Rouben Mamoulian, poorly juxtaposes narrative and music and reactionary theme; and the cast, Roger Smith again and a blithe Shirley Jones, is purely summer stock. Cagney is the only strength of this weakest of vehicles.

The theme that persistently dogged Cagney throughout his career—that violence corrupts—was given a final, redundant reprise in *Shake Hands with the Devil* in 1959. In the Thirties and Forties, in films such as *Public Enemy* and *The Roaring Twenties*, the violent side of the Cagney persona was linked inextricably to the ills of the social system, and the dehabilitating influences of the environs. A new phase began with *White Heat* and Cagney's tendency towards violence became identified with mania, as in *Kiss Tomorrow Goodbye, A Lion Is in the Streets, Love Me or Leave Me* and *Tribute to a Bad Man* —even *West Point Story* and *Mister Roberts*.

So too with *Shake Hands with the Devil* where Sean Lenihan (Cagney), a surgeon turned underground fighter with the IRA in 1921, is obsessed by his desire for Irish independence. So haunted is he with the struggle for complete sovereignty that he will not compromise his ideals, even when a settlement treaty is offered. At the film's climax, he threatens to execute a member of the royal family (Dana Wynter), even though a truce has been signed. His comrades, all fellow members of the IRA underground, beg him not to shoot her. He shouts that they are all traitors and as he spins around to fire the killing shot, he is himself cut down by a bullet from the gun of Kerry O'Shea (Don Murray), an American who had tried to stay aloof from the Irish Rebellion. Like Edmond O'Brien in *White Heat*, O'Shea had been Cagney's friend; he is also his executioner. "Those who shake hands with the devil often have trouble getting their hands back" was the old Irish proverb used as a basis for the film's title. In other words, violence corrupts or corruption is inextricably linked to violence—that is the idea proposed by the deaths of Cody Jarrett, Ralph Cotter, Hank Martin and Sean Lenihan.*

Shake Hands with the Devil is an inconsistent, clumsy film, as is evident from the accents that shuttle back and forth between brogue and English. Cagney is one of the worst offenders, though the sight of him in long, white flowing surgeon's robes lecturing on medicine to a class of juniors (after all, he once had doctor ambitions), is almost enough to chase away memory of the blunders. When he sheds his gown and his physician pretence, the film begins to move. The story opens with a placid cemetery funeral that is interrupted by a brigade of British Black and Tans. The pallbearers scatter in all directions and the coffin crashes to the ground, breaking open and revealing a load of smuggled guns. As the story compounds, Cagney evolves slowly from a seemingly gentle doctor to a rabid warrior. He is a pitiless old soldier, a grisly fighter; his performance is the backbone of a faint-hearted film, and he is gen-

---

* Cagney wrote a rambling public relations explanation of his involvement in *Shake Hands with the Devil* that is worth quoting in full, even though it seems contradictory in part. "Twenty-five years ago I was a hoofer," he wrote. "Somebody stuck a gun in my hands and I've been living cinematically by the gun ever since. Some people think I was born with a gun in my hand.

"The truth is, I hate violence. In the last few years I've rejected hundreds of possible film parts because I want to get away from violence. So now, I'm back with the gun in *Shake Hands with the Devil*.

"This time I'm not playing a gunman. I'm a revolutionary. I'm one of the band of hard men, dedicated men who fought the battle to bring peace and freedom to Ireland. It's not just a man with a gun, it's a man with a gun and a purpose.

"The gun is incidental to the purpose. In *Shake Hands With the Devil* I'm a revolutionary and the gun is part of my professional equipment, as much a part of it as the stethoscope I carry as a doctor, which is the revolutionary's daytime profession. What is important to me is that the character has reality and validity; he's the prototype of the men who fought in 1921 to free Ireland.

"I'm interested in this difference between *Shake Hands With the Devil* and other roles in which I've carried a gun, not merely artistically, but personally.

"During my career, thousands of words have been written about me. Most of them dwelt on the fact that I am, by vocation, a farmer; that off screen I lead a quiet life and don't get into trouble.

"But none of these stories has anywhere near the impact of one of my pictures. People get an impression of me from the screen that sticks much more thoroughly than anything they read."

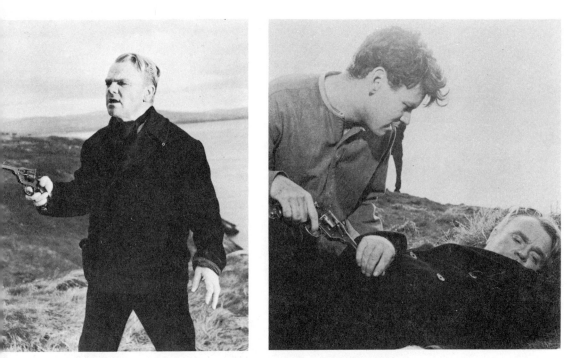

In SHAKE HANDS WITH THE DEVIL with Don Murray (right)

erously assisted by tiny but sonorous performances from a range of crack bit players, members of the Abbey Theatre and other Dublin-based companies.

By *The Gallant Hours* in 1960, Cagney was beginning to show visibly his physical age. And there were rumours of retirement. He was greying, jowled and heavier around his middle. Columnists began to report that he would never make another film. But the actor was a personal admirer of Admiral William F. ("Bull") Halsey (just as he personally admired the subjects of his other screen biographies) and he agreed to do the film.

"This film is a labour of love and gratitude to a man who, when the chips were down, performed for us," he told a reporter. *The Gallant Hours* is the story of a five-week period in the life of Admiral Halsey, who commanded U.S. naval forces in the critical Second World War battle of Guadalcanal in 1942. The film was directed by Cagney's old friend Robert Montgomery.*

---

* Cagney had appeared on television for Montgomery also, on September 10, 1956, for "Soldiers from the Wars Returning" on TV's "Robert Montgomery Presents." The story of an Army Sergeant (Cagney) assigned to escort home the body of a soldier killed in the Korean War, received complimentary but reserved reviews. Cagney disclaimed any long-term interest in television: "It's a high tension business. I have tremendous admiration for the people who go through this sort of thing every week. But let's face it, some of them are in the hospital half of the time."

In THE GALLANT HOURS

The Gallant Hours resurrected Cagney Productions, though in name only, to share billing with Montgomery Productions. Cagney's son Jimmy and Montgomery's son Bob had cameo parts in the film and Montgomery appeared briefly also. The film chooses to concentrate on the private agony of Halsey's responsibility as a commander rather than battle scenes and war footage; and Cagney correspondingly delivers a solemn, introspective performance. "There is no braggadocio in it, no straining for bold or sharp effects. It is one of the quietest, most reflective, subtlest jobs that Mr. Cagney has ever done," wrote Bosley Crowther. Cagney's Halsey (critics pointed out a physical resemblance) was a quiet, compassionate man, yet given to outbursts of emotion and temper.

The two-hour-long film is filled with reflective moments: Halsey, standing alone on deck contemplating the waves of the ocean and the future ahead; or Halsey, pacing worriedly, awaiting battle news. Cagney's profile is abundant in detail. At one point during a conversation with officers, he stops his stream of orders to pick a hair from his teeth. The gesture, slight and quick, is lost to the undiscriminating eye, but it is indicative of the heed Cagney paid to the smallest nuance of his characterisation.

The film unfolds in a documentary style, in flashback, beginning at the time of Halsey's retirement and proceeding to
divulge the past via the officer's reminiscences and actual newsreel footage. The narration is the weakest, most obvious element of the film. As Japanese seamen converse in one scene,
for instance, the storyteller intones melodramatically, "In case
you do not understand what is being said . . ." and then continues to reveal the self-evident plot. The Roger Wagner Cho-
rale sings pseudo-glorious hymnals at all the wrong moments,
punctuating grave crises with discomfiting bombast, and the
pacing, the two hours of nothing but small talk and conscience,
is unforgivably slow, slow, slow. One scene unknowingly betrays
Cagney's deterioriating physical condition. Four navy officers are
spread out on a beach, sun bathing, dressed in their swim-suits.
Halsey (Cagney) runs up to the group (he is off-camera; the
audience sees only the navy men wave to him as he approach-
es) and enters the frame, back to the camera. He swiftly clothes
himself in a full-length beach robe. Then he turns and seats
himself among the four. The implication is distressing but certain: the "tough guy" is fat.

Again, more rumours of imminent retirement. But Cagney
was tempted to a fitting motion picture swan song by a phone
call from director Billy Wilder and he signed for *One, Two,
Three* in 1961. ("The chief reason that Wilder made *One, Two,
Three* was that he wanted to work with Cagney," according to
Tom Wood, author of "The Bright Side of Billy Wilder, Primarily.") Filmed entirely on location in West Berlin and at the
Bavaria Studios in Munich, *One, Two, Three* showed that Cagney, over sixty, was still hyper-energetic. Chubby, his face almost bulbous, looking like Mr. Magoo when hatted, Cagney's
performance belied his age. One shot in the film follows his
feet as he climbs a flight of steps en route to a meeting with
Soviet diplomats. The movement of his legs is self-conscious-
ly bouncy, upbeat, rhythmical, dance-like; it was the dancer
Cagney mounting those stairs. Even frenetic Billy Wilder himself had difficulty controlling and capturing the kinetic, faster-
than-ever Cagney style. And Cagney had equal difficulty adapt-
ing to Wilder's mode. One sequence required over fifty takes.
The scene called for Cagney to "deliver at triphammer speed
several pages of complicated monologue that he had been
given only the day before." Cagney was supposed to rattle off
the long speech while selecting an assortment of clothes items
designed to remake Communist Horst Buchholz into an accept-
ably-dressed American-style youth (sample of the talk—to a

suit salesman: "Too loud! Too quiet! This is all right, but take the padding out of the shoulders. Belt in the back! I thought that went out with high button shoes!")

The actor stumbled several times on the line, "Where's the morning coat and striped trousers?" The usually patient Wilder blew his temper. Other actors began to miss their cues. Not until after some fifty-odd takes later, did the scene go right. (Said Cagney: "The mechanics of learning . . . One line can bug you. I did a play once with Mary Boland. One night she blew a line. The next night, worrying about her line, I blew my own following line. After that, I had trouble with the line every night. It's the rhythm.").

One, Two, Three is literally the fastest-paced film that Cagney ever made—it is the figurative, supreme embodiment of Cagney's own fleet person, the only movie of his career to have matched the rapidity of his persona. The film explodes with gag after gag, joke after joke, punch-line after punch-line—it is Billy Wilder's most lickety-split comedy, a rushing stream of one-liners. Though many of the cold war jokes are dated and obsolete (Cagney: "I wouldn't touch the Russians with a ten-foot Pole and I wouldn't touch the Poles either") they come so fast and furious that there is no time for pause. The picture is constructed on a *motif* of speed: even the title indicates pacing, timing and motion.

One, Two, Three is a series of chase scenes, a running battle of wits and a chain succession of shouting matches. Cagney is the racing soul of the film. He stomps, bellows, bullies and wheedles his way through the script, a performance so relentless and abrasive that some critics found it offensive. "Cagney, I fear, has done Wilder an ill service," wrote the "Saturday Review" critic. "He shouts his way through the entire movie, bellowing and bowling over all opposition. After a while, I found myself flinching every time he gathered his breath. A man just can't keep that up without strain to the vital organs."

The film is an appropriate last curtain call, thematically and dramatically, for the actor who initially found stardom as America's *Public Enemy*. Cagney plays C. P. MacNamara, a Pepsi-Cola executive in West Berlin, who must babysit a spoiled Southern teenager named Scarlet (Pamela Tiffin) and head off the girl's marriage to a young Marxist East Berliner (Horst Buchholz) if he wants to please his bosses and safeguard his own industry-climbing ambitions. MacNamara is a modern-day Tom Powers, older and wiser (unlike Tom Powers, the modern businessman avoids "criminal" mistakes, makes millions and

With Lilo Pulver and Hanns Lothar in ONE, TWO, THREE

escapes without onus), gentlemanly-dressed in suit, tie, hat
and cane: but ruthless, gangsterly pursuing his ambitions, the
businessman's equivalent of the "Public Enemy."

The part is Fifties Cagneyesque: he is a "tough guy," a
toughness made respectable by old age and position. Though
he is married (to Arlene Francis, for 16 years) his marriage is
sour (in other words, no woman is his suitable lifemate), in
time-honoured Cagney tradition. MacNamara cheats on his wife
and lies to her; he dallies with his blonde secretary (Lilo Pulver) during office hours.

His farewell role is a sardonic recapitulation of his greatest
films; the humour derives largely from other Cagney films. Besides the wall clock cuckoo that waves flags and sings "Yankee
Doodle Dandy," there is the brash young military policeman
(Red Buttons) who performs a brisk Cagney imitation ("Oo-
kay, buster!"). Cagney himself cocks his arm, holds a grapefruit
threateningly in his hand and warns Otto Ludwig Piffl (Horst
Buchholz) menacingly: "How would you like a little fruit for
desert?" And there are other cinematic references, too. A ho-

tel is named Hotel Potemkin and Cagney, in one burst of des-
peration, cries out, "Mother of Mercy, is this the end of Little
Rico?". The jokes are just jokes: gone is the glowing Thirties
Cagney persona and in its place is Wilder's ultimate con man
—the con man as a military-industrial complex henchman. The
wit does not recreate the warm feelings of the earlier works,
however, but merely recalls an intellectual memory of the
Warners past, thus capitalizing on the star's lifelong image.

"Plenty of speed, but not much pace," observed Penelope
Gilliat, enunciating the most frequent objection to a film generally considered one of Wilder's least. For those, however, who
find bearable the overzealous, patriotic, political content, the
ice-cold amoral tone, and who can swallow some of the more
unpalatable, sexual jokes, *One, Two, Three* does offer one of
Cagney's most eruptive performances. Unequalled zip.

After *One, Two, Three*, Cagney announced his retirement:
unequivocally, unalterably. Through the Sixties, he never wa-
vered in his determination to stay out of feature films and away
from the public limelight. "In this business you need enthusiasm," he told one reporter. "I just don't have it for acting any-
more. After all, acting is not the beginning and end of everything." He became a farmer in professional earnest, raising cattle with a vengeance on his Dutchess County, New York estate
and dividing his time between several homes on the east and
west coasts. "While I was shooting *One, Two, Three*" he told
Charles Champlin, "I loaned my boat to three of my pals and
their wives for a cruise, and while they were out they had a
picture taken of the six of them standing on deck holding drinks
and toasting me. They sent me a print of it and they wrote on
it, 'Thank God you are gainfully employed.' And didn't they
look smug and happy.

"It showed up on a day when we were shooting some last
interiors at Goldwyn. And it was a beautiful day, a gorgeous
day. I was standing outside, catching the sun and the blue sky
and the clouds, and the assistant director came out and said,
'We're ready for you now, Mr. Cagney.' Well, I went back inside that black cavern and right then I said to myself, 'That's
it, baby,' and it was. No more. I'm owed $1500 in bets from
pals who said I wouldn't stick to it. One guy at 500-1 odds;
wait'll I catch up with him. I was always whaddya call it, a
journeyman actor, I never gave a damn about the rest of it.
Do the job and run. I don't need the applause. My feeling always was that there was so much more living to do, outside
the industry. By the time I'd finished each job, I'd have my

reservations to get out of here. There was all the nonsense going on here, and I figured the days aren't long enough for doing all the things that are fun and interesting."

Cagney's ventures into the performing arts were few and far between after 1961, and limited to narration. In 1962, he went to work for government propaganda purposes, in a film produced by CBS entitled *Road to the Wall*. It was a crude documentary, since declared inoperative by the Department of Defense, except for historical purposes. The film documented a number of famous Communist take-overs and subsequent party purges, and warned Americans to be vigilant. "This is a one-way street," cautioned Cagney in brittle tones, explaining that the road to the execution wall was inevitable under Communist rule. "We intend that the world should be free."

The actor did not appear in front of the camera for his role, however, leading to speculation that the old "gangster" was putting on weight in leaps and bounds, or, rather, that threatened his leaps and bounds. "Mr. Five-by Five," Pat O'Brien called the retired star in his autobiography. But a nationally syndicated newspaper story in 1973, the first interview with Cagney in nearly a dozen years, denied the rumours that he was "grossly fat" and claimed that he still tap-danced for exercise daily, no doubt polishing some of the very routines he executed in vaudeville 50 years previous.

The actor perhaps best remembered for defining acting in sheer physical terms became only a disembodied voice-over for the dribblings of a career in the Sixties as he continued to serve as narrator. On November 24, 1966, he lent his voice for "General Electric Theatre's" *Ballad of Smokey the Bear*, produced in co-operation with the U.S. Department of Agriculture. Cagney played Big Brother Bear in the animated fantasy; the production was enthusiastically received by most television critics. Jack Gould of the "New York Times" was severe: "Smokey, whose voice was provided by Barry Pearl and the big brother bear, for which James Cagney was the voice, were not endowed with too much personality, either in the lines they had to say or in the design of their faces." The cartoon feature was aired twice again, in May, 1968, and in the spring of 1969. For Cagney, the project was an extension of his lifelong interest in conservation.

In 1968, he supplied the voice-over for friend-producer A. C. Lyles' *Arizona Bushwhackers*, an unexciting B western starring Howard Keel, Yvonne De Carlo and Marilyn Maxwell. The story concerned captured Confederate soldiers who served in the U.S. Army out west; only a modest credit among the titles offered a clue to the fact that the unexceptional words which introduce the film were spoken by James Cagney.

In 1973, Cagney narrated (but again did not appear before the camera) the prelude to a special Academy Awards tribute dedicated to the memory of the late Edward G. Robinson. Through the years, producers have tried to lure him to a comeback in front of the cameras. He was offered a small fortune to play Alfred Doolittle for George Cukor's production of *My Fair Lady*. He refused. Other offers poured in, including a part in Samuel Bronston's never-realised *The French Revolution* in 1965 and Jack Lemmon's *Kotch* in 1972. He steadfastly turned down everything.

In March, 1974, he made a rare public appearance, even submitting to a press conference and several interviews, when he was honoured by the American Film Institute with the second-ever Life Achievement Award (the first such tribute was given director John Ford, one year earlier). A gala, celebrity-studded dinner in Hollywood, hosted by Frank Sinatra, attended by California Governor Ronald Reagan, plus the top luminaries of filmdom's dwindling constellation of stars, was the occasion for an evening-long sequence of film clips, take-offs and testimonials to filmdom's premier "tough guy." In the audience also were Mrs. Billie Cagney, sister Jeanne Cagney, and many of the old Warners gang—Ralph Bellamy, Mae Clarke, Frank McHugh and Allen Jenkins. Cagney, seeming embarrassed but in healthy condition—white-haired, slightly heavier, with the ringing voice intact—sat quietly at ringside for most of the salute, then bounded up on stage with a few, jaunty dance steps at the end to accept his award. His voice trembled and he had to fight back the tears—especially when he announced that his brother Bill, incapacitated with a serious illness, couldn't be present for the event. But, like a trouper, he finished his speech—quoting poet John Masefield and thanking his many friends—and then disappeared quickly back into his hermitage, as the applause reverberated loud and long.

In retirement, the actor became, by his own admission, a dabbler in poetry, an amateur artist and a wealthy landowner-farmer. A sample of his poetry? "Writing verses I cannot help/ As a pig furrows her brood to whelp/Each must come in its given time/So there's naught to do but write and rhyme." Long a frustrated artist, Cagney took up the hobby of painting seriously, studying with Sergei Bongart, a Santa Monica artist. He refused all offers to reproduce or sell his works. "How could I

Above, receiving the Life Achievement Award from George Stevens Jr., director of the American Film Institute. Below, at the banquet with Mr. and Mrs. Ronald Reagan and Mrs. "Billie" Cagney

Gentleman farmer, taken during the Fifties

face those really good artists who've given their whole lives to it and may still be having a hard time making a living?" he told a reporter. "I'm a tyro with a little name value. No thanks; it's not right."

His devotion to soil conservation led him to narrate several radio programmes on the subject, and he once addressed students of the University of Maine on the topic. When, in 1955, he was awarded an honorary doctorate in the humanities at Rollins College, Winter Park, Florida, school officials were pleasantly surprised by a lengthy, fact-filled acceptance address on the subject of—not Hollywood but soil conservation.

A diligent researcher in the Thirties once unearthed a studio questionnaire which was filled out by the young Cagney during his first days on the Warners lot. Under the heading "Ambition" Cagney had scrawled: "To retire to the backwoods permanently." Three decades later, James Cagney resigned from Hollywood forever and achieved his ambition.

4

'Tough Guy'

Charm and the Split Personality of Sex

"No one can blame me for getting a bit annoyed with this business of striking women in every one of my pictures. It has been going on for some time now. In each succeeding picture, I approach such scenes with a sinking feeling. The film audiences seem to have found it novel when I first did it in The Public Enemy. *They clamoured for more. The writers of all my pictures have written it into the scripts and the directors have followed it up by directing it into the pictures."*

JAMES CAGNEY

"I am not the characters I play. I believe that, in order to do anything well, you must have perspective, a certain amount of objectivity, of detachment. This is necessary in order to give a clear portrait of a character. If I were a 'tough guy,' I couldn't play one even as well as I hope to do. It has been more valuable to me to stand on the sidelines and, with a certain degree of impersonality, register the reactions I have noted. The idea of playing oneself is essentially fallacious. The fact that I am supposed to be a tough guy in real life doesn't bother me in the least. It's amusing. It doesn't matter."

JAMES CAGNEY

His professional show business debut as a female impersonator was a somewhat ironic beginning for Cagney the actor. Later a leading man in Hollywood, he became movieland's paradoxical heart-throb (a sex-symbol star—though he himself was happily married and free from rumour of scandal), a cinema male known mainly for his tendency by reputation to bop women in the face with an arrogant fist.

His attitude was actually dual: he could be soft or hard. He would often accentuate his kisses with a fake punch that mocked the warmth of his feeling. He could be tender one moment, distrustful the next. And, significantly, not only with women—but with men also. With some men he scrapped; others

Movieland's paradoxical heart-throb of the Thirties

he loved. His film affairs of friendship were as often with males as females. This split personality—this rare ability to communicate and sustain a relationship on the screen with men or women—popularised Cagney with male moviegoers (who either identified vicariously with his woman-slapping or just appreciated his masculinity) and female moviegoers both, an unusual distinction for any movie star, especially a man.

(In fact, many critics argued, Cagney was actually more popular among male audiences. "Variety" reported on one occasion: "The populace, at least that portion attending the Strand, are now expectant of this player socking all and sundry including all the women in the cast. There's even a distinct tremor of disappointment through the house when no wallop is forthcoming. . . . And Cagney probably has no more partial gathering than the mob which gathers at the Strand whenever they hang out his name. The boys start to gather early and a peek at 12:30 noon will reveal a good sized assemblage of 90 percent male. That element which delays deliveries to see a picture and drops over from Eighth Avenue and West, goes in a big way for the manner in which James handles his film women.")

Cagney's relations with women were stormy. The Cagneyesque courtship was characteristically a bout, a romeo's game of matched wits and oneupmanship with optional recourse to physical punishment. Many of Cagney's women, like Mae Clarke in *The Public Enemy* or *Lady Killer*, were simply punching bag specimens. Some few others, such as Joan Blondell in films like *Blonde Crazy*, fought back. Cagney treated women suspiciously always—even at the expected and programmed moment in each of Cagney's films when "She" walked onto the scene and Cagney surveyed her with an admiring gaze, cool approval and a smile. Audiences were conditioned to know that it wasn't exactly love at first sight. More often (as in *St. Louis Kid, Taxi!* or *The Strawberry Blonde*) it was love/hate at first sight. Cagney first distrusted and even despised the woman. Later, she won him over, proved herself equal in her womanhood to his manhood. But such a woman was—in Cagney's films—rare. Equally rare was his dedication or marriage to any woman: when Cagney was wed, as in *Footlight Parade, White Heat* or *One, Two, Three*, his marriage was duly depicted as estranged and cheerless (only the independents and *Yankee Doodle Dandy* are exceptions) as if to verify his essential identity as a hard-to-tame bachelor.

Cagney only liked "tough" women, the Cagney/Warners films

postulated in the Thirties and Forties. Mild Margaret Lindsay, for example, an actress with a sniffly, haughty temperament, was an inferior match for the actor in films such as *Lady Killer* or *Frisco Kid*. Other "weak" women were comparably mediocre love interests in *Picture Snatcher, Oklahoma Kid, Each Dawn I Die* and other films. The Cagney persona demanded a woman who was strong and unyielding, a woman who could stand up to the Cagney braggadocio. In *The Public Enemy* Gwen Allen (Jean Harlow) explained the enticing charm behind the star.

"You are different, Tommy," she tells him, cradling his head in her arms, "Very different. And I've discovered it isn't only a difference in manner and outward appearances. It's a difference in basic character. The men I know . . . and I've known dozens of them . . . oh, they're so nice, so polished, so considerate. . . . Most women like that, Tommy, I guess they're afraid of the other kind. I thought I was, too. But you're so strong. You don't give, you take. Oh Tommy, I could love you to death."

It was a perfect capsule summation of his sexual persona.

Joan Blondell—called "a perfect punch bag for his clenched, explosive talent" by Kenneth Tynan—was easily Cagney's "toughest" female co-star, and the best. In the seven Cagney-Blondell films, she holds her own, Cagney's equal, one of the few actresses ever to stand up victoriously and indomitably to Cagney's manliness. Like Cagney, Blondell was hard-shelled but sentimental, rowdy but winsome. Cynical and flip, their screen relationship set the foundations for the later partnerships of Bogart and Bacall and, in a lighter vein, Tracy and Hepburn. They were the most popular male-female screen team of the early Thirties.

The kernel of expression for all three screen duos was verbal words-as-love. Physical love-making was only implied (partially because of cinematic convention), symbolically represented by the back-and-forth, artful, witty, pseudo-antagonistic and suggestive debate. Cagney and Blondell were the first twosome to refine and popularise the exercise of romantic rivalry and double-edged repartee.

From the first, their careers and style were intertwined. Both began in vaudeville and both graduated to Broadway. On stage together in New York's "Maggie the Magnificent," they received good reviews and landed parts in "Penny Arcade." When Warners bought the stage property from Al Jolson, Cagney and Blondell went along as part of the deal. Their very

With Joan Blondell in SINNER'S HOLIDAY

first film was also their first film together: *Sinner's Holiday* in 1930, the screen version of "Penny Arcade," in which Blondell plays a gum-chewing, wise-cracking carnival dame who agrees to provide murderer Harry Delano (Cagney) with an alibi, for a price. Blondell is already Cagney's peer in *Sinner's Holiday*, glowering with vengeful fury at the slightest hint of doublecross and sniggering with laughter the next moment when her upper hand is acknowledged. Their scenes together in *Sinner's Holiday*—Cagney trying to bluff his way past Blondell's discriminating looks, Blondell menacingly out for her own best interests—have the same, favourably gruff give-and-take quality which later becomes their trademark.

In three subsequent films together—*Other Men's Women, The Public Enemy* and *The Crowd Roars*—Blondell played secondary parts; their reputation as a screen team rests largely with three films besides *Sinner's Holiday*: *Blonde Crazy, Footlight Parade* and *He Was Her Man.* At their peak in 1931's *Blonde Crazy,* Cagney is tricky and Blondell is nonchalant, especially in the casual but cunning love scenes. "You worship nothing but dough," Blondell tells Cagney after one advance, eyeing Cagney in a wistful tease. "Aw, c'mon, we're getting too serious," answers Cagney, his voice disinterested. "Let's dance." The seriousness of romance is scolded throughout *Blonde Crazy* and Cagney, who loses Blondell to a "respectable businessman," tells her with good-natured sportsmanship when she quits his company, "I wish you all the luck in the world—name the first one after me." Their implicit care for each other, caught mostly by the tender animation of their eyes, is resolved by an ending in which they are re-united. The whole playful flirtation works because Blondell is never at a disadvantage. When she slaps Cagney after he lures her into a hotel room he tells her with mock admiration, "I'd like to have you slap me like that every day." Unimpressed by his bluff, she slaps him again and with a pert, determined smile, she stalks off. But if she eludes "Blonde Crazy" Cagney throughout the narrative, she nevertheless capitulates in the final moments and vows to stay beside him (this, according to the standardised, contrived Hollywood formula).

Footlight Parade, in 1933, brought back the duo, combining Blondell's soft, scheming secretary Nan Prescott with Cagney's beleaguered Chester Kent, theatrical producer. Again, it is Blondell's smartness that is so appealing: Kent, trusting and

In the early Thirties, with Richard Barthelmess, Joan Blondell, "Billie" Cagney and William Cagney

slow-to-learn, is being cheated by his co-producers; Blondell, discovering the swindle, blackmails the two crooks and gaily delivers the payment to Cagney. She is his aide, his confidante, his friend, hoped-for lover and unknowing guardian angel. She unmasks the pretentious Vivian Rich (Claire Dodd), who is out for Kent's money, disguising her slum background with fraudulent high society airs. "As long as there are sidewalks you'll have a job," Blondell tells her, accenting the insult with a smug, pleased smile. She trades barbs, grumbles cynical and uncaring asides, swaps ideas excitedly with Cagney and steals around every corner of *Footlight Parade*'s plot, nourishing its weaknesses. Enterprising and granite-hard, she resembles nothing so much in style as a female Cagney.

He Was Her Man may be the best Cagney-Blondell film, just as surely as it is the last and most unusual. The most serious and thoughtful example of their teamwork, *He Was Her Man* is the story of Flicker Hayes (Cagney), a petty gangster who is being pursued by double-crossed rivals bent on murder; Hayes falls in love while escaping with a former prostitute (Joan Blondell), who herself is on the way to marry a kindly Portuguese fisherman (Victor Jory). Slow, almost ponderous, but directed patiently and steadily by Lloyd Bacon, *He Was Her Man* is an oddly sentimental film which rests on Cagney's assured, warm-hearted characterisation set against Blondell's portrait of a forlorn, untrusting woman in distress. They are attracted to each other gradually but inevitably until Hayes, seeking to save Rose (Blondell) from the gunman's bullet, ultimately spurns her in a heroic display of bravado. "You're just trying to let me down easy," she tells him, painfully measuring the words (the waiting assassins are in full view), suspecting his sacrifice. "I hope you get the breaks right down the line always. You've got to believe that. I'm for you all the way." Stone-faced, he says goodbye, and rides off with the killers to the edge of a nearby cliff. "Nice day for it," he says to the grim thugs. "Nice day for what?" rasps one of the men. "The wedding," he answers. As the words escape, he is shot down; in the distance, church bells chime to announce the wedding of Rose and the fisherman. Though the film wanders into *cliché* (the buxom, affectionate mother of the fisherman, for example, is a stock, one-dimensional character), it happily does not stray too far; the film is to be recommended for Blondell's astute, sympathetic characterisation as a prostitute (still the reason why the film is not shown on American television). Both Cagney and Blondell deliver heart-rending performances, honestly wrenching tears at the finale of this obscure film, all but unknown to present-day audiences.

He Was Her Man was Blondell's last feature with Cagney. He never again found such a durable and appropriate female co-star. After Blondell, Cagney's women were, for the most part, tidy, meek and uninspiring; scriptwriters and directors were painfully at a loss over what to do with a woman in a Cagney film who wasn't feisty. Olivia de Havilland in *Strawberry Blonde* flickered briefly; Bette Davis in *The Bride Came C.O.D.* was overly caustic; Viveca Lindfors in *Run For Cover* was embarrassingly subordinate. Like Mae Clarke in *The Public Enemy*, women, subjected to Cagney's increasingly secure status as a "tough guy" male movie star, became "things" to be pushed and shoved around—witness the brutal treatment accorded Virginia Mayo in *White Heat*, Doris Day in *Love Me or Leave Me*, Irene Papas in *Tribute to a Bad Man* or Arlene Francis in *One, Two, Three*. Each, in turn, are physically or emotionally dominated by Cagney, by the brusque manner that had gained wide acceptance among audiences over the years. Besides Blondell, few strong women rose to challenge Cagney's male mastery (those like Virginia Mayo in *White Heat*, who were temporarily fiery and gutsy, eventually suffered his domination). Only infrequent women such as Loretta Young in *Taxi!*, who defiantly opposes Cagney's orders, or the worldwise Ann Sheridan of *Torrid Zone*, who dogs his every step, punctured the Cagney front.

Ann Sheridan is really the only actress after Blondell to rival Cagney in his ever-imbalanced battle of the sexes. "One of the great screen teams was James Cagney and Ann Sheridan," argues David Shipman in his "The Great Movie Stars." "It wasn't written up at the time and, as far as is known, legions of fans didn't write in to ask Warners to reunite them. Indeed, they were only really teamed together twice, in two not very notable films, *City for Conquest* and *Torrid Zone*. They complemented each other perfectly, he all bombast and bounce, she more knowing, sharp and disillusioned." Actually, Sheridan made three films with Cagney—*Angels with Dirty Faces, City for Conquest* and *Torrid Zone*. Because her role in *Angels with Dirty Faces* is relatively small, *City for Conquest* and *Torrid Zone* are the better films on which to judge their collaboration. In *City for Conquest* she plays Peggy Nash, a slum girl with big eyes for fame and fortune, who goads boy-friend Danny Kenny (Cagney) into a boxing career while she herself pursues a career as a professional dancer. Hair pulled back and eyebrows arched, looking alternately innocent and sophisticated, she smoothly manipulates events to her own satisfaction. On board the Staten Island Ferry, she leans longingly over the boat railing and, in a daydreaming voice, urges boy-friend Kenny to make a name for himself in the world. "Oh, c'mon," Cagney answers, "Get off that express and take a local." "But Danny," she insists in a convincing voice, "I don't want you to do it for me. I only want you to do it for yourself." They are well-paired—she the romanticist, he the realist. She wins him over to her view but loses him altogether when he is blinded in the ring. She plays the entire last ten minutes of the film in tears, sustaining her blurry eyes with elegant and believable reserve during a Carnegie Hall concert, and through a tearful, prolonged reunion with Kenny at the end.

Torrid Zone trades tragedy for comedy, successfully though, proving that Sheridan was equally capable at matching Cagney for laughs. Wry and deadpan, her voice betraying only a slight edge of emotion, she traded barbs with Cagney and co-star Pat O'Brien with a skill and female presence missing in Cag-

With Ann Sheridan in TORRID ZONE

ney's films since *Blonde Crazy.* "Why don't you send that mind of yours out and have it dry cleaned?" asks an exasperated Cagney in *Torrid Zone.* "What's the use?" replies Sheridan, a faint smile telegraphing her response: "Look at the company I'm in." Cagney eventually falls in love with Sheridan (of course) and then grudgingly pays her the ultimate Cagneyesque compliment: "You know, you'd be a pretty nice guy if you weren't around so much at the wrong time." Expressed in explicitly male terms, the phrase underlines the implicit sexual thesis of all Cagney/Warners (and Cagney/Hollywood) works: Only a woman who is tough (tough like Cagney/tough like a man) is a fitting mate for the male hero. Cagney's super-masculine stance lent credence and support to an ethic that is still in force: women in the movies must live up to the man's standards— not vice versa. Cagney's cinema was plainly a man's world.

Sweethearts were not always the main women in Cagney's films, though, for his "mother" played a repeatedly important role. No other American actor has been so closely haunted by his nearest kin. Cagney's successor "tough guy" of the Forties, Humphrey Bogart, was rarely seen on the screen with his mother. Two instances spring to mind—in a bitter, wretched reunion in William Wyler's *Dead End* (1937), and in 1942's funny *All Through the Night.* The enigmatic Bogart persona denied emphatically the existence of a "mother"; Bogart was cold, rootless, independent, a loner. Bogart depended on the distance he kept from his audience as a factor of his appeal. But Cagney's appeal depended conversely on the innately sympathetic qualities projected by his persona and on the implicit notion that he was a "regular guy," with feelings, ideas and problems common to the populace at large. Cagney was an alienated figure but, unlike Bogart, he was never an isolated figure. For Cagney, the appearance of his "mother" in his films represented roots: the past, a tradition and the hope of future. And, importantly, drawing on the tender associations mythically linked to motherhood, the omnipresence of Cagney's mother was the one indispensable bond between star and audience that exonerated the nastier actions of the Cagney character.

"In *Public Enemy,*" bragged producer Darryl F. Zanuck, "I gave Cagney one redeeming trait. He was a no-good bastard but he loved his mother, and somehow or other you felt a certain affection and rooting interest for him even though he was despicable." But before *Public Enemy,* in 1930's *Sinner's Holiday,* Cagney's first film, his "mother" already played a key role, evidencing that from the start the screen Cagney was allied with his mother in the mind's eye of audiences. In *Sinner's Holiday*, Cagney bends on his knee and weeps openly in his mother's lap, begging her forgiveness for the murder he has committed. "I didn't mean to, Ma," he sobs. "I couldn't help it. Honest I couldn't. Don't leave me. You've got to believe me. You've got to help me. I'm scared, Ma." The scene is unusually touching for what is otherwise a commonplace Thirties melodrama—and Cagney is predictably "forgiven" by his understanding mother (in the same sense that audiences, appreciating the sentiment of the sequence, also "forgive" Cagney his indiscretion). Like Ma Jarrett of *White Heat* (1949) twenty years later, the mother of *Sinner's Holiday* exerts a bizarre psychotic control over Cagney. Helpless, he follows her instructions every whit, even when she maliciously plots the false arrest of her daughter's lover.

Cagney's screen mother re-appeared frequently after *Sinner's Holiday*—in *The Public Enemy, The Irish in Us, Each Dawn I Die, Yankee Doodle Dandy* and *White Heat*. In each case, Cagney's devotion and attachment to his mother is a focal point of the plot; in each case the relationship is depicted as close and familial. Cagney's mother is not only his maternal relative but also his friend and aide. Their relationship, simple and wholesome enough to compel incessant hugs and kisses before the camera, is also almost a fanatical affection. Even in *The Irish In Us*, a jovial film with barely an inkling of the neuroses of *White Heat*, the seed of Cagney's maniacal affinity for his film mother can be detected: pretending disinterest in a girl-friend, Cagney tells his mother jokingly, "I'm not the marrying kind. What do I need with a wife? I've got you, haven't I? You're my sweetheart." The double-edged meaning of the presence of Cagney's mother would, perhaps, have even surprised Darryl F. Zanuck. Even the little goody in *The Public Enemy* accepts graft from her son, such as the keg of beer in the middle of the table, demonstrating how neurotic-psychotic many of the mothers are. In this way, *Sinner's Holiday, Public Enemy* and *White Heat* all show the perversion of the close American family (perhaps unintentionally), not how wonderful such a family is.

His early "mother films" formed a foundation for *White Heat*, in which the love of Cody Jarrett (Cagney) for Ma Jarrett (Margaret Wycherly) swells to an insane proportion. Critics such as Bosley Crowther who didn't comprehend Cagney's filmic development berated *White Heat*, unable to accept Cody Jarrett's seemingly implausible dependence on his mother.

But the inclusion of the character of Ma Jarrett in *White Heat* is a carefully groomed schematic ploy dating for its validity all the way back to *Sinner's Holiday* and Cagney's unholy alliance with Ma Delano. The "tough" woman/mother dependent complex, predicted in its extreme form in *Sinner's Holiday* but found in variation in many of Cagney's films, is fulfilled in *White Heat*: Ma Jarrett synthesises all of the "best" character traits of Cagney's women, producing a female who is strong (manly) and motherly. Cagney's mother is such an important figure to the story of *White Heat,* in fact, that she symbolically becomes a man when Cody (Cagney) is sentenced to prison. Designated by Cody as titular head of the mob, she runs the Jarrett gang in Cody's absence with an iron control and firm command, not unlike Cody's own domination, until she is shot dead by a treacherous bullet in the back. Cagney's Freudian-like mother fixation in *White Heat* is never so overt as at the screaming finale—Cody howling, "Made it, Ma! Top of the World!"—with its perverted salute to the sway of motherhood.

Ma Jarrett's violent death in *White Heat* (though the death occurs off-camera, it is the first and only time in film that Cagney's mother dies) marked the end of prominence for Cagney's film mother. The disappearance of his screen mothers coincided with his Fifties maturation. As Cagney put on weight and greyed a little, the idea that he was too old to have a mother naturally replaced the earlier implication that he was an overgrown mama's boy. But the point had already been scrupulously made by years of conscious groundwork carried over by memory: this boy gone wrong, witness his mother's confidence, was really okay.

Typically, Cagney's closeness to his mother was complemented by warm relationships with other family members (interrupted only by fights with his brothers in *The Public Enemy* and *The Crowd Roars*—his intra-family quarrels are invariably with the men of the clan). If the family was absent from the plotline, Cagney could rely usually on the attentions of a "surrogate mother," a representative older woman at whom he directed the rapt devotion of a boyish son, as in *He Was Her Man* and *Devil Dogs of the Air*. The "surrogate mother" becomes the whole focus of *Johnny Come Lately* when, ignoring the advances of the ingenue love interest, Cagney played separate and exquisite "love" scenes with Grace George, Hattie McDaniel and Marjorie Main—all middle-aged women.

To audiences, Cagney's screen family doubtless represented stability, unswerving support in crisis and firm friendship in the time of need. It was reassuring to audiences that Cagney, headstrong and problem-prone, was cared for by a mother and family. Two of Cagney's films—*The Irish In Us* and *Yankee Doodle Dandy*—capitalised wholly on the family ethic. Both films—about Irish-American families—celebrate and honour the institution of the family. Both films extol the virtues of family togetherness, a tradition which is heavily Irish-Catholic—like Cagney—as well as American.

But Cagney's most outstanding contribution to the American cinema is his frank articulation of the intimate relationship between men. Traditionally, the American screen is the haven of conventional romanticism ("boy-girl business," as Cagney once termed it), love stories between women and men. It is one of the unwritten taboos of American filmdom (only recently amended to accommodate the changing values of the Sixties) that women do not consort with women on celluloid and men do not consort with men, at least not on familiar terms. Howard Hawks's films are among the few exceptions to the rule. Cagney's films likewise are a special case. He worked best with men, partly because the men of the Warners stock company seemed to outlast the starlets in contract life; and he developed a persuasive, working relationship with a number of versatile actors—such as Alan Hale, Allen Jenkins, Stuart Erwin, Guy Kibbee and George E. Stone. Though men figure centrally in all Cagney films (and sometimes, during the Warners years, major actors such as George Raft or Humphrey Bogart were co-starred opposite Cagney deliberately to heighten box-office interest), two male actors in particular were an influence on his career. The first was Frank McHugh, the chubby, likeable Warners character actor; the second was Pat O'Brien, described by one critic as "the cinema's most skilled exponent of the rapid-fire delivery."

McHugh played beside Cagney, as his friend and side-kick, in eleven films. Traditionally, the "side-kick" is assigned to provide comic relief. But unlike the side-kicks popularised by association with John Wayne or Gene Autry, McHugh's role *vis à vis* Cagney was always explicitly that of a serious comrade. Though McHugh also provided comic relief—he had an odd, squeaky, whining voice that invited laughter—he was loyal and devoted, less a "second banana" (such as someone like Gabby Hayes) than an accomplice. A real-life bond between Cagney and McHugh contributed to their affinity on the screen; the off-screen friendship embellished the on-screen

With Ruby Keeler, Joan Blondell, Frank McHugh and Dick Powell in
FOOTLIGHT PARADE

friendship. As young, struggling actors on Broadway during the
Twenties, they were fast chums. (O'Brien, also Cagney's close
friend off-screen, was McHugh's room-mate in those days.)

McHugh is the poky counterbalance to Cagney's intense
rhythm. In *Footlight Parade*, he plays a whimpering choreographer with interminable complaints. Cigar in mouth, he lazily
sings the female half of a dance number nestled comfortably
in the arms of Dick Powell, in order to demonstrate the step.
Cagney is the opposite, barking orders and moving in locomo-
tive fashion. In *The Roaring Twenties*, McHugh is naive and
bumbling, an antidote to the ruthless Cagney. Foremost, Mc-
Hugh was forever loyal. When he died in the course of a Cagney film, he died violently and his death always signalled a
sharp turn of events for the worse (as in *The Crowd Roars* or
The Roaring Twenties); when McHugh was alive, he support-
ed Cagney with above-call devotion (as in *Here Comes the
Navy, Footlight Parade, City for Conquest* or *The Irish in Us*),
pledging his allegiance even when everyone else in the script
deserted Cagney.

During the formative Warner years, McHugh was an inte-
gral and almost constant component of Cagney's films; in his
absence, other Warners stock company seconds (Allen Jenkins,
Alan Hale, George E. Stone, etc.) supplanted him, though Mc-
Hugh's service was more convincing owing to his personal in-
timacy with Cagney. The trustworthy sidekick's last appearance

with Cagney was in 1953 as Rector in *A Lion Is in the Streets*, but McHugh's part, oddly, called for him to play the "heavy."

Pat O'Brien, however, was Cagney's finest co-star, and also a "tough guy" actor known for his crisp, spitfire delivery. O'Brien joined Cagney for *Here Comes the Navy* in 1934, the year Joan Blondell left the team (a tough man substituting for a tough woman), and O'Brien and Cagney made eight films together concluding with *Torrid Zone* in 1940. It is one of the very few recorded instances in American film history of two male film stars—both essentially dramatic actors rather than comedians—of parallel stature, sharing billing and developing a screen relationship over a period of time in a series of films. The pairing was the most sustained and candid male relationship ever experienced in the American cinema to date.

There was a symbolic dichotomy in the relationship that was pure and exciting. O'Brien represented enlightened authority and Cagney signified rebellion. O'Brien played a policeman (*The Irish in Us*), a priest (*Angels with Dirty Faces, The Fighting 69th*), a military commander (*Here Comes the Navy, Devil Dogs of the Air*) and an imperialist banana plantation manager (in *Torrid Zone*—American authority expressed in its expansionist form). Liberal and well-meaning, he was the perfect foil for Cagney's contempt for authority, a better contrast, for example, than the blatant authoritarianism of someone like Warners regular Barton MacLane. O'Brien was "top dog" but unsubtle plot devices always revealed Cagney as the "moral" victor. For example, Cagney always "won the girl." O'Brien, bland and sexless, was never rewarded with the elusive sweetheart.

Tension sustained the duo—the tension between authority and rebellion. In other parts, independent of Cagney, O'Brien was a competent but relatively uninteresting actor. When rubbed like sandpaper against the friction of the Cagney persona, he was polished and sparkling. ("Many people think all I ever appeared in were service pictures," he complained in his autobiography, alluding perhaps to the memorable Cagney-O'Brien films, "except those who think I only played priests, or those who have the impression I only acted football coaches or prison wardens. Actually, while I did play these parts, most of my roles had nothing to do with the above, not that they weren't great parts.")

In *Boy Meets Girl* (a film produced after Cagney's third Warners walkout), the two were badly miscast in a film originally designed for Marion Davies but re-written to accommo-

date O'Brien and Cagney. They played "idea men" in Hollywood, colleagues and cohorts, who behaved in concert throughout. The parts literally as well as figuratively echoed each other. "New!" exclaims Cagney in the film. "Brand new!" repeats
O'Brien. "How!" says Cagney. "And how!" says O'Brien. A
hoped-for change of pace became instead a failed try at broad
comedy.

Here Comes the Navy, their first film together, set a pat-
tern for their later roles in tandem, especially *Devil Dogs of
the Air* (the air version of *Here Comes the Navy*) and
The Fighting 69th (the land version of *Here Comes the
Navy*). But though *Devil Dogs of the Air*, featuring Cagney as
a braggart flying ace and O'Brien as his officer-pal, and *The
Fighting 69th*, with Cagney as a coward coached by priest
O'Brien, are relatively pallid imitations of the original, *Here
Comes the Navy* is solid fun.

All the familiar elements of the Cagney-O'Brien situation
are introduced in *Here Comes the Navy*. At the outset, Cagney is a "swell guy" until he meets O'Brien, a Navy officer who
bests him in a dance-hall brawl and "steals" his girl. Cagney
joins the Navy to "get even," conflict arises, Cagney falls from
grace and shipmates describe him as a "wrong guy." The conflict is attributable (as is customary in Cagney-O'Brien films)
to the struggle between Cagney and O'Brien over the attentions of a woman, in this case O'Brien's sister (Margaret Lindsay). At the conclusion, Cagney executes a brave, life-saving
deed to recoup favour with his friends, salvage his personal
honour, make amends with O'Brien and win the girl. Warners
varied the formula only slightly for the future Cagney-O'Brien
films of a military composition. Critics complained about the
familiarity of the plots of *Devil Dogs of the Air* and *The Fighting 69th* but they forgave the repetition for the better films,
Ceiling Zero, Angels with Dirty Faces and *Torrid Zone*.

Angels with Dirty Faces is prime Cagney-O'Brien. As Father Jerry Connelly, the boyhood chum-turned-priest of gangster
Rocky Sullivan (Cagney), O'Brien acted his best part opposite Cagney, a hard-core role with a discernible trace of sympathy. Both men feign outer toughness but they cannot help
but show their mutual respect and genuine liking for each other. In a soft, pleading voice, Father Connelly asks Rocky to
give up crime because he is an idol to the neighbourhood kids.
"Whatever I teach them, you show me up," implores O'Brien.
"You show them the easiest way." But Rocky refuses, and Connelly vows to campaign against crime, even against his old

With Gloria Stuart and Pat O'Brien in HERE COMES THE NAVY
With Ann Sheridan and Pat O'Brien in ANGELS WITH DIRTY FACES

friend. "Go to it," Rocky tells him. Like the best of enemies, they shake hands passionately and part, the moment of their accord made vivid by the obvious feeling they have for each other. This scene is only one of several that set up the incredible ending. Rocky, waiting for the electric chair, is begged by Father Connelly to act cowardly at his execution in order to deflate the hero worship of the slum kids. "You're asking me to crawl on my belly—the last thing I do in life. Nothing doing," answers the visibly nervous gangster. But in his defiant answer is still the hint of possible surrender and that unconcealed fondness for the old friend of his youth. En route to extermination, Rocky cries and screams in terrifying, blood-curdling fright—the scene is disclosed in shadows. Hearing him, O'Brien's face freezes into a half-smile. Rocky has gone to death as a villain in the eyes of the Dead End kids, but he is a hero to the neighbourhood priest, and, possibly, to audiences also.

Torrid Zone in 1940 was their last film together and also their most unashamedly wacky. O'Brien is at his most profane as Steve Case, the cigar-addict banana plantation manager who is beset by a revolutionary named Rosario, a female card shark (Ann Sheridan), and his old wife-stealing pal, Nick Butler (Cagney). O'Brien tries hard to disguise his affection for Cagney but he fails miserably. At the same time that he accepts a string of collect telegrams from Butler—"Meet me down at the boat, sweetheart!"—he angrily issues orders that no more are to be received. He crumples the telegrams furiously, spits a long series of insults about Butler and then schemes madly to keep the maverick administrator on hire as a plantation manager. The deal is swung, the chase is on to capture the bandit rebel, and in the benevolent climax of the tale (an ending United Fruit would not appreciate today), O'Brien gets Cagney, Cagney gets Sheridan, and Rosario gets away. O'Brien and Cagney are wonderfully in their stride in *Torrid Zone*. One moment they are at each other's throats and the next they are laughing and kidding as if nothing at all had happened. In the way they walk and converse, eye each other warily and size up their hostile surroundings, they convey an unabashed pleasure at their own cleverness, and a healthy enthusiasm besides about their zaniest vehicle.

Eventually, O'Brien tired of his type-casting (*vis à vis* Cagney) and he complained publicly about his image. "Jimmy is grand to work with," he told a reporter in the Thirties. "I think one picture a year with Cagney would be fine. But, as it is, I've been with him in every uniform—the army, the navy, the police, the marines, the air corps—and it's always a case of me falling in love with his girl, or him falling in love with mine. It gets tiresome." The advent of the Forties and *Torrid Zone* spelled the end of the partnership. O'Brien continued in films and played the title role in *Knute Rockne* later in 1940 (the personal favourite of all his roles, and his best, according to many misguided film critics); he then left Warners as Cagney did, acting in films for other studios, particularly R.K.O., and he even organised his own independent production outfit for a spell. O'Brien performed a stint on television in the Sixties, and extensive work in summer stock throughout the decade.

If O'Brien was somewhat sensitive about his alliance with Cagney, it could be largely because Cagney always received top billing, and the better roles. But the Cagney-O'Brien partnership had subtle and delicate qualities which greatly recommend it and even make it an important contribution to the American cinema. The two actors captured the essence of the friendship that exists between many American men, an accomplishment in the cinema that has been repeated occasionally (Jon Voight and Dustin Hoffman in *Midnight Cowboy*, for example; or Hawks's films) but not often. In their banter and warm camaraderie there was much of the uneasy, competitive oneupmanship that constitutes the core of many male relationships. "New York Times" writer Frank S. Nugent called them "You hit me and I'll hit you" films, and this kind of seesaw slap-happy dynamic aptly describes their films together.

The undercurrent of the rivalry was love. Their films are indeed stories about love between men, the sort of profound and honest evidence of male friendship that Hollywood rarely produced. War ners writers exploited the recognisable, bosom friendship between the two men and Cagney and O'Brien, with tact and insight, improved the relationship. Thus it was not unusual for O'Brien to put his arm around Cagney lovingly or to hug him unabashedly (as in *Ceiling Zero, The Irish in Us* or *Torrid Zone*). So do the two refer to each other (jokingly—but with truthful double meaning) as "dear" or "sweetheart" (as in *Here Comes the Navy, Torrid Zone, Ceiling Zero* and *Devil Dogs of the Air*).

Cagney's friendship with McHugh in *Here Comes the Navy* extends so far that the actor simply, plaintively blows Cagney a kiss as Cagney leaves the U.S.S. Arizona for transfer, during one segment of the film. A nearby sailor, unnerved by the spectacle, asks laconically, "Oh swift, what are you two guys, a couple of violets?" That action and response, so delight-

fully natural and casual, is almost an afterthought, practically
a reflex. Within the wholly male context of a Cagney film, such
feelings are readily understood and acceptable.

Because Howard Hawks is generally considered an especial
director of male themes (he directed Cagney in *The Crowd
Roars*, and Cagney and O'Brien in *Ceiling Zero*), his contribution to the Cagney ethos is an intriguing matter. Hawks was
unquestionably one of Cagney's most sympathetic directors. *The
Crowd Roars* (scripted in part by Hawks from an original story
by the director) is one of the finest of the early Thirties Cagney films. In *The Crowd Roars*, more than any of his early
works, Cagney veers away from a tendency (encouraged by
Warners) towards over-theatricality and, in the process, emerges as a more human character. Cagney is cast as Hawks's ideal
man: a skilled, independent adventurer (racing driver) who
responds with one of his most empathetic performances. The
scenes in which, jobless and unshaven, he wanders downcast
through the racetracks seeking employment as a driver are especially gripping. And when he breaks down sobbing into the
arms of his old girl-friend (Ann Dvorak), at the climax, the
tableau is poignant.

Likewise, *Ceiling Zero* is one of the best Cagney-O'Brien
films, if not *the* best. Adapted from a popular play of the period, Hawks (and the scriptwriters) stripped the duo of some
of their more artificial antagonisms and instead concentrated
on a likelier, more honest—if still uneasy—working relationship.
As Cagney talks on the phone early in the film, for instance,
O'Brien's hand drifts almost lazily to the back of Cagney's
neck and halts there affectionately, briefly. The two actors exchange winks, looks and knowing smiles at each other's innu-
endoes and private jokes. In these scenes, and in the overall
mood of *Ceiling Zero*, Hawks's sensitive understanding of the
characters and their essential masculinity is evident.

But to attribute the primary thrust of these two films solely to Hawks—and not partly also to the Cagney persona and
the established working relationship of Cagney and O'Brien—
is misleading. Though Hawks's precise measure of control over
The Crowd Roars and *Ceiling Zero* is difficult to ascertain,
it is fair to assume that Warners, as always the case with its
directors, meddled extensively in production decisions and influenced choice of star and script. Cagney's image was well
on its way to being a fixture by the time Hawks first directed
the actor in 1932. Thus, though Hawks's contribution was considerable (it is remarkable how well these two relatively un-

known Hawks's works fit the themes and emphases of the director's entire career), Cagney's own contribution was surely significant.

The evolution of Cagneyesque motifs during the Warners years goes a long way towards explaining the later, older Cagney, particularly regarding the actor's attitude towards women and his association with men in his films. The tried and tested meaning of Cagney's sexuality in the Thirties and Forties clarifies, in the Fifties, his disposition toward Virginia Mayo in *White Heat,* Irene Papas in *Tribute to a Bad Man* (1956) and Arlene Francis in *One, Two, Three* (1961). It explains, in advance of the occurrence, the reason why Cagney's co-stars are so often really men: Edmond O'Brien in *White Heat,* Dan Dailey in *What Price Glory?* (1952), John Derek in *Run for Cover* (1955), and Stephen McNally in *Tribute to a Bad Man.* The Warners Cagney can be deciphered, with modern translation, into the post-Warners Cagney.

When critic Andrew Sarris, in his "An American Cinema," quotes approvingly the "Time" magazine reviewer who said Raoul Walsh is the only American director, evidenced by *White Heat,* who could get away with putting Cagney on his mother's lap, it is startlingly obvious that Sarris never saw *Sinner's Holiday,* Cagney's first feature, in which the famous lap scene is duplicated almost exactly, nearly twenty years earlier, and with agreeable results—handsome testimony that certain Cagneyesque qualities, in this case sexual, were inherent in the man. It is equally transparent that it was not Walsh in this instance who dictated the Cagney persona but quite the contrary: the substance *and* the style are suggested by the actor.

5

Persona

Cagney as Symbol and Image

"Cagney, even with submachine-gun hot in hand and corpses piling at his ankles, can still persuade many people that it was not his fault. By such means he made gang law acceptable to the screen, and became by accident one of the most genuinely corrupting influences Hollywood has ever sent us. Cagney brought organised crime within the mental horizons of errand boys, who saw him as a cavalier of the gutters—their stocky patron saint."

KENNETH TYNAN

From *Sinner's Holiday* to *Yankee Doodle Dandy,* James Cagney, in collaboration with Warner Brothers, constructed and sustained a screen persona which came to govern the remainder of his career, and affected in very distinctive ways his meaning to audiences. Though he is remembered foremost as a screen gangster, Cagney only played a hoodlum in one-fourth of his films, an extraordinary indication of the effectiveness of his few "criminal" appearances. But though his performances as a mobster were relatively few, his characterisation as a "tough guy" was constant, the most prominent feature of the Cagney persona (abandoned only, with qualification, for *Great Guy, Something to Sing About, Yankee Doodle Dandy, Johnny Come Lately* and *The Time of Your Life*). It was his toughness—his spunk, wit, resiliency, and charm—that insured his popularity, a popularity due partly to the implicit thematic connotations, ideas affiliated with the Cagney persona, which the actor inspired.

As a symbol, the Cagney persona communicates both positive and negative connotations. At worst, Cagney presents the liberal guise of fascist instincts: the drive to be on top, to go solo, to dominate women, to buy one hundred new suits, to succeed—the competitive, individualist, capitalist ethic. At best, he represents an optimistic faith in circumstances, hope in the

180

future, a gritty refusal to be dominated in any situation and a stubborn resistance to accepted social standards and *mores* that is exemplary.

There is a special aura of tension which surrounds his Warners works, a tension which is founded on the dynamic contradictions of his character, as a symbol and otherwise. The tension not only derived from outside pressures—such as Hays Office coercion, the specifications of Warners filmmakers or the general influence of the times (the Depression, F.D.R., the New Deal, etc.)—but it also stemmed from Cagney's personal evocation of his screen persona, replete with traits which seemingly disputed his "tough guy" studio-arranged nature—smiling congeniality, warmth and humour. His persona (and his image) was a study of contradictions, of many and different engrossing qualities which occasionally clashed disconcertingly.

A quartet of films from Cagney's earliest Warners period, all directed by Roy Del Ruth, appropriately illustrate what happened, for instance, when the actor's gangsterism was translated into light comedy—pitting the hoodlum Cagney (which Warners was reluctant to de-emphasise) against the comedian Cagney. The effect was a not entirely satisfactory stress. Ostensibly comedies, the four—*Blonde Crazy* (1931), *Taxi!* (1932), *Winner Take All* (1932) and *Lady Killer* (1933)—are an imprecise, neurotic juxtaposition of comedy and drama, damaged by a too-scrupulous concentration on Cagney's desperado personality. Cagney attempts to flirt with Joan Blondell in *Blonde Crazy*, for example, but he is continuously rebuked by a series of slaps in the face which intrude harshly on the otherwise logical and amicable plotline (thereby, theoretically, supplying action and cruelty—criminal *motifs*—to what is otherwise a romantic story). In one scene, trying to interest Blondell in his manly charms, Cagney offers her a share of his train berth. She demurs, and in a sudden comment adds, "I musn't let you go before I tell you how much I care for you, Bert dear." She then slaps him—loud and evidently hard. Stretched to symbolic length, her action is explicitly punitive, an unsubtle reminder without cause that Cagney is at base a mere crook. The same action is repeated several times in the film, without reason or warning, courtesy of the assumed, rowdy requisites of Cagney's gangster image.

(Not that *Blonde Crazy* is without its charms. Engaging, despite its drawbacks, like Cagney's other Del Ruth comedies, *Blonde Crazy* depends on its strain between comedy and drama as a strength as well as a weakness, giving the film an alluring experimental complexity, as well as a certain suggestion of spontaneity. Molly Haskell is one contemporary critic who has rediscovered the merit of the movie, which portrays the exploits of two clever con artists on a cross country spree. "The film's casual and continuous triumph," wrote Haskell in "The Village Voice," "is the rapport between Cagney and Blondell—buddies, would-be lovers, he calling her 'honey,' going up ironically on the second syllable, she self-reliant and soft, giving as much as she gets and more. Blondell's beauty as a 'broad' is that she can outsmart the man without unsexing him. Cagney's beauty as a male is that he can be made a fool of without becoming a fool. They flesh out the spare Warners script . . . with intimations of love, life, confidence, and sexual equality that only reinforce all one's suspicion that they don't make movie stars—or men—like they used to.")

In *Taxi!*, the story shifts from a glance at a taxi war and Cagney's light love affair with Loretta Young to an almost manic depiction of Cagney's urge to revenge his brother's killing. The first half of the movie is reasonable, straightforward narrative, and entertaining. The second half of the film, with its intense focus on Cagney's temper (an aspect of the gangster) is sorely strained. (*Taxi!* is the first film which featured the explosive temper of the Cagney persona, later typically identified with Cagney in all of his roles—the famous Cagney temper surfaced repeatedly until the maximum outburst at the end of *White Heat*.)

In *Winner Take All*, the competition between Cagney's discordant tendencies is subtly symbolised by his choice between city girl Joan Gibson (Virginia Bruce) and country girl Peggy Harmon (Marian Nixon). The city woman is cold, haughty and insensitive, embodying the worst qualities of a metropolitan existence; she is like a gunman's moll. The country woman is, contrarily, sweet and kind, a homespun, affectionate type. After throwing himself after Gibson, Jim Kane (Cagney) returns at the film's end to the arms of country girl Harmon. Yet the contradictions were not always so easily resolved.

Lady Killer further traces the delicate dividing line between the thuggish aspects of the Cagney persona and the gentler qualities of his screen character. Cagney plays a reformed "Fingerman" who becomes a Hollywood film star, the newest "tough guy" discovery. In a central scene, he attends a gala birthday party in honour of his actress friend, star Lois Underwood (Margaret Lindsay). Because she jokingly requests monkeys and elephants and a Swiss band for her birthday gifts,

With Marian Nixon in WINNER TAKE ALL

Cagney triumphantly delivers monkeys and elephants into the midst of the party. Bedlam ensues. The animals run wild, Cagney laughs uproariously, but Lindsay is hysterical, nearly in tears. Intended to be funny, the scene has a bitter, unresolved edge which infects the integrity of the overall production. The bitterness of the scene is caused by Cagney's irrational nastiness, unmotivated in the light context of the scene. A coda scene, written into the script, in which the guests laugh also when they finally understand the joke, does not appear in the finished film.

Blonde Crazy, Taxi!, Winner Take All, and *Lady Killer* are quintessential Cagney Thirties films, but they are all partially marred by this dependence on Cagney's image as a hard-boiled he-man. These four early Warners films evidence all of the qualities subsequently associated with the mature Cagney persona—his child-like emotions, spontaneity and, importantly, his aggressive, sometimes violent attitude about life. Cagney's characteristics remained fairly constant throughout the Thirties, overlapping into the Forties and Fifties; and the recurrent Cagneyesque qualities were nicely suited to capturing and holding a wide audience appeal.

In *Lady Killer*, he attacks a policeman after he is thrown in jail, but he catches himself and apologises, "I'm sorry." A near-identical situation occurs in *The Roaring Twenties*, when gangster Eddie Bartlett (Cagney) savagely attacks his former friend and partner Lloyd Hart (Jeffrey Lynn) because Hart has run away with the gangster's "true love." Bartlett slugs Hart, but then stops abruptly, mumbles "I'm sorry," and walks away. The Cagney apologia recurs in virtually all of his films. His apology is carried to extreme, symbolic lengths by his face-saving martyrdoms in *Ceiling Zero* (1935), *The Fighting 69th* (1940) and *Captains of the Clouds* (1942), but comparable acts of redemption happen in nearly every Cagney story. These scenes are obligatory scenes—vital components of the Cagney persona required to neutralise the less appealing aspects of the law-breaker. Reform (of a gangster) is good drama, a transition which happens in thousands of movies, but Cagney institution-alised the reclamation and parlayed the gimmick into an ex-pected, appreciated and vital part of his persona.

Most importantly, Cagney's enormous popularity as a Warn-ers star stemmed also from the always-evident implication that he represented the "little guy," from the strong belief gener-ated among critical circles and fans that the Cagney persona was intended to typify the average American. This implication came partly from Warners—mostly from Cagney himself, who always described his persona in a strictly American context. He usually played a New Yorker, for example, occasionally a spe-cifically small neighbourhood Brooklynite. He spoke American slang and he evinced American mannerisms. He was often out-of-work. He was earthy. He dressed sharply only when he could afford it. He was lower class. He was hard times and bad luck but spit-grin-and-fight-back. And, he was outrageously masculine in his every action. "He was and continues to be so brilliantly right in his interpretation of a particular type of American male," wrote the "New York Times," "a type that has been spawned in large numbers out of the slum districts of New York and Chicago that it is a natural thing to suspect that he is not acting at all."

Cagney sometimes played a working man (taxi-driver in *Taxi!*, construction worker in *Here Comes the Navy*, truck driver in *St. Louis Kid*) but more often he played simply an independent man, a "dog eat dog" type as he calls himself in *Frisco Kid*. Like many Warners films, Cagney's films not on-ly championed the underdog but they also occasionally mocked the rich. It was not unusual for Cagney to begin his films as a crook and, by the end of the story, become an accepted mem-ber of high society (as in *Hard to Handle* or *Winner Take All*). Along the way, the upper crust and big businessmen are exposed as either fools or bandits. And ambition is interpreted as morally unrewarding.

The "fight your way to the top" metaphor, berated in many Cagney films, is at its most literal in *City for Conquest.* In the film, Cagney, bowing to Ann Sheridan's urging to "have ambition" and "be somebody," fights his way in the boxing ring up the economic and social ladder, only to be tragically blinded by his opponent's trickery in the "big fight" at the end. Many of his films carried such implicit social criticism, the hallmark of most Warners works, but their statements were often compromised. In films like *Here Comes the Navy* or *Devil Dogs of the Air,* the military comes under attack from the Cagney character. (The attack is always directed at the hard-ruled code of military discipline; when, for instance, Cagney is decorated in *Here Comes the Navy* for extinguishing a deck fire and saving the lives of his comrades, he sarcastically rejects his medal. "I did it to save myself and I want them to know that." He tells a Board of Inquiry, "I don't like the Navy and I never have.") But Cagney's disagreements are characteristically resolved by promotion in rank at the finale, resulting, in the words of one critic of the day, in a final impression that Cagney is really nothing more than an "amiable recruiting poster" for the military regiments.

In *Each Dawn I Die,* for further example, the judicial system and correctional institutions are exposed when Cagney plays an innocent journalist who is wrongly incarcerated—but at the film's end he shakes hands forgivingly with the warden as he leaves the prison. In films such as *Taxi!* and *St. Louis Kid* (1934), the compromises are even more evident. *Taxi!* concerns the brave efforts of small-time taxi-cab drivers to resist the strong arm tactics of a larger, rival taxi firm, pressures that eventually cause the death of an older, popular cabbie (Guy Kibbee) and Cagney's own brother (Ray Cooke). Warners obscured the taxi struggle as the movie progressed and substituted instead a love story and revenge angle. There is very little correlation between the beginnings of the tale, which lead in dramatic build-up to the ominous possibility of an all-out taxi war, and the later segments, in which Cagney blindly pursues personal vengeance.

St. Louis Kid is similarly compromised. In that film, Cagney plays a scab driving trucks through picket lines during a milk war. The Cagney character is unconscionable, cheery and joking as he ignores the strike. Coming in 1934 at the time of a national "milk trust" scandal, the picture could have been timely and influential. Typically, Warners chose instead to focus on another amorphous love story and the added entanglement of a false murder rap.

The (compromised) critical attitude toward American society embodied in such Cagney films leads to speculation as to the actor's possible impact on the orientation of his films. At least one hint exists, for example, that Cagney himself fought for something other than standard Hollywood fare for *Taxi!* Marxist film critic H. A. Potamkin wrote in a 1933 issue of "Closeup" magazine: "A film like *Taxi!* was not borne along its logical *motif* of the struggle between the taxi-trust and the privately owned taxi. I understand Cagney wanted such a story but it was rejected as being labour v. capital!" Another contemporary account echoed Potamkin's analysis: "*Taxi!* could have been a superb picture. As it was, its plot, which started out in a series of fast events surrounding a taxi war with union-trouble, was wanly pushed over into boy-girl romance. Cagney was furious that the dramatic significance of the whole idea was deliberately sabotaged by influence from the Hays Office, whose policy fears any mention of industrial controversy. But even in retrospect—Cagney the taxi-driver was an ominous and solid character."

(Bill Nichols, in the British "Screen" magazine, writes that the Film and Photo League, "conceived as part of an international worker's cinema movement," was involved in the production of *Taxi!* and Nichols includes the film as his only example of a full-length feature affiliated with the League. Nichols also lists Cagney as among the League's "claimed advisors or associates." His contention, however, is preposterous, as can be determined by a mere viewing of the film—hardly a political tract. Warners would be astonished by the claim. The connection—as with any possible personal connection between Cagney and the League—impossible to document or prove—was at best informal, unofficial, and, judging from the result, entirely ineffective.)

Politically-oriented film journals lamented the reactionary message of many of Cagney's films, blaming Warners for the politics and simultaneously praising Cagney, based on their highly subjective interpretation of his cinematic character, for his inferentially progressive political stance. "Greater than the tragedies he has enacted," wrote a critic for "New Theatre and Film," "is the very tragic situation whose protagonist he himself is—to be such an artist and to have almost every achievement crippled at its climax by the conditions of the industrial background which pays him well but which he cannot control. Everything good he has done has been in an accidental frame. All the memorable moments are fragmenting, in spite of the main direction, and increasingly unrelated to a central pattern. There is nothing so disastrous to the morale of an artist of Cagney's calibre as to have every excellence of his work at the grudging mercy of a chance director or a haphazard choice of the editorial department, or the shears of the cutting room."

Critics and fans of the Thirties would find themselves much in agreement with the further assessment of the "New Theatre and Film" writer, who translated the natural grit of the Cagney persona into progressive political terms. "James Cagney," he concluded, "one of the pre-eminent American artists in any field, finds himself in a situation which one can only imagine must be quite intolerable. A living definition of the American working class—the most vital, creative personification of the energy, courage, cleverness and fatalism of vast numbers of American workers, he finds himself not only hamstrung by the contracts of his producers as far as 'art' goes, but what is worse, he finds himself forced into testimonials against the best possibilities of that class from which he springs and whose heroic representative he could be."

As the tone of Cagney's 1936 independent features proves (*Great Guy, Something to Sing About*), Cagney's personal political orientation was decidedly liberal during the Thirties and the early years of his immense popularity. Though it is difficult to argue that he was further to the left on the political spectrum than Warners (his independent *Great Guy*, for example is thematically similar to Warners' *Bullets or Ballots,* also filmed in 1936) it is fair to say he preferred and even agitated for liberal political themes. His politics (as reflected in his films) eventually changes severely, but as late as 1940 (in the face of Hitler, and World War Two) he appeared in a radio production of Dalton Trumbo's "Johnny Got His Gun," playing the role of an armless, legless war veteran—a basket case who symbolised the moral outrage at the world's looming militarism. From liberalism to pacifism to idealism—not an unlikely succession. In the Forties, Cagney strove to advance his own idealistic, romanticised vision of life with such whimsical and sentimental offerings by Cagney Productions as *Johnny Come Lately* and William Saroyan's *The Time of Your Life.* But Cagney Productions was plagued by low box office receipts (the times were not ripe for good faith, reformism and whimsy) and problems of financing and distribution. It became increasingly obvious that Cagney would have to try for a full comeback as the financially lucrative (and more readily "acceptable") "tough guy." On May 6, 1949, Cagney signed for *White Heat*. His detailed 57-page contract guaranteed $250,000 per picture for one feature per year for three years; a time limit of a fourteen weeks shooting schedule was established; story approval rights was obtained; "star billing" and "star dressing room" were assured. And an "escape" clause allowed for Cagney to submit his own stories, if he so desired, and to make two Cagney Productions films on his own. Twenty years—and light years of import—after *Public Enemy*, the actor was back in business as a gangster reborn.

The Cagney of the Fifties was a painfully different "tough guy" than the Cagney of the Thirties. The mature Cagney persona was shorn of its politically progressive implications, divested of its more complex overtones, and narrowly clarified to modern-day explication. If the Thirties and Forties were relative periods of experimentation for Cagney, then the Fifties was clearly resignation, the conditional surrender to the more simplistic facets of the "tough guy" image that he had fought —by walkout, lawsuit and independent production—since *The Public Enemy*. The decade began with Raoul Walsh's *White Heat* and concluded with Billy Wilder's *One, Two, Three*. Despite the nihilist explosion ending *White Heat*, no sensible critic or person of political interest would argue that either of these films are politically progressive, as so many would have argued in the past about others of Cagney's films. And indeed, nearly his entire output of the Fifties, in marked contrast to his output of the Thirties, conveys an acceptance (however reluctant) of his new image as a super-hardened middle-aged gangster.

Politically and thematically, *White Heat* is an astonishing denial of the normally progressive Warners themes which, during the Thirties, customarily suggested that gangsters were inevitable products of the lower class, wronged by a social system which created conditions from which it was difficult to rise. *White Heat* changed everything. Cody Jarrett (Cagney) is mad, not impoverished. His deranged mind is beset by violent, maddening headaches and he has a psychotic mother-complex. Unlike the classic Warners formula, enunciated in *Public Enemy* and *Little Caesar*, there is little explanation of Cody's upbringing, tiny rationale for his behavior. There is no sympathetic explanation for his development into a ruthless killer. In the twisted, bizarre context of the story, there are no good guys. Even the cops are demented, like Hank Fallon (Ed-

As Cody Jarrett in WHITE HEAT

mond O'Brien), who is himself caught up hysterically in the robbery and escape schemes plotted by Cody; the lawmen of *White Heat* tinker like lunatics with sophisticated, modern "tracking" devices and hatch improbable strategies designed mercilessly to nail Cody dead.

Cody is simply a remorseless murderer. He even munches a hot dog absent-mindedly at one point as he plugs a double-crosser through a car trunk. But—and this is the unmistakable thrust of the film—Cody Jarrett's most hideous actions are made palatable, almost enjoyable, by the sheer audacity and exhibitionism of Cagney's tremendous performance, and by the inescapable memory of all that he has been and meant to audiences before *White Heat*.

John Howard Lawson, one of the "Hollywood Ten," viewed *White Heat* in federal prison while jailed for alleged connections with the Communist Party. Lawson, a Marxist, watched the film at a Saturday night showing with other prisoners and wrote that the "anti-social message" of the film made an "unforgettable impression." Sensing the "new" Cagney, Lawson articulated a perceptive explanation of the updated (*vis à vis White Heat*) significance of the Cagney persona.

"There are many decent, well-intentioned people in prison; many who recognise that the forces which drove them to vice or crime are inherent in our present social system," he wrote. "Related to this partial understanding is a deep bitterness, a feeling that the individual has no chance in a jungle society unless he adopts the way of the jungle.

"*White Heat* idealises this code of the jungle and advertises it as a way of life. It made a strong impression on the prison inmates, especially on the younger men. There were long discussions after the showing: one would insist that Cagney is characterised as a madman in the picture. But Cagney is a famous actor. The prison audience—and this is probably true of any audience—associated the fictitious character with Cagney's reputation. The spectators saw him as an attractive symbol of toughness, defending himself against a cruel and irrational society; at least, it was said, 'he has the guts to stand up and fight back!'

"This emphasis on the individual's total depravity in a depraved society rejects the possibility of rational social co-operation. Man is doomed to prowl alone a beast in the jungle. However, there is one way in which the killer instinct can be utilised or sublimated: it can perform a necessary and even a 'holy' purpose, if it is subjected to absolute authority, disciplined to serve the needs of war."

Cagney Productions, the last defence against the drift of the Fifties as enunciated by *White Heat*, gradually abandoned Cagney's independent features. Only two more, both thematically progressive in intent, were produced during the Fifties: the anti-violent anti-corruption *Kiss Tomorrow Goodbye* (1950), a companion piece to *White Heat* which reacted against the excessive bloodbaths of that production; and *A Lion is in the Streets* (1953), a story based loosely on the life of Huey Long, which condemned the tyranny of demagogic politicians. However, Cagney's studio work of the Fifties—films such as *Love Me or Leave Me* (1955), *Mister Roberts* (1955) and *Tribute to a Bad Man* (1956)—all paid respect to the full-grown

Reading "The Wall Street Journal" in ONE, TWO, THREE

and transformed Cagney persona: a character not really unlike Cody Jarrett, who is old, mean and surly—a social misfit,
but clearly to be esteemed, sympathetic in an inexplicable way. From *The Public Enemy* (a social outcast gangster)
to *White Heat* (a berserk gangster) to *One, Two, Three* (a
frenetic gangster-ish executive) Cagney's image is brought to
full-circle consummation. Anti-system slum child Tom Powers
becomes pro-system corporate-climbing C. P. MacNamara.

Cagney is so super-American in the film that he is cast as
a Coca-Cola industrialist, but his ruthlessness is reduced to businessmen's standards (he is a societal gangster). As the soft
drink company's chief executive in West Berlin, C. P. MacNamara (Cagney), plotting to rise up the company ladder in
any way possible, defends American life, "Americanises" an
over-zealous Communist youth (Horst Buchholz) and bellow-
ingly wheels and deals his way, in true gangster fashion, over
every obstacle in sight—but enjoyably so, that's important.

All the tried and true traits of the Cagney persona are in evidence, the same qualities which are so magnetic in Roy Del Ruth's Thirties quartet of films. For instance: Cagney delivers orders in authoritative, rapid-fire lingo, as if he is the leader of a mob. He has a lurid eye for the pretty secretary, forty years his junior, and behaves contemptibly to his wife (Arlene Francis), so poorly in fact that she nearly leaves him, taking the children away with her at the end of the film. He redeems himself just in time at the end by apologising—that valuable, old trait of contrition is still important to the success of the Cagney persona. He is no longer a killer but he no longer has to be. He is established; his reputation is made. And the hint nevertheless persists that, in the brutal competition of free trade, there may yet be a reason to resort to weaponry. Thus are all the characteristics of the younger Cagney put to the service of the older Cagney persona—patriotic, rightist and complacent.

Since Cagney's personal political perspective was once so avowedly liberal (one widely circulated fan magazine in the Thirties described his politics as "radical"), the connection between his films and his ideology, and the ideology of his films, is fascinating to trace. For just as John Wayne, politically conservative and anti-Communist, has left a concrete political legacy by his films, not only in the obvious *Green Berets* but in the traditional *The Searchers* and *She Wore a Yellow Ribbon,* so too with Cagney is there an association between his real life and the life reflected by his films. Particularly well-known in the Thirties were his feelings for the poor and the underprivileged. "If you've never been poor," the original slum kid of filmdom once told an interviewer, "you're automatically a stranger to more than half of the men and women in the world. You're cut off from them. You have no idea why they're hard as nails where they're hard and soft as fools where they're soft" —perhaps as good a summary of the Cagney screen persona as has been ever expressed.

The facts of Cagney's occasional political involvement are fascinating. He donated generously of his time and money to humanitarian and left-liberal causes; he also participated in some political organising activity in Hollywood. Most historians of this era in Hollywood, for example, put him among the leaders of the "actor's rebellion" against the "Merriam Tax." During the 1934 California gubernatorial campaign, the big Hollywood movie studios were actively backing Frank E. Merriam, the conservative Republican candidate for governor, versus Upton Sinclair, the noted muck-raker and radical. The movie moguls were understandably frightened by Sinclair's proposed EPIC (End of Poverty in California) programme and also by his outspoken criticism of Hollywood movie-making.

Not only did certain studios produce fake newsreels for theatrical distribution which showed tramp armies ready to cross the California border if Sinclair were elected, but, led by Louis B. Mayer of M-G-M and newspaper magnate William Randolph Hearst, the producers raised "a campaign fund of half a million dollars (for Merriam), partly by assessing their high-salaried employees one day's salary." Although most actors, directors, writers and producers paid their one day's salary into the Republican campaign chest, according to one knowledgeable account, "Cagney and Jean Harlow refused, and led a revolt against the tax."

Sinclair lost, due greatly to such power broking, but significantly "his campaign and the producers' tax on studio personnel, coincided with the rise to power of the Screen Actor's Guild and the fight of the Screen Writer's Guild for recognition." Cagney, embroiled in his own contractual disagreements at Warners, became involved early in the union struggles and in the organisation of the Screen Actor's Guild. Later he served as president of the Guild for a period. Once he told a reporter with some pride that SAG was begun to aid the "little guy." Cagney evidently first joined the union at a key meeting in 1933. "James Cagney, Gary Cooper, James Dunn, Otto Kruger and Ann Harding joined on that memorable night," chronicled "Films" magazine in 1940, in a well-documented history of the union, "and no doubt the magic of their names had much to do with the fact that membership jumped from 81 to four thousand in six weeks."*

Cagney's public involvement with the "Merriam tax" and the Screen Actor's Guild led indirectly to two additional episodes in his career in which his political disposition was awarded an unexpected national spotlight. In August of 1934, Cagney was accused by a California grand jury, meeting in Sacramento, of being a Communist sympathiser who had given financial support to the Communist Party. According to police officials in Sacramento, a letter written by Ella Winter (wife of author Lincoln Steffens) was seized in a raid on the Sacramento Communist Party headquarters; allegedly to Caroline Se-

* Actually, SAG was not absolutely a democratic union, dedicated mainly or solely to assisting the "little guy"; name stars benefitted more from SAG representation than extras and bit players, who were categorised out of the decision-making control.

cher, a local Communist official, the letter said, "Cagney was fine this time and is going to bring other stars up to talk with Stef about Communism." Cagney promptly denied the charges; he said he had never offered any money to the Communist Party and he explained further that he was "against all isms except Americanism."

"If Ella Winter wrote such a letter as has been reported found by the police and which I can hardly believe she did, then she had no right to do so, because I had never expressed any intention of coming to the aid of anyone trying to upset our government," Cagney announced to the press. "I am proud to call myself a 100 percent American. This old country of ours has been pretty good to me. I started with nothing, worked hard and today am very comfortable. I believe that nowhere else is there the same glorious opportunity for anyone willing to work hard as in America. It certainly would be ridiculous for me to align myself with any communistic, socialistic, Nazi, white shirts, silver shirts or any other un-American movement because I would be the first to suffer should these radical movements and agitations succeed."

Steffens backed up Cagney; the charges stemmed, he said, from Cagney's charitable donations to relieve the misery of the San Joaquin Valley cotton strikers the previous year.

In 1940, Cagney was again accused of being a Communist. This time the denunciation came from John R. Leech, former "chief functionary" for the Los Angeles Communist Party, in testimony before another California grand jury. Leech named Cagney, Humphrey Bogart, Clifford Odets, Fredric March, Jean Muir and others "as communist members, sympathisers and contributors." Leech claimed Cagney was a "member and a contributor" of the Communist Party; he said Bogart contributed $50 monthly. A swift and stern denial came from William Cagney, representing brother James, who said that the 1940 charges derived also from Cagney's contributions to the San Joaquin Valley Strike "but that was a humanitarian cause, and Jimmy's contributions always are for deserving causes."

The actor travelled to Washington for hearings conducted by House Representative Martin Dies, chairman of the Subcommittee investigating un-American activities. He testified that he had given money to the San Joaquin Valley strikes, to the Salinas lettuce strike, the Motion Picture Relief Fund, the Hollywood Guild, the Scottsboro Boys' Defense Fund, the Community Chest, and other organisations "whose work I have never considered un-American." Charges that Hollywood is permeated with Communism are "so exaggerated they are ridiculous," Cagney told reporters. Dies summarily cleared Cagney and the others. Obviously relishing the charges, the "New York Times" printed the accusation on page one and its retraction on page 21.

For Cagney, like most Americans, the Second World War (and the advent of McCarthyism) meant an embrace with patriotism. He appeared in war newsreels. In August, 1942, he raced "exhibitions" at the Roosevelt Raceway to sell war bonds. He donated his Martha's Vineyard estate to the Department of the Army for practice manoeuvres. In 1944, he spent three months entertaining American troops in the European theatre, including "twelve shows a week as an Irish jig and clog dancer." In March, 1942, Cagney did a three-week whistle-stop junket with some of Hollywood's biggest names to raise money for the war effort. The performers included Bing Crosby, Laurel and Hardy, Groucho Marx, Cary Grant, Bob Hope, Pat O'Brien, Frank McHugh, Joan Blondell, Claudette Colbert, Bert Lahr, and Charles Boyer. "The show was so big," recalled Frank McHugh, "that someone like Marlene Dietrich could join us for a few days, as she did in Washington, and you wouldn't know she was there." Cagney performed *Yankee Doodle Dandy* routines for the crowds.

With the Second World War, represented by his *Yankee Doodle Dandy*, Cagney's personal politics took a gradual but unswerving turn to the right. The actor recalls today that his political persuasion began to change at about the same time as friend-actor Ronald Reagan, later Republican governor of California.

In his book "Tracy and Hepburn: An Intimate Memoir," Garson Kanin recounts the story of how Cagney's wealth eventually came to determine the increasingly conservative view of his politics. Once good friends, Cagney and Spencer Tracy ultimately almost stopped talking to each other—over Tracy's disappointment at Cagney's shifting political disposition. Their friendship "practically fell apart." Cagney had grown extremely rich as a result of unceasing work and judicious investments. ('No actor,' Tracy said, 'has a right to be *that* rich!') Spencer observed that the richer Jimmy became, the more right wing and intolerant he became politically. In their youth, Cagney had been more left wing than Spencer, who, throughout his life, steered a middle political course . . .

"The war came, and McCarthyism, Red Channels and blacklisting, along with all the ugly apparatus of the super-patriots

in vindictive action with questionable motives. On many issues,
Tracy and Cagney found themselves seriously at odds. The
phone calls grew shorter, the time between visits longer and
eventually they saw little or nothing of each other."

Cagney's postwar work indicates a change in thought and
self-conception that really originates with *White Heat* and cul-
minates with *One, Two, Three*. It made him increasingly patriotic, conservative, and, ironically, anti-Communist—very different from the Cagney of the Thirties. By the time of *Road
to the Wall*, a 1962 documentary for the Department of Defense (produced under contract to the now defunct CBS Films
Inc.) narrated by Cagney, the theatrical dimension of the
"tough guy" is stripped bare; the anti-Communist, patriotic, conservative message of *Road to the Wall* puts in straightforward
manner the Hollywoodish "Red Scare" themes of *One, Two,
Three*.° "James Cagney Narrating" is the dignified title which
introduces the film, giving some notion of the importance the
Department of Defense attaches to the prestigious Cagney name
in this instance. Declared obsolete by Defense officials in 1972
except for historical purposes, *Road to the Wall* is a bloody
newsreel of Communist purges and a bluntly-phrased exhorta-
tion to Americans to beware of all Communists everywhere.
"Each new threat must be met, force with force, as in Korea,"
argues Cagney's animated voice early in the documentary with
the cold war logic that was widespread in the early Sixties.
"It was rather common practice at that time to use name per-
sonalities to narrate our films," declares Paul Murdock of the
Defense Department. "No unusual circumstances surrounded Mr.
Cagney's contribution to the film."

But "no unusual circumstances" notwithstanding, *Road to the
Wall* banks on Cagney's stature as a movie star, his implied,
symbolic "toughness," for its meaning to the average American.
The film is leagues closer in content to *One, Two, Three* or
White Heat, the older and "wiser" Cagney, than to *The Public
Enemy* or *Great Guy* or even *Yankee Doodle Dandy*. The humanitarian overtones of Cagney's films of the Thirties and Forties have been transformed into the blatantly rightist-patriotic
politics of the Fifties and early Sixties—Cagney has changed
and the world has, too.

° The comparison might convincingly be made between Cagney's role in
Road to the Wall and *Vietnam! Vietnam!*, John Ford's army-sponsored documentary
on the war in Vietnam. See Joseph McBride's article, "Drums along the Mohawk"
in "Sight and Sound," Autumn 1972.

6

The Actor as Auteur

The Artistic Influence of the Performer

"During the shooting of M-G-M's Love Me or Leave Me, *Jimmy surprised everybody one day by demanding an unusually early lunch break. No one understood why until after lunch when a young player who had been blowing his scenes all morning returned to the set letter perfect. Cagney had spent the lunch break rehearsing the boy quietly in his dressing room."*

LOUELLA O. PARSONS

"The old tradition still continues in Hollywood. The idea there is 'to buy the body.' They do not think of intelligence. They do not buy you for what you can do. They buy you for your body, and in spite of so many dismal failures, they have not learned the lesson that the body does not make a picture. All that makes a picture is a player with intelligence. But they have the idea, you see, that it is the body that makes the picture. Good acting is thinking, and unless there is some intelligence behind the picture, some imagination and sincerity, you have nothing. And the public is the first to detect it. In the end you don't fool the public."

JAMES CAGNEY

The creative influence of the actor on the cinema has become increasingly a subject for heated debate, while the argument over the position of the film director has ground to a halt. The "director as auteur" theory finally has found at least partial approval in every critical circle. And as the director has emerged as the artistic centre, the prime hero of the cinema. the director has also joined hands with the critic in dismissing the actor's accomplishments.

If Alfred Hitchcock's famous snide pronouncement, "All actors are cattle," is not to be taken totally seriously (but not to be dismissed as a joke either), impresario Josef von Sternberg expresses a more typical directorial attitude, scoffing at the proposition that an actor (the term is used here to mean "actress" also) can be central to the filmmaking process. In "Fun in a Chinese Laundry," Sternberg contends "that the actor in films cannot function as an artist . . . he is little more that one of the complex materials used in our craft."

Sternberg's elitist views have much support among highbrow film critics, but fan magazines steadfastly cling to their belief that actors are the most important element in the movies. And, much more significantly, it should not be forgotten for a moment that the Hollywood industry itself has always emphasised "movie stars" above other elements in films, especially in the Thirties and Forties, the so-called "Golden Age" of the studio system.

In 1930, H. A. Potamkin, a leading theorist among film critics, erected a critical foundation for the present snobby disregard for the contributions of movie stars to the cinema when he argued that "the 'star' system exaggerates the performer above his place as human instrument and thereby damns the film." In a lengthy essay in "Closeup" magazine entitled "The Personality of the Player: A Phase of Unity," Potamkin wrote: "To confuse the category of an art like acting with one like painting is an evidence of a failure to recognise the submissive character of the player: he is an instrument! Assuredly, he is an instrument of greater importance than the mechanical instruments of the cinema because in a film of human content he is also the content and the final experience. That is just where the will of the player enters. Either he must be pliable in his submissiveness or intelligently receptive. In the latter case, receptivity becomes the expression of a conception of acting. In the expression of the conception lies the understanding of the structure of the character in his place in the structure of the film."

Potamkin's theory of acting, like that of von Sternberg's, leads necessarily to the belief that, because the performer is "submissive" to a greater degree than the other participants in film-making, the performer is therefore something less than an artist. Only actor "poets" such as Chaplin and Buster Keaton, who wrote, directed, and starred in their own films, are accorded widespread recognition as "auteur" artists of the first rank. But this conventional approach to actor-in-film criticism seems to forget certain essential points about film-making which suggest a different conclusion: that the actor is not inherently more "submissive" than directors or writers.

If it is true, for example, that an actor sometimes flounders without the proper director, then it is equally true that a director is often pitiably ineffectual without the proper actor. The problem becomes even more interesting at middle ground when the contributions of an especially talented and charismatic actor sometimes meet and surpass the contributions of a particular director. How is this achieved? How can so many movies be explained in which all that is remembered is some stunning acting performance, even as the story, setting, theme and—yes, direction—fades into the memory?

Whether or not an actor can be a genuine "auteur," in the widely-accepted critical sense, is really a moot, provocative point in many ways. The "Actor as Auteur" concept is proposed here as a model against which to explore an explanation of the actor's influence. What must be realised is that the actor's part in the creation of a film has been greatly underrated in the past. The auteur theory can be revised and reproposed with actors in mind: under certain circumstances, an actor may influence a film as much as a writer, director or producer; some actors are more influential than others; and there are certain rare few performers whose acting capabilities and screen personas are so powerful that they embody and define the very essence of their films. If an actor is responsible only for acting but is not involved in any of the artistic decisions of film-making, then it is accurate surely to refer to the actor as a semi-passive icon, a symbol that is manipulated by writers and directors. But actors who not only influence artistic decisions (casting, writing, directing etc.) but demand certain limitations on the basis of their screen personas, may justly be regarded as "auteurs." When the performer becomes so important to a production that he or she changes lines, adlibs, shifts meaning, influences the narrative and style of a film and altogether signifies something clear-cut to audiences despite the intent of writers and directors, then the acting of that person assumes the force, style and integrity of an auteur.

James Cagney was such an actor. His independent films, particularly, express a clear and personal life vision, beginning in the Thirties, with optimistic, progressive films such as *Great Guy,* and ending in the Fifties, with less hopeful tales such as *A Lion Is in the Streets.* Other actors have delved into independent production, but few have managed their films along such a personal course, outlining such a strong and consistent thematic outlook, composing films with such closely-related style and detail. Cagney Productions steered the Cagney persona, built through the approving eyes of Cagney himself, without the obstacle of studio interference; the obvious parallel again is with Chaplin and Keaton, both of whom worked best as their own employers. Cagney himself must have appreciated the comparison when he told an interviewer in 1936, "The motion picture industry, like every monopoly, must act in restraint of trade to succeed. I don't blame them, but that is the situation. I shall organise my company and make pictures. Chaplin, Pickford, Fairbanks and Harold Lloyd had to do the same thing. They were forced to do it. It's the game. I am satisfied." Grand National first and then Cagney Productions stubbornly fought to banish the notion of a Cagney "vehicle": the snug, action-oriented, plenty-of-punches picture with Cagney cast as a lone gangster, graduate of poverty row or lady killer. Yet, even in Cagney's Warners works, or in his studio films of the Forties and Fifties, Cagney fought for and won a formidable measure of respect for his talents, and some discernible degree of control over his movies.

Whether he rewrote his dialogue (as he frequently did), sat in on story conferences, advised casting, contributed ideas for scene design (on one occasion), or even wrote music, his impact on the average production was enormous. The names of his directors blur in deference to the memory of Cagney's performances, a subconscious but very real measure of his authority as an actor. A "Cagney vehicle"—that truly revealing phrase—is a picture in which the display of Cagney's talents dominates other aspects of the film. Not accidentally so, for by his singular honesty of impersonation, Cagney salvaged many otherwise dull and average melodramas with brilliantly energetic performances. The record of his years at Warners is largely the transcript of Cagney's victory over such ordinary films, his gift for prevailing above the most nondescript plots, and his skill at preserving the Cagney persona in the process. Just as Chaplin towed his famous tramp person through film after film, without altering the basic character make-up, so too did Cagney keep fundamentally intact the Cagney persona throughout three decades of film acting. Critics have recognised Chaplin's accomplishment but Cagney has fared poorly and belatedly among those who distribute such kudos.

For example, "Closeup" magazine wrote in 1932 that "students of the theatre are not particularly thrilled by the thought of emulating Greta Garbo and Clark Gable, Jimmy Cagney and Edward G. Robinson, Joe E. Brown and Tallulah Bankhead," an early indication of the less-than-serious respect accorded Cagney's prowess as an actor throughout his career.

Even his Hollywood peers have been slow to acknowledge his artistry. Despite his many Oscar-calibre performances, Cagney has been honoured with an Academy Award only once, for his role as George M. Cohan in *Yankee Doodle Dandy*, a tour de force which veered drastically from Cagney's usual gangster stereotype and capitalised on Second World War fervour besides in order to garner enough votes. (Hollywood players frequently win only when they veer from "playing themselves," when they don a wig and make-up disguise, like Marlon Brando in *The Godfather*.) Once before, Cagney was nominated for an Oscar while in the Warners stable—for his portrayal of Rocky in 1938's *Angels With Dirty Faces*. Spencer Tracy received the Academy prize instead that year for his portrayal of bleeding-heart Father Flannagan in *Boys Town*, suggesting that gangsters are not prizewinners (especially when compared to priests) by Hollywood standards. Cagney received the New York Film Critics' prize for *Angels*, however, though it took him nine ballots to obtain enough votes.

When, in 1955, Cagney was again nominated—for his blustering, bullying performance as "The Gimp" in *Love Me or Leave Me*—he lost out to Ernest Borgnine's *Marty*, generally considered a more "acceptable" and poignant characterisation. The "New York Times's" Frank S. Nugent once insightfully explained Cagney's dilemma: "Mr. Cagney has the faculty of being taken for granted. Although he is not in the least public-enemyish off the screen, he has done so well in the role that producers entered a happy conspiracy to keep him there. His few breaks for freedom—*Boy Meets Girl* among them—have not been successful, whether through Cagney's fault or our inability to adjust ourselves to seeing him without an armpit holster."

His artistry is so under-appreciated partly because the actor built his early career, and thus his reputation, alongside inauspicious directors and indistinguished writers in films often so urban and seemingly commonplace that "serious" critics scoffed at them. Cagney's most frequent directors during the Warners years were the little-known workhorses of the Warners lot: Lloyd Bacon, William Keighley and Roy Del Ruth. Under more skilled directors, such as Michael Curtiz (*Angels With Dirty Faces, Yankee Doodle Dandy*), Cagney excelled, but under the workaday taskmasters, he meticulously constructed the persona and style that became his forte. Significantly, each of the three—Bacon, Keighley and Del Ruth—began their respective careers in show business as actors; likewise, all three are best recalled for their work with the Warners ensemble of performers. None of the three directors are famed as particular stylists.

Lloyd Bacon, for example, was best known as the "fastest" director in Hollywood; he was an especial favourite of Warners executives because he always maintained tight budget control of his films. While, occasionally, Bacon could be visually interesting, as in the atmospheric opening shots of *Frisco Kid*, he was more familiar as the lean and spare director of films such as *Picture Snatcher* and *Here Comes the Navy*, each scene looking suspiciously as if it had been shot speedily, single take. Bacon could be a thoughtful and brooding director, when aided by tight material and good actors (as with John Barrymore in the silent *Sea Beast*) but, saddled by inferior material (as with the story that became Cagney's *Boy Meets Girl*), he was merely (and understandably) business-like.

Bacon's economical style is reflected by his reputation as the holder of the studio record for scenes completed in one day (eight hours)—forty-seven for *Knute Rockne* (1940). His approach to the craft of film-making gave the actors in his films free rein to interpret their roles: indeed, there was little time for anything else. Cagney worked in nine films under Bacon, ranging from *Picture Snatcher* in 1933 to *The Oklahoma Kid* in 1939. The nine Cagney-Bacon films have a singular sameness of hue: a professional but uncomplicated manner of exposition, an unmistakable fondness for the Cagney persona and a disguised sense of spontaneity. Bacon's *The Irish in Us*, for example, is so devoid of purposeful plot that it plays merely on the effusive goodwill of the Warners acting troupe—Pat O'Brien, Frank McHugh, Allen Jenkins, and Cagney—seeming suspiciously like one extended improvisation (and Jenkins later confirmed that there was a great deal of experimenting while shooting was in progress). It is not difficult to imagine the trustworthy director Bacon, one hand on his wallet and an eye keened to the studio clock, giving his players liberal sway, and working methodically to capture the results meanwhile—which is why his final product is so deceptively free-wheeling.

"We did pictures like *Picture Snatcher* in fifteen days," Cagney once recalled, "and this is perhaps why people today think they move so fast." Cagney told "Films and Filming" in 1959 that Bacon's method during the filming of *Picture Snatcher* (an indication of the freedom given Cagney to define his roles) was practically hands-off and come-what-may. "Lloyd Bacon actually shot rehearsals," Cagney said, "(In a scene with

Ralph Bellamy and Patricia Ellis) I heard the cue come and I walked through the door, went up to the desk and did the necessary. As I was working out what I was going to do for the scene and got all the business done I heard Bacon say 'Cut. Give me that one.' So I said I was rehearsing. He said 'Fine. Over there.' And we started on the next scene."

William Keighley, before he came to Hollywood, had been a stage director, his work including the Cagney-Blondell Broadway production of "Penny Arcade." He joined the Warners company in the Thirties, first as a "dialogue director" for the Cagney-Bacon films *Picture Snatcher* and *Footlight Parade*. Like Bacon, Keighley cheerily declared himself for "good entertainment" for the masses rather than artistic triumphs for the few, according to one definitive Thirties interview. The ex-stage director filmed five Cagney features, beginning with *G-Men* (1935) and concluding with *The Bride Came C.O.D.* (1941); and all five of the Cagney–Keighley films are swift-paced yarns with a polished emphasis on action and dialogue: like Bacon, Keighley was a quick, dependable director known primarily as an "actor's director." Both Keighley and Bacon are relatively unresearched directors—neither are mentioned in Andrew Sarris's authoritative "The American Cinema" (although, interestingly, Manny Farber in his "Negative Space" alludes briefly and positively to the Cagney-Keighley films, commending the contributions of both actor and director to *Each Dawn I Die*). Keighley was the grittiest, the most hard-boiled of the three directors, infinitely more capable of developing a slugfest or a gunfight—as in *G-Men* or *Each Dawn I Die*—than a romance (consider the relative failure of *The Bride Came C.O.D.*). Known also as a "talk" expert, Keighley's dialogue raced by so fast and furious that it often seemed careless or incidental, a quality of near-improvisation that he shared in common with Bacon, though Keighley always kept a firmer grip on the goings-on. Under their directorial hands, Cagney flourished.

Roy Del Ruth, the last of Warners' hard-working trio, directed six Cagney films, including the four (*Blonde Crazy, Lady Killer, Taxi!* and *Winner Take All*) which were such propellants to the actor's career in the early Thirties. Like Bacon and Keighley, Del Ruth characteristically applied his directorial acumen toward acting: he sometimes stressed acting above the narrative of his films, concentrating on colourful little vignettes, and Damon Runyonesque characterisations. In this category, for example, is Clarence Muse's black helpmate Rosebud from *Winner Take All*, Guy Kibbee's lecherous old hotel guest of *Blonde Crazy*, and the shadowy talent scouts of National Movie Studios in *Lady Killer*. More urbane and inclined to humour than either Bacon or Keighley, Del Ruth was always tempted to yield his camera to certain fleeting exchanges within his films and gloss over the remainder—which is why the Cagney-Del Ruth films sometimes seem so disjointed, a marriage of excellent tidbits and moments of the routine. When Del Ruth turned almost exclusively to musical comedy later in his career—directing Cagney in the Fifties in *West Point Story* and *Starlift*—he also abandoned his occasionally captivating attention to nuance, becoming merely a competent if average Hollywood director in his sunset years. But in the Thirties —as with Bacon and Keighley—Del Ruth was smart enough to allow Cagney an unusual freedom within the confines of his vehicles, to toy with his own characterisations, to invent within the limits.

Because his directors were frequently liberal overseers, and because of his own bargaining position as a "movie star," Cagney also sometimes influenced the technical decisions which shaped his films. For *City for Conquest*, for example, Cagney submitted drawings which were eventually used for a scene design. For *Captains of the Clouds*, Cagney wrote new stanzas to the Canadian war song "Bless 'Em All," which he eventually sang in a bar-room duet with Alan Hale.

Cagney always kept his eye on the casting department. He boosted the careers of Doris Day, Don Dubbins and Roger Smith for example, by arranging for his directors to hire the performers (for *Love Me or Leave Me, These Wilder Years, Never Steal Anything Small*, and *Man of a Thousand Faces*). Director Joseph Pevney recalls that Cagney's most helpful assistance for *Man of a Thousand Faces* came in the area of casting. Cagney suggested Roger Smith for the part of Lon Chaney Jr., and sister Jeanne for the role of Chaney's sister; Jeanne also played in *Yankee Doodle Dandy, The Time of Your Life* and *A Lion Is in the Streets* with brother James. Cagney Productions enlisted old friend Frank McHugh for *A Lion Is in the Streets*. And it was Cagney who persuaded Grace George to the screen in *Johnny Come Lately;* it was he also who invited Sylvia Sidney to make her Hollywood comeback in *Blood on the Sun*.

Even when working with veteran Raoul Walsh, in *White Heat*, for example, Cagney ventured suggestions which later became memorable and important moments in the film. "Well, we got a little into the picture," he told "Films and Filming" in 1959, "I said to the director, Raoul Walsh, 'Raoul, let's try something. I don't know whether we'll get away with it or not: after the boy's first fit, Mama will be seated there and she will rub my head. And then I'll sit on her lap, for just a second, and put my arm around her and then walk away.'" Thus did he augment a mood and theme and characterisation in *White Heat* that many fans and critics later ascribed to the influence of director Walsh.

Cagney wrote dialogue, added words and phrases, distinctive sayings, which embroidered his characterisations with a unique and personalised flavour. In *Footlight Parade* for example, an intended punch line was faulty—director Lloyd Bacon and the writer were stumped. "What was that foreigner's name—the guy who built the monster he couldn't stop?" Cagney was supposed to ask. "Frankenstein," Joan Blondell would answer. "Shake hands with old man Frankenstein," Cagney was supposed to respond, according to the script. But something was plainly wrong; as written, the scene was simply not funny. Cagney impulsively changed the punch line to "shake hands with his Aunt Emma" and, according to a contemporary, "even the electricians laughed. The scene was saved."

"Empty lines are his most violent hate on the set," reported a Thirties fan magazine, "Any number of directors can tell a tale of how Cagney has said, 'No dice. The guy's only speaking words.' Then Cagney has introduced some by-play for business worth a thousand words. Like the time, for instance, when he adlibbed and administered a kiss to the startled Loretta Young (*Taxi!*) instead of aiming a long speech filled with silly love talk at her. The director let Jimmy's version stay."

In William Wellman's *Other Men's Women* (1931), Cagney plays the tiniest of parts; but, when he enters in a short dance-hall scene and hands his coat to a checker, he talks rapidly as he removes his garment, improvising, adding whole phrases and sentences unaccounted for in the script. In *Taxi!*, a scene was written expressly for Cagney after the Warners executives discovered that the Irish street boy could converse in Yiddish. The sequence calls for Cagney, playing a taxi-driver, to settle a cross-cultural argument between an Irish policeman and a Jew. Cagney smooths things over in Yiddish. The script stipulates a momentary exchange, but the scene as filmed is extended when Cagney double-talks in his rapid fashion, padding the sequence with unprovided dialogue. For *Jimmy the Gent*, Cagney appeared nearly bald, with a stark, close-

ly-trimmed haircut, for the first day of shooting—just the sort
of slight physical variation Cagney would frequently employ to
enrich a characterisation. Director Michael Curtiz, taken aback,
was nevertheless forced to begin shooting on schedule.

Warren Duff, scenarist for Warners' *Frisco Kid, Angels
with Dirty Faces* and *Each Dawn I Die,* has called Cagney
the "perfect writer's actor." "Every writer enjoys writing for
an actor who will not just speak the lines but will bring the
character to life," Duff said. "Cagney's almost intuitive understanding of the character he plays, plus his intelligent approach to creating it, guarantees the role's interpretation. This,
of course, is gratifying to the writer."

Cagney's acting style can practically be catalogued, so familiar are his physical gestures—the jabbing finger; the toe-
spring walk; the nervous, flailing arms; the twitching legs; the
pinched, jerking mouth; and the Cagney laugh, a fancy high-
pitched, rolling guffaw that admitted childish pleasure at everything. The Cagney laugh was omnipresent. In *Winner Take
All,* for example, after being jilted by Virginia Bruce, Cagney
throws a triumphant laugh over his shoulder as he skips merrily off camera. In *Blonde Crazy* he laughs crazily each time
he is slapped by Joan Blondell. In *White Heat,* above the suicidal explosion which kills Cody Jarrett is heard a wild, maniacal laugh. Cagney delivers his lines always with a smile or
grimace—his face is ever mobile. And he cries with ease (as
in *The Crowd Roars, Roaring Twenties* or *White Heat*). He
is still the only male American film star (besides James Stewart)
to have consistently and successfully incorporated crying into
his repertoire of emotions.

His incredible versatility—not only his willingness but his
capability to vary his roles—was reinforced and assisted by the
fact that Cagney did all of his own physical stunts (including
the vaudeville variety: singing, dancing, sketching before the
camera and occasionally tinkering on the piano). His most
strenuous physical workouts came during his three boxing films
—*The Irish in Us, Winner Take All,* and *City for Conquest*—
in which Cagney sparred with former contenders for training,
and then performed all of his own boxing before the camera.

He told a reporter during *City for Conquest*: "Some wise
guys think all movie fights are faked. I'd like to have had them
with me. I trained hard for this, with Harvey Perry—otherwise, I couldn't have taken it. Had five weeks of road-work,
up at 5:30 every morning. Worked up by easy stages to ten
miles, with sparring partners riding alongside on bicycles. It

made me feel like knocking their heads off, which I tried to do in the ring. That's what they hoped I'd try. I took the works —bag punching, wind sprints, rope skipping, shadow boxing, wrestling. Mushy Callahan, ex-welter-champ of the world, the technical director, says I trained as hard as any pro ever did for the title. I was baked out, steamed out, tired out—reduced ten pounds, slept ten hours every night. It made me feel great."

Cagney's acting style, as Kenneth Tynan has observed in his famous essay on the actor, was unique; he presented a type that can best be summed up as the "anti-hero." Cagney was really the first. Gable, the smiling chiseller; Bogart, the charismatic loner; Brando, the brooding misfit; and James Dean, the rebel—all owe a hefty measure of their tradition to Cagney. He was direct, unpretentious, clean-cut. He was flamboyant but not excessive. Way back in 1930, before anyone else had conceived of the kind, Cagney introduced the home town boy villain, the toughie with a heart of gold, the likeable mutineer. He was not the first simply because he was the original but because he caught on like no one had before him. Almost every American male performer since Cagney's heyday can trace the lineage of his style to the actor's influence.

(Consider Cagney's influence on contemporary film-makers also, as indicated by the remarks of Elia Kazan, who acted with Cagney in *City for Conquest,* and who, as the director of Brando in *A Streetcar Named Desire* and *Viva Zapata,* and James Dean in *East of Eden,* has been one of the most formative directors of the modern decades. "I learned something from Jimmy Cagney—he taught me quite a lot about acting," Kazan told "Movie" magazine, "Jimmy taught me some things about being honest and not overdoing it. He even affected my work with Brando a little bit. I mean—'Don't show it, just do it!'")

Cagney himself has always been diffident and practical towards his "art," a word that amuses him. "Acting was a job to be done, and I liked doing it," he told a reporter in 1974. "Apparently, whatever equipment I had seemed to lend itself to the job, and it worked, and inasmuch as it worked and the pay was good, why not? I had no idea of performing high art. The axiom for me has been this very self-evident truth: that you're only as good as the other fellow thinks you are because he buys the tickets. You leave that all to him; you don't sit in judgment on your own work. You hope it's right, and if it isn't, too bad." "There's not much to tell you about acting," he reportedly advised his brother William, at the beginning

Giving brother Bill some acting tips in 1933

of Bill's short-lived Hollywood acting career, "but this: Never settle back on your heels. Never relax. If you relax, the audience relaxes. And always mean everything you say."

Two essential constituents of the Cagney performance have always defined his approach: rhythm and mime. "Never relax"—the motto aptly explains the energy which is at the core of Cagney's performances. The hypnotic fascination for the actor comes in part from the speed in which he does everything—the fleet, rapid-fire manner in which he talks and acts. The speed is translated by stamina and endurance and rote into rhythm: his sentences are short and staccato-like; his movements are quick and choppy. The effect is blurred, of constant motion and almost musical tempo. Like the tick-tock of a watch, timing is all-important to Cagney's performances—he was a master at timing—and repetition becomes cadence, the crux of his delivery. This is why Cagney's films all seem so uniformly swift-paced: the velocity is Cagney. His movements are orchestrated: he punches one-two, jabs one-two, speaks one-two. *One, Two, Three* is his perfect swan song because the entire film is constructed rhythmically. The musical backing pulsates, things happen in pairs and threes and Cagney's orders are given in curt and methodical meter.

For Cagney, all movement is or should be an extension of rhythm. "All actors should dance," he told Jack Lemmon during the filming of *Mister Roberts*. And, known as a fanatic who skipped lunch hours regularly to practice his dance steps, Cagney's passion for dance, and his assertion that all actors should be versed in footwork, give further documentation to Cagney's devotion to rhythm. "A gutter boy with the grace of dancing" Otis Ferguson called him. In his strut and manner, there was surely the gait of a dancer omnipresent, and the melodic implication of music, and ballpoint shuffle.

Cagney's other certain, primary weapon in his arsenal of acting is mimicry. Busby Berkeley's opinion that Cagney was an "expert mimic" is echoed by Joseph Pevney, director of *Man of a Thousand Faces*, who says that Cagney "made numerous suggestions in the areas of pantomime and dancing" during the filming of the Lon Chaney biography.

Critic-director Peter Bogdanovich visited the retired Cagney in 1972 and reported in "Esquire": "During the course of a small dinner party in Brentwood, he also proved to be an extraordinary raconteur. He doesn't just tell a story, he acts it out, playing all the parts, with remarkable precision and an economy of gesture that is as subtle and revealing as most of his professional performances. He gave us some memorable impressions that night of people he'd worked with—a gentle Hungarian-like director Charles Vidor (Cagney had the accent down perfectly and thoughtfully pantomimed holding a cigarette from below, with thumb and forefinger, which immediately caught the flavour of the man), a not-so-gentle Hungarian director like Michael Curtiz (two hilariously unprintable stories here), and the absolute essence of John Ford (in this context, he gave a great one-word description of the Irish, of whom Cagney is one: "Malice").

"He did several others for us, including a 'hop-headed' pimp he observed in his Hell's Kitchen childhood standing on a corner, nervously cracking his knuckles and jacking his pants up with his arms—a mannerism he remembered and immortalised in *Angels With Dirty Faces*. One of the guests asked him how he had developed his habit of physically drawn-out death scenes, and Cagney told how he'd once seen a film of Frank Buck's, in which the hunter was forced to kill a giant gorilla. The animal died in a slow, amazed way that gave the actor his inspiration and which he played out for us in a few, riveting moments of mime."

Cagney himself once denounced "living-the part mumbo-jumbo" as "the purest bunk!": "All I try to do is to realise the man I'm playing fully," he wrote, confirming his affinity for mime, "then put as much into my acting as I know how. To do it,

I draw upon all I've ever known, heard, seen or remember."
In *Mister Roberts*, for instance, Cagney imitated an old friend,
the president of a Massachusetts bank, for his role as the dom-
ineering boat skipper. "I asked myself," wrote Cagney, "Who
do I know who's like this skipper? How would he talk? For
a long time, I'd been aping one of my best friends, the president of a Massachusetts bank. I'd been telling stories about
him featuring his New England accent, so I stole my bank
president-pal's way of talking for my *Mister Roberts* role. This
will probably come as news to him.

"I don't mean that making one role different from another is altogether a matter of personal tricks, of copying mannerisms or imitating accents. As an actor, you have to find
out what the fellow you're playing is all about. You must work
him out in your mind. Just hitting upon an accent I could
use wasn't understanding the Captain in *Mister Roberts*. Jack
Ford saw him as the most pathetic man on the ship, entirely
alone and not knowing how to exert his authority. He was a
lonely soul, removed from everybody and everything. I agreed."

For his part as Martin Snyder, "The Gimp," in *Love Me or
Leave Me*, Cagney visited his doctor brothers (Harry and Ed)
and other physicians to ask advice about limps, because the
real-life "Gimp" had a notoriously lame walk. After receiving
conflicting advice, Cagney decided to make his limp "as un-
repellant and usable as possible. I still don't know whether
his real life limp is worse than the one I used in the film or
not. But I do know that when people who are so afflicted grow
tired they limp more, and when they are rested, they limp less;
so I figured that I could vary that limp as I saw fit, and in
that way keep it from being monotonous. Ironically, when the
picture was released, I heard that the original Gimp complained that I'd limped on the wrong leg." Cagney added, after one sequence in *Love Me or Leave Me*, that he apologised
to director Charles Vidor for neglecting to limp. But, Vidor
informed the actor, with a surprised look, that he had limped
like a trouper throughout the entire scene. "By that time my
limp had become so automatic with me that I did it without
knowing it."

Cagney detailed his affection for mimicking people in a rambling, autobiographical article entitled "How I Got This Way,"
published by the "Saturday Evening Post" in January, 1956.

"New York's East Side was full of colourful people while
I was growing up," he wrote, ". . . Many had unusual mannerisms of body or speech. I studied them, and from time to

time I've used them. Maybe these mannerisms I've collected and have used are one of the reasons that, along with Jimmy Stewart, Clark Gable and Cary Grant, I seem to be a target for mimics. Most impersonators think that they are taking me off when what they're really doing is imitating me imitating a character I knew back in the neighbourhood where I grew up.

"There was one guy, for example, who had a trick way of handling his body while he was engaged in a sidewalk debate. He held his elbows against his sides as he argued, and he made his points by poking his finger at you. When he met you, he never said, 'Hello, how are you?' He'd ask, 'What do you hear?' or 'What do you say?' In 1938, when I made *Angels With Dirty Faces* I dredged this character out of my past and used him.

"There was another fellow who stood on a corner in my neighbourhood. He'd hitch up his trousers and he'd combine that with a nervous twitching of his neck and shoulders. I used his mannerisms in another movie. Because of the Cagney impersonators, most of the public thinks that I'm really like this pants-hitching neck-jerker.

"I've used one of my pop's favorite gestures in a movie too. Pop had an affectionate thing he did with his four sons; he'd put one hand behind the back of our necks, ball his other fist as if he were about to clout us, then say, 'If I thought you meant it—' It was always good for a laugh, for afterward he'd put his arm around us. I used that gesture in a film I made with Loretta Young (*Taxi!*).

"Most mimics inject a chronic hoarseness into my voice. The truth is, I'm not usually hoarse at all. That hoarseness they reproduce was part of my George M. Cohan characterisation in *Yankee Doodle Dandy*. As Cohan grew older, his voice grew husky and it had a kind of breathy quality it didn't have when he was younger. I didn't use that breathiness when I played the younger Cohan, but I did use it for the sequences when he was older. The whole thing was a trick of make-believe; nevertheless, the impersonators have latched on to the older Cohan's voice as being mine."

Each Cagney film was thus individualised. A representative example of how the Cagney persona can rescue minor films, elevating them to the stature of great entertainment, can be found in *Strawberry Blonde*, a pleasant-enough yarn which is recommended by Cagney's whole-hearted acting. A sugar-sweet ending is in the making in the film as co-star Olivia de Havilland publicly confides to sheepish husband Cagney that she is pregnant. It is an awkward moment. Both are embarrassed. Cagney kisses her impetuously and she protests, blushing because they are in public. "When I want to kiss my wife, I'll kiss her anytime," he exclaims, sweeping his arm outward, "anyplace," gesturing broader, "anywhere," his arms sweeping the horizon. "That's," he punctuates the word with an emphatic fingerpoint, "the kind of hairpin I am." A wide smile underlines his obvious satisfaction, and the scene carries, courtesy of the boundless Cagneyesque charm.

In his major films, Cagney's consummate acting skill rises nobly to the test. Kenneth Tynan described his performance in *White Heat*: "Cagney staggered even his devotees by acting it up to the hilt with a blind conviction which was often terrifying; he never let up . . . One cannot unlearn the sequence in which Cagney, attempting to ward off a mutiny in the mob, succumbs to one of his recurring blackouts and drags himself to the cover of a bedroom, moaning in deep thick sighs like a wounded animal." *White Heat* is still the rawest, most seductive and frightening gangster film ever made, unmatched in American film history for its wholeness of savagery. And *Yankee Doodle Dandy* is still the penultimate Hollywood musical. Back to back, these two films alone testify without contradiction to Cagney's stunningly diverse and incomparable talents.

"The style in that amazing film was the man himself," wrote Tynan of *White Heat,* concurring with other critics who often complained that his films disintegrated when Cagney left the frame.

The tragic, unavoidable footnote to Cagney's career must be that the "tough guy" never gained an opportunity to devote his time fully to serious drama—perhaps to additional Shakespeare or private projects—because Cagney always had other aspirations besides gangster films and musicals. Early in his career, he talked about the possibility of performing Irish drama in repertory with Pat O'Brien and other Irish actor-friends. An article by John T. McManus in the "New York Times" entitled "James Cagney Dreams of O'Casey" described the obstacles of such an undertaking by likening Cagney's Warners employment to that of the average worker: "Like the white-collar worker who, just for the vicarious thrill of it, pores over heaps of world-tour pamphlets before sighing and going off on his two-week vacation in the Catskills, James Cagney toys frequently with the idea of playing Irish drama." Cagney planned a touring stock company that would have included

Robert Montgomery, J. M. Kerrigan, William Gargan, Barry Fitzgerald, Edward McNamara and O'Brien. He talked of beginning with J. M. Synge's "Playboy of the Western World" but the plans never materialized.

One of the several times that he announced his retirement, Cagney told friend Jim Tully, for a November 24, 1935, article in "The New York Herald," entitled "He Tired of Slapping Ladies," that he was going to fulfill a lifelong ambition by going to join the famous Irish Players at the Abbey Theatre in Dublin. "No one can blame me for getting a bit annoyed with this business of striking women in every one of my pictures," he told Tully. "It has been going on for some time now. In each succeeding picture, I approach such scenes with a sinking feeling. The film audiences seem to have found it novel when I first did it in *The Public Enemy*. They clamoured for more. The writers of all my pictures have written it into the scripts and the directors have followed it up by directing it into the pictures."

The tragic irony of Cagney's career is that, while still young, he was marketed mainly as a "tough guy" and that is the mould to which he returned time and again in his prosperous middle-age. His few, bold attempts at independent production—Grand National and Cagney Productions—succumbed to untimely deaths in the imbalanced, competitive market. The gentler nature of the Cagney persona—that which was described by Nicholas Ray as a "great serenity"—was truly explored in only five films (*Great Guy, Something to Sing About, Yankee Doodle Dandy, Johnny Come Lately, The Time of Your Life*). That he was restricted and restrained by circumstances and contractual binds from developing the wonderful alter ego he offered just once, in the forgotten *Johnny Come Lately*, is one of the most lamentable truths of the American cinema. It is surely not unfair to recall, alongside his magnificent performances and his tremendous stature as an actor, his unfulfilled promise also of even further levels of greatness.

Filmography

SINNER'S HOLIDAY (1930). Melodrama about the bad-seed son in a family which runs a penny arcade; as Harry Delano, the errant son. *Dir:* John G. Adolfi. *Sc:* Harvey Thew, George Rosener ("Penny Arcade," the play by Marie Baumer). *With* Grant Withers, Evalyn Knapp, Joan Blondell, Lucille LaVerne, Noel Madison, Otto Hoffman, Warren Hymer, Purnell B. Pratt, Ray Gallagher, Hank Mann. *Prod:* Warner Bros. 60m.

DOORWAY TO HELL (G.B.: A HANDFUL OF CLOUDS) (1930). Drama about an underworld bootlegging czar who tries to quit the rackets; as Steve Mileaway, the crime chieftain's sidekick. *Dir:* Archie Mayo. *Sc:* George Rosener ("A Handful of Clouds," the story by Rowland Brown). *With* Lew Ayres, Charles Judels, Dorothy Mathews, Leon Janney, Robert Elliott, Kenneth Thomson, Jerry Mandy, Noel Madison, Bernard "Bunny" Granville, Fred Argus, Ruth Hall, Dwight Frye, Tom Wilson, Al Hill, Eddie Kane. *Prod:* Warner Bros. 77m.

OTHER MEN'S WOMEN (1931). Sketchy drama concerning a love triangle involving two railroad workers, one of whom is married; as Ed, a train worker. *Dir:* William A. Wellman. *Sc:* Maude Fulton, William K. Wells (the story by Maude Fulton). *With* Grant Withers, Mary Astor, Regis Toomey, Joan Blondell, Fred Kohler, J. Farrell MacDonald, Lillian Worth, Walter Long, Bob Perry, Lee Morgan,

With Richard Purcell, Dorothy Mathews and Lew Ayres
in DOORWAY TO HELL

Kewpie Morgan, Pat Hartigan. *Prod:* Warner Bros. 70m. The original title was *The Steel Highway*, discarded after previews.

THE MILLIONAIRE (1931). Comedy about a retired millionaire who seeks escape from boredom; as Schofield, an insurance salesman. *Dir:* John G. Adolfi. *Sc:* Julian Josephson, Maude T. Powell ("Idle Hands" by Earl Derr Biggers). *With* George Arliss, Evalyn Knapp, David Manners, Bramwell Fletcher, Florence Arliss, Noah Beery, Ivan Simpson, Sam Hardy, J. Farrell MacDonald, Tully Marshall, J. C. Nugent, Charles Grapewin, Charles E. Evans, Ethel Griffies, Ben Hall. *Prod:* Warner Bros. 82m. The film was re-made by Warners in 1947, as *That Way with Women,* with Sydney Greenstreet and Dane Clark.

THE PUBLIC ENEMY (G.B.: ENEMIES OF THE PUBLIC) (1931). Drama of the rise and fall of two boyhood pals from the slums who become involved in the liquor rackets of the early Thirties; as Tom Powers, the "Public Enemy." *Dir:* William A. Wellman. *Sc:* Kubec Glasmon, John Bright, Harvey Thew ("Beer and Blood," the story by Glasmon and Bright). *With* Jean Harlow, Edward Woods, Joan Blondell, Beryl Mercer, Donald Cook, Mae Clarke, Mia Marvin, Leslie Fenton, Robert Emmett O'Connor, Murray Kinnell, Ben Hendricks Jr., Rita Flynn, Clark Burroughs, Snitz Edwards, Adele Watson, Frank Coghlan Jr., Frankie Darro, Robert E. Homans, Dorothy Gee, Purnell Pratt, Lee Phelps, Helen Parrish, Dorothy Gray, Nanci Price, Ben Hendricks III, George Daly, Eddie Kane, Charles Sullivan, Douglas Gerrard, Sam McDaniel, William H. Strauss. *Prod:* Warner Bros. 74m.

SMART MONEY (1931). Comedy-drama about a gambling country barber who travels to the big city to seek his luck with higher stakes; as Jack, the barber's assistant and friend. *Dir:* Alfred E. Green. *Sc:* Kubec Glasmon, John Bright, Lucien Hubbard, Joseph Jackson (from

Left, with Edward G. Robinson in SMART MONEY. Right, in TAXI!

an original story by Hubbard and Jackson). *With* Edward G. Robinson, Evalyn Knapp, Noel Francis, Morgan Wallace, Paul Porcasi, Maurice Black, Margaret Livingston, Clark Burroughs, Billy House, Edwin Argus, Ralf Harolde, Boris Karloff, Mae Madison, Walter Percival, John Larkin, Polly Walters, Ben Taggart, Gladys Lloyd, Eulalie Jensen, Charles Lane, Edward Hearn, Eddie Kane, Clinton Rosemond, Charles O'Malley, Gus Leonard, Wallace MacDonald, John George, Harry Semels, Charlotte Merriam, Larry McGrath, Spencer Bell, Allan Lane. *Prod:* Warner Bros. 90m.

BLONDE CRAZY (G.B.: LARCENY LANE) (1931). Comedy about two con artists on a romantic and swindle-scheming whirl; as Bert Harris, the "brains" of the pair. *Dir:* Roy Del Ruth. *Sc:* Kubec Glasmon, John Bright (their original story). *With* Joan Blondell, Louis Calhern, Noel Francis, Guy Kibbee, Raymond Milland, Polly Walters, Charles (Levinson) Lane, William Burress, Peter Erkelenz, Maude Eburne, Walter Percival, Nat Pendleton, Russell Hopton, Dick Cramer, Wade Boteler, Ray Cooke, Edward Morgan, Phil Sleman. *Prod:* Warner Bros. 73m. The film retained its original title, *Larceny Lane,* for British release.

TAXI! (1932). Comedy-drama of a metropolitan taxi war, the romance of one of the cab drivers and the hackman's maniacal search for a racketeer who kills his brother; as Matt Nolan, leader of the independent cabbies. *Dir:* Roy Del Ruth. *Sc:* Kubec Glasmon, John Bright ("The Blind Spot," the play by Kenyon Nicholson). *With* Loretta Young, George E. Stone, Guy Kibbee, David Landau, Ray Cooke, Leila Bennett, Dorothy Burgess, Matt McHugh, George MacFarlane, Polly Walters, Nat Pendleton, Berton Churchill, George Raft, Hector V. Sarno, Aggie Herring, Lee Phelps, Harry Tenbrook, Robert Emmett O'Connor, Eddie Fethersone, Russ Powell, Ben Taggart, Cotton Club Orchestra. *Prod:* Warner Bros. 70m. The working titles of the film were *The Blind Spot* and *Taxi, Please!*

THE CROWD ROARS (1932). Drama about a star racing driver who causes an estrangement with his brother, the speedway death of a friend, and his own racetrack downfall; as Joe Greer, the auto champ. *Dir:* Howard Hawks. *Sc:* Kubec Glasmon, John Bright, Niven Busch (the story by Hawks and Seton I. Miller). *With* Joan Blondell, Ann Dvorak, Eric Linden, Guy Kibbee, Frank McHugh, William Arnold, Leo Nomis, Charlotte Merriam, Regis Toomey, Harry Hartz, Ralph Hepburn, Fred Guisso, Fred Frame, Phil Pardee, Spider Matlock, Jack Brisko, Lou Schneider, Bryan Salspaugh, Stubby Stubblefield, Shorty Cantlon, Mel Keneally, Wilbur Shaw, James Burtis, Sam Hayes, Robert McWade, Ralph Dunn, John Conte, John Harron. *Prod:* Warner Bros. 85m. The film was originally titled *The Roar of the Crowd,* then *The Roaring Crowd.*

WINNER TAKE ALL (1932). Comedy about a prizefighter who must choose between a rustic woman's affections and the flirtatious attentions of a high society dame; as Jim Kane, the pugilist. *Dir:* Roy Del Ruth. *Sc:* Wilson Mizner, Robert Lord ("133 at 3," the magazine story by Gerald Beaumont). *With* Marian Nixon, Virginia Bruce, Guy Kib-

Left, with Ann Dvorak in THE CROWD ROARS
Right, with Mary Brian in HARD TO HANDLE

bee, Clarence Muse, Dickie Moore, Allan Lane, John Roche, Ralf
Harolde, Alan Mowbray, Clarence Wilson, Charles Coleman, Esther
Howard, Renee Whitney, Harvey Perry, Julian Rivero, Selmer Jack-
son, Chris Pin Martin, George Hayes, Bob Perry, Billy West, Phil
Tead, Rolfe Sedan, John Kelly, Lee Phelps, Jay Eaton, Charlotte Mer-
riam. *Prod:* Warner Bros. 68m.

HARD TO HANDLE (1933). Comedy concerning the various enter-
prises of a fast-talking promoter; as Lefty Merrill, the con artist. *Dir:*
Mervyn LeRoy. *Sc:* Wilson Mizner, Robert Lord (the story by Houston
Branch). *With* Mary Brian, Ruth Donnelly, Allen Jenkins, Claire Dodd,
Gavin Gordon, Emma Dunn, Robert McWade, John Sheehan, Matt
McHugh, Louise Mackintosh, William H. Strauss, Bess Flowers, Lew
Kelly, Berton Churchill, Harry Holman, Grace Hayle, George Pat
Collins, Douglass Dumbrille, Sterling Holloway, Charles Wilson, Jack
Crawford, Stanley Smith, Walter Walker, Mary Doran. *Prod:* Warner
Bros. 75m. The working title of the film was originally *Bad Boy*, then
The Inside.

PICTURE SNATCHER (1933). Comedy-drama about a former mob-
ster turned "picture snatcher" for a disreputable tabloid; as Danny
Kean, the novice photographer. *Dir:* Lloyd Bacon. *Sc:* Allen Rivkin,
P. J. Wolfson (the story by Danny Ahern). *With* Ralph Bellamy, Patri-
cia Ellis, Alice White, Ralf Harolde, Robert Emmett O'Connor,
Robert Barrat, George Pat Collins, Tom Wilson, Barbara Rogers,
Renee Whitney, Alice Jans, Jill Dennett, Billy West, George Daly,
Arthur Vinton, Stanley Blystone, Don Brodie, George Chandler, Ster-
ling Holloway, Donald Kerr, Hobart Cavanaugh, Phil Tead, Charles

King, Milton Kibbee, Dick Elliott, Vaughn Taylor, Bob Perry, Gino Corrado, Maurice Black, Selmer Jackson, Jack Grey, John Ince, Cora Sue Collins. *Prod:* Warner Bros. 76m.

THE MAYOR OF HELL (1933). Drama about the problems which arise when a well-intentioned hoodlum becomes supervisor of a reformatory and turns government of the school over to the boys; as Patsy Gargan, the reform-minded gangster. *Dir:* Archie Mayo. *Sc:* Edward Chodorov (the story by Islin Auster). *With* Madge Evans, Allen Jenkins, Dudley Digges, Frankie Darro, Farina, Dorothy Peterson, John Marston, Charles Wilson, Hobart Cavanaugh, Raymond Borzage, Robert Barrat, George Pat Collins, Mickey Bennett, Arthur Byron, Sheila Terry, Harold Huber, Edwin Maxwell, William V. Mong, Sidney Miller, George Humbert, George Offerman Jr., Charles Cane, Wallace MacDonald, Adrian Morris, Snowflake, Wilfred Lucas, Bob Perry, Charles Sullivan, Ben Taggart. *Prod:* Warner Bros. 85m. The film was re-made by Warners as *Crime School* in 1938, starring Humphrey Bogart.

FOOTLIGHT PARADE (1933). Musical comedy about the multiple predicaments of a talented producer who stages theatrical prologues for movie theatres; as Chester Kent, the beleagured impresario. *Dir:* Lloyd Bacon, Busby Berkeley. *Sc:* Manuel Seff, James Seymour (musical numbers by Sammy Fain, Irving Kahal, Harry Warren, Al Dubin). *With* Joan Blondell, Ruby Keeler, Dick Powell, Guy Kibbee, Ruth Donnelly, Claire Dodd, Hugh Herbert, Frank McHugh, Arthur Hohl, Gordon Wescott, Renee Whitney, Philip Faversham, Juliet Ware, Herman Bing, Paul Porcasi, William Granger, Charles C. Wilson, Barbara Rogers, Billy Taft, Marjean Rogers, Pat Wing, Donna Mae Roberts, Dave O'Brien, George Chandler, Hobart Cavanaugh, William V. Mong, Lee Moran, Billy Barty, Harry Seymour, Sam McDaniel, Fred Kelsey, Jimmy Conlin, Roger Gray, John Garfield, Duke York, Donna La Barr, Marlo Dwyer. *Prod:* Warner Bros. 100m.

LADY KILLER (1933). Comedy-drama about a movie usher turned con man turned Hollywood movie star who has some unexpected difficulty shaking his criminal past; as Dan Quigley, filmdom's ex-"finger man." *Dir:* Roy Del Ruth. *Sc:* Ben Markson, Lillie Hayward ("The Finger Man," the story by Rosalind Keating Shaefer). *With* Mae Clarke, Leslie Fenton, Margaret Lindsay, Henry O'Neill, Willard Robertson, Douglas Cosgrove, Raymond Hatton, Russell Hopton, William Davidson, Marjorie Gateson, Robert Elliott, John Marston, Douglass Dumbrille, George Chandler, George Blackwood, Jack Don Wong, Frank Sheridan, Edwin Maxwell, Phil Tead, Dewey Robinson, H. C. Bradley, Harry Holman, Harry Beresford, Olaf Hytten, Harry Strong, Al Hill, Bud Flanagan (Dennis O'Keefe), James Burke, Robert Homans, Clarence Wilson, Sam McDaniel, Spencer Charters, Herman Bing, Harold Waldridge, Luis Alberni, Ray Cooke, Sam Ash. *Prod:* Warner Bros. 76m. The working title of the film was *The Finger Man.*

JIMMY THE GENT (1934). Fast-moving comedy of the rivalry between two pseudo-respectable firms which specialise in hunting up missing heirs to large fortunes; as Jimmy Corrigan, the more "ungentlemanly" of the two shysters. *Dir:* Michael Curtiz. *Sc:* Bertram

Milhauser (the story by Laird Doyle, Ray Nazarro). *With* Bette Davis, Alice White, Allen Jenkins, Arthur Hohl, Alan Dinehart, Philip Reed, Hobart Cavanaugh, Mayo Methot, Ralf Harolde, Joseph Sawyer, Philip Faversham, Nora Lane, Joseph Crehan, Robert Warwick, Merna Kennedy, Renee Whitney, Monica Bannister, Don Douglas, Bud Flanagan (Dennis O'Keefe), Leonard Mudie, Harry Holman, Camille Rovelle, Stanley Mack, Tom Costello, Ben Hendricks, Billy West, Eddie Shubert, Lee Moran, Harry Wallace, Robert Homans, Milton Kibbee, Howard Hickman, Eula Guy, Juliet Ware, Rickey Newell, Lorena Layson, Dick French, Jay Eaton, Harold Entwistle, Charles Hickman, Olaf Hytten, Vesey O'Davoren, Lester Dorr, Pat Wing. *Prod:* Warner Bros. 67m. The working title of the film was *The Heir Chaser*, then *Always a Gent*, then *Blondes and Bonds.*

HE WAS HER MAN (1934). Melodrama of the sensitive romance between a gangster on-the-run from rivals and an ex-prostitute on her way to a mail order marriage; as Flicker Hayes, the doomed thug. *Dir:* Lloyd Bacon. *Sc:* Tom Buckingham, Niven Busch (the story by Robert Lord). *With* Joan Blondell, Victor Jory, Frank Craven, Harold Huber, Russell Hopton, Ralf Harolde, Sarah Padden, J. M. (John) Qualen, Bradley Page, Samuel S. Hinds, George Chandler, James Eagles, Gino Corrado, George Pat Collins. *Prod:* Warner Bros. 70m. The film's working titles were *Without Honor*, then *Without Glory.*

HERE COMES THE NAVY (1934). Comedy-drama about the hostility between a brash seaman and his superior officer; as Chesty O'Connor, the misfit and latent hero. *Dir:* Lloyd Bacon. *Sc:* Ben Markson, Earl Baldwin (the story by Ben Markson). *With* Pat O'Brien, Gloria Stuart, Frank McHugh, Dorothy Tree, Robert Barrat, Willard Robertson, Guinn Williams, Maude Eburne, Martha Merrill, Lorena Layson, Ida Darling, Henry Otho, Pauline True, Sam McDaniel, Frank LaRue, Joseph Crehan, James Burtis, Edward Chandler, Leo White, Niles Welch, Fred "Snowflake" Toone, Eddie Shubert, George Irving, Howard Hickman, Edward Earle, Gordon (Bill) Elliott, Nick Copeland, John Swor, Eddie Acuff, Chuck Hamilton, Eddie Fetherstone. *Prod:* Warner Bros. 86m. First of eight Cagney-O'Brien pictures, the working title of the film was *Hey, Sailor.*

THE ST. LOUIS KID (G.B.: A PERFECT WEEK-END) (1934). Comedy-drama about a truck driver on the St. Louis to Chicago run who becomes involved in a dairyman's strike; as Eddie Kennedy, the scab trucker. *Dir:* Ray Enright. *Sc:* Warren Duff, Seton I. Miller (the story by Frederick Hazlitt Brennan). *With* Patricia Ellis, Allen Jenkins, Robert Barrat, Hobart Cavanaugh, Spencer Charters, Addison Richards, Dorothy Dare, Arthur Aylesworth, Charles Wilson, William Davidson, Harry Woods, Gertrude Short, Eddie Shubert, Russell Hicks, Guy Usher, Cliff Saum, Bruce Mitchell, Wilfred Lucas, Rosalie Roy, Mary Russell, Ben Hendricks, Harry Tyler, Milton Kibbee, Tom Wilson, Alice Marr, Victoria Vinton, Lee Phelps, Louise Seidel, Mary Treen, Nan Grey, Virginia Grey, Martha Merrill, Charles B. Middleton, Douglas Cosgrove, Monte Vandergrift, Jack Cheatham, Stanley Mack, Grover Liggen, Frank Bull, Wade Boteler, Frank Fanning, Gene Strong, Edna

Bennett, Clay Clement, James Burtis, Eddie Fetherstone, Joan Barclay. *Prod:* Warner Bros. 67m.

DEVIL DOGS OF THE AIR (1935). Flimsy comedy concerning the
romantic rivalries between two boyhood chums, one a Marine Flying
Corps lieutenant and the other a roughneck flyer; as Tommy O'Toole,
ace stunt flyer. *Dir:* Lloyd Bacon. *Sc:* Malcolm Stuart Boylan, Earl
Baldwin ("Air Devils," the story by John Monk Saunders). *With* Pat
O'Brien, Margaret Lindsay, Frank McHugh, Helen Lowell, John Ar-
ledge, Robert Barrat, Russell Hicks, William B. Davidson, Ward Bond,
Samuel S. Hinds, Harry Seymour, Bill Beggs, Bob Spencer, Newton
House, Ralph Nye, Selmer Jackson, Bud Flanagan (Dennis O'Keefe),
Gordon (Bill) Elliott, Don Turner, Dick French, Charles Sherlock,
Carlyle Blackwell Jr., Martha Merrill, David Newell, Olive Jones,
Helen Flint, Joseph Crehan. *Prod:* Cosmopolitan Productions for
Warner Bros. 86m. Working titles of the film include *Air Devils, All
Good Soldiers Have Wings, Flying Leathernecks* and *The Flying
Marines.*

G-MEN (1935). Action drama of the early exploits of the Federal
Bureau of Investigation; as James "Brick" Davis, attorney who joins the
FBI ranks after a college buddy turned special agent is murdered by
gangsters. *Dir:* William Keighley. *Sc:* Seton I. Miller (the book "Public
Enemy No. 1" by Gregory Rogers). *With* Ann Dvorak, Margaret Lind-
say, Robert Armstrong, Barton MacLane, Lloyd Nolan, William Har-
rigan, Edward Pawley, Russell Hopton, Noel Madison, Regis Toomey,
Addison Richards, Harold Huber, Raymond Hatton, Monte Blue,
Mary Treen, Adrian Morris, Edwin Maxwell, Emmett Vogan, James
Flavin, Stanley Blystone, Pat Flaherty, James T. Mack, Jonathan Hale,
Ed Keane, Charles Sherlock, Wheeler Oakman, Eddie Dunn, Gordon
(Bill) Elliott, Perry Ivins, Frank Marlowe, Gertrude Short, Marie
Astaire, Florence Dudley, Frances Morris, Al Hill, Huey White, Glen
Cavender, John Impolito, Bruce Mitchell, Monte Vandergrift, Frank
Shannon, Frank Bull, Martha Merrill, Gene Morgan, Joseph De Stefani,
George Daly, Ward Bond, Tom Wilson, Henry Hall, Lee Phelps, Marc
Lawrence, Brooks Benedict. *Prod:* Warner Bros. 85m. The working
title of the film was *The Farrell Case;* the film was re-released in 1949
on the FBI's twenty-fifth anniversary.

THE IRISH IN US (1935). Pleasant comedy about three contrary
sons in an Irish family, plus a zany boxer; as Danny O'Hara, the way-
ward son, manager of long-shot prize fighters. *Dir:* Lloyd Bacon. *Sc:*
Earl Baldwin (the story by Frank Orsatti). *With* Pat O'Brien, Olivia
De Havilland, Frank McHugh, Allen Jenkins, Mary Gordon, J. Farrell
MacDonald, Thomas Jackson, Harvey Perry, Bess Flowers, Mabel
Colcord, Edward Keane, Herb Haywood, Lucille Collins, Harry Sey-
mour, Sailor Vincent, Mushy Callahan, Jack McHugh, Edward Gargan,
Huntly Gordon, Emmett Vogan, Will Stanton. *Prod:* Warner Bros. 84m.

A MIDSUMMER NIGHT'S DREAM (1935). Lavish adaptation of
William Shakespeare's classic comedy; as Bottom. *Dir:* Max Reinhardt,
William Dieterle. *Sc:* Charles Kenyon, Mary McCall Jr. (the play by
William Shakespeare). *With* Dick Powell, Joe E. Brown, Jean Muir,
Hugh Herbert, Ian Hunter, Frank McHugh, Victor Jory, Olivia De

Left, in DEVIL DOGS OF THE AIR
Right, with Margaret Lindsay in FRISCO KID

Havilland, Ross Alexander, Grant Mitchell, Nini Theilade, Verree Teasdale, Anita Louise, Mickey Rooney, Dewey Robinson, Hobart Cavanaugh, Otis Harlan, Arthur Treacher, Katherine Frey, Helen Westcott, Fred Sale, Billy Barty. *Prod:* Warner Bros. 132m.

FRISCO KID (1935). Drama concerning the rise to power of a rowdy sailor among the coarse citizenry of San Francisco's Barbary Coast; as Bat Morgan, the tough seaman. *Dir:* Lloyd Bacon. *Sc:* Warren Duff, Seton I. Miller (their story). *With* Margaret Lindsay, Ricardo Cortez, Lily Damita, Donald Woods, Barton MacLane, George E. Stone, Addison Richards, Joseph King, Robert McWade, Joseph Crehan, Robert Strange, Joseph Sawyer, Fred Kohler, Edward McWade, Claudia Coleman, John Wray, Ivar McFadden, Lee Phelps, William Wagner, Don Barclay, Jack Curtis, Walter Long, James Farley, Milton Kibbee, Harry Seymour, Claire Sinclair, Alan Davis, Karl Hackett, Wilfred Lucas, John T. (Jack) Dillon, Edward Mortimer, William Holmes, Don Downen, Mrs. Wilfred North, Charles Middleton, Joe Smith Marba, Landers Stevens, Frank Sheridan, J. C. Morton, Harry Tenbrook, Lew Harvey, Eddie Sturgis, William Desmond, Jessie Perry, Edward Keane, Edward Le Saint, Robert Dudley, Dick Rush, John Elliott, Helene Chadwick, Bill Dale, Dick Kerr, Alice Lake, Vera Steadman, Jane Tallent. *Prod:* Warner Bros. 77m.

CEILING ZERO (1935). Aviation drama of civilian flyers who risk dangerous "ceiling zero" weather to deliver the post; as Dizzy Davis, the woman-chasing pilot whose amorous entanglements cause the death of a fellow aviator. *Dir:* Howard Hawks. *Sc:* Frank Wead ("Ceiling Zero," his play). *With* Pat O'Brien, June Travis, Stuart Erwin, Henry Wadsworth, Isabel Jewell, Barton MacLane, Martha Tibbetts, Craig Reynolds, James H. Bush, Robert Light, Addison Richards, Carlyle Moore Jr., Richard Purcell, Gordon (Bill) Elliott, Pat West, Edward Gargan, Garry Owen, Mathilde Comont, Carol

Hughes, Frank Tomick, Paul Mantz, Jimmy Aye, Howard Allen, Mike Lally, Harold Miller, Jerry Jerome, Helene McAdoo, Gay Sheridan, Mary Lou Dix, Louise Seidel, Helen Erickson, Don Wayson, Dick Cherney, Jimmie Barnes, Frank McDonald, J. K. Kane, Jayne Manners, Maryon Curtiz, Margaret Perry. *Prod:* Cosmopolitan Productions for Warner Bros. 95m.

GREAT GUY (G.B.: PLUCK OF THE IRISH) (1936). Comedy-drama about the campaign by a deputy in a metropolitan Bureau of Weights and Measures to halt fraudulent market practices; as Johnny Cave, the intrepid crusader. *Dir:* John G. Blystone. *Sc:* Henry McCarthy, Henry Johnson, James Edward Grant, Harry Ruskin (additional dialogue by Horace McCoy) ("The Johnny Cave Stories" by James Edward Grant). *With* Mae Clarke, James Burke, Edward Brophy, Henry Kolker, Bernadene Hayes, Edward J. McNamara, Robert Gleckler, Joe Sawyer, Ed Gargan, Matty Fain, Mary Gordon, Wallis Clark, Douglas Wood, Jeffrey Sayre, Eddy Chandler, Henry Roquemore, Murdock MacQuarrie, Kate Price, Frank O'Connor, Arthur Hoyt, Jack Pennick, Lynton Brent, John Dilson, Bud Geary, Dennis O'Keefe, Robert Lowery, Bobby Barber, Gertrude Green, Ethelreda Leopold, Bruce Mitchell, James Ford, Frank Mills, Ben Hendricks Jr., Kernan Cripps, Bill O'Brien, Lester Dorr, Harry Tenbrook, Lee Shumway, Gertrude Astor, Vera Steadman, Mildred Harris, Bert Kalmar Jr., Walter D. Clarke Jr. *Prod:* Grand National. 75m.

SOMETHING TO SING ABOUT (1937). Loose musical comedy about a city bandleader who becomes a Hollywood movie star, somewhat against his will; as Terry Rooney, the Manhattan bandleader. *Dir:* Victor Schertzinger. *Sc:* Austin Parker (the story by Schertzinger). *With* Evelyn Daw, William Frawley, Mona Barrie, Gene Lockhart, James Newill, Harry Barris, Candy Candido, Cully Richards, William B. Davidson, Richard Tucker, Marek Windheim, Dwight Frye, John Arthur, Philip Ahn, Kathleen Lockhart, Kenneth Harlan, Herbert Rawlinson, Ernest Wood, Chick Collins, Duke Green, Harland Dixon, Johnny Boyle, Johnny (Skins) Miller, Pat Moran, Joe Bennett, Buck Mack, Eddie Allen, Bill Carey, The Vagabonds, Elinore Welz, Eleanor Prentiss, Pinkie and Pal, Frank Mills, Duke Green, Larry Steers, Eddie Kane, Edward Hearn, Dottie Messmer, Virginia Lee Irvin, Dolly Waldorf, Robert McKenzie, Alphonse Martel, BoPeep Karlin, Paul McLarand. *Prod:* Grand National. 84m. The film was re-issued as *Battling Hoofer* in 1947 by Screencraft Pictures.

BOY MEETS GIRL (1938). Comedy about two Hollywood scenarists who make a star of a baby named "Happy"; as Robert Law, one half of the zany writing team. *Dir:* Lloyd Bacon. *Sc:* Bella Spewack, Sam Spewack (their play). *With* Pat O'Brien, Marie Wilson, Ralph Bellamy, Frank McHugh, Dick Foran, Bruce Lester, Ronald Reagan, Paul Clark, Penny Singleton, Dennie Moore, Harry Seymour, Bert Hanlon, James Stephenson, Pierre Watkin, John Ridgely, George Hickman, Cliff Saum, Carole Landis, Curt Bois, Otto Fries, John Harron, Hal K. Dawson, Dorothy Vaughan, Bert Howard, James Nolan, Bill Telaak, Vera Lewis, Jan Holm, Rosella Towne, Loi Cheaney, Janet Shaw, Nanette Lafayette, Peggy Moran, Eddy Conrad, Sidney Bracy, William Haade, Clem Bevans. *Prod:* Warner Bros. 80m.

ANGELS WITH DIRTY FACES (1938). Drama of the return of a notorious gangster to his childhood neighbourhood; as Rocky Sullivan, the hoodlum who is an idol to a local gang of youths. *Dir:* Michael Curtiz. *Sc:* John Wexley, Warren Duff (the story by Rowland Brown). *With* Pat O'Brien, Humphrey Bogart, Ann Sheridan, George Bancroft, Billy Halop, Bobby Jordan, Leo Gorcey, Bernard Punsley, Gabriel Dell, Huntz Hall, Frankie Burke, William Tracy, Marilyn Knowlden, Joe Downing, Adrian Morris, Oscar O'Shea, Edward Pawley, William Pawley, John Hamilton, Earl Dwire, Jack Perrin, Mary Gordon, Vera Lewis, William Worthington, James Farley, Chuck Stubbs, Eddie Syracuse, Robert Homans, Harris Berger, Harry Hayden, Dick Rich, Steven Darrell, Joe A. Devlin, William Edmunds, Charles Wilson, Frank Coghlan Jr., David Durand, Bill Cohee, Lavel Lund, Norman Wallace, Gary Carthew, Bibby Mayer, Belle Mitchell, Eddie Brian, Billy McLain, Wilbur Mack, Poppy Wilde, George Offerman Jr., Charles Trowbridge, Ralph Sanford, Wilfred Lucas, Lane Chandler, Elliott Sullivan, Lottie Williams, George Mori, Dick Wessell, John Harron, Vince Lombardi, Al Hill, Thomas Jackson, Jeffrey Sayre. *Prod:* Warner Bros. 97m. The working title of the film was *Battle of City Hall*.

THE OKLAHOMA KID (1939). Unserious western drama concerning outlaw rule in newly-settled Oklahoma; as Jim Kincaid, the "Oklahoma Kid," who fights to rid the territory of desperadoes, and to clear his own name. *Dir:* Lloyd Bacon. *Sc:* Warren Duff, Robert Buckner, Edward E. Paramore (the story by Paramore and Wally Klein). *With* Humphrey Bogart, Rosemary Lane, Donald Crisp, Harvey Stephens, Hugh Sothern, Charles Middleton, Ward Bond, Edward Pawley, Lew Harvey, Trevor Bardette, John Miljan, Arthur Aylesworth, Irving Bacon, Joe Devlin, Wade Boteler, Ray Mayer, Dan Wolheim,

In THE OKLAHOMA KID, at right with Rosemary Lane and Donald Crisp

Bob Kortman, Tex Cooper, John Harron, Stuart Holmes, Jeffrey Sayre, Frank Mayo, Jack Mower, Al Bridge, Don Barclay, Horace Murphy, Robert Homans, George Lloyd, Rosina Galli, George Regas, Clem Bevans, Soledad Jiminez, Ed Brady, Tom Chatterton, Elliott Sullivan, Joe Kirkson, William Worthington, Spencer Charters. *Prod:* Warner Bros. 85m.

EACH DAWN I DIE (1939). Drama concerning a falsely-imprisoned newsman's fight to prove his innocence; as Frank Ross, the journalist who becomes embittered by his jail experience and allies with a "lifer." *Dir:* William Keighley. *Sc:* Norman Reilly Raine, Warren Duff, Charles Perry (the novel by Jerome Odlum). *With* George Raft, Jane Bryan, George Bancroft, Maxie Rosenbloom, Stanley Ridges, Alan Baxter, Victor Jory, John Wray, Edward Pawley, Willard Robertson, Emma Dunn, Paul Hurst, Louis Jean Heydt, Joe Downing, Thurston Hall,. William Davidson, Clay Clement, Charles Trowbridge, Harry Cording, John Harron, John Ridgely, Selmer Jackson, Robert Homans, Abner Biberman, Napoleon Simpson, Stuart Holmes, Maris Wrixon, Garland Smith, Arthur Gardner, James Flavin, Max Hoffman Jr., Walter Miller, Fred Graham, Wilfred Lucas, Vera Lewis, Emmett Vogan, Earl Dwire, Bob Perry, Al Hill, Elliott Sullivan, Chuck Hamilton, Nat Carr, Wedgewood Nowell, Frank Mayo, Dick Rich, Lee Phelps, Jack Wise, Granville Bates. *Prod:* Warner Bros. 92m.

THE ROARING TWENTIES (1939). Drama of the underworld exploits of a bootlegging napoleon; as Eddie Bartlett, former garage mechanic, whose kingdom of liquor topples for the unrequited love of a woman. *Dir:* Raoul Walsh. *Sc:* Jerry Wald, Richard Macaulay, Robert Rossen (the story by Mark Hellinger). *With* Priscilla Lane, Humphrey Bogart, Jeffrey Lynn, Gladys George, Frank McHugh, Paul Kelly, Elisabeth Risdon, Ed Keane, Joseph Sawyer, Abner Biberman, George Humbert, Clay Clement, Don Thaddeus Kerr, Ray Cooke, Vera Lewis,

Left, with George Raft, in EACH DAWN I DIE. Right, with Frank McHugh and Humphrey Bogart in THE ROARING TWENTIES

Murray Alper, Dick Wessel, Joseph Crehan, Norman Willis, Robert Elliott, Eddy Chandler, John Hamilton, Elliott Sullivan, Pat O'Malley, Arthur Loft, Al Hill, Raymond Bailey, Lew Harvey, Joe Devlin, Jeffrey Sayre, Paul Phillips, George Meeker, Bert Hanlon, Jack Norton, Alan Bridge, Fred Graham, James Blaine, Henry C. Bradley, Lottie Williams, John Deering, John Harron, Lee Phelps, Max Wagner, Nat Carr, Wade Boteler, Creighton Hale, Ann Codee, Eddie Acuff, Milton Kibbee, John Ridgely, James Flavin, Oscar O'Shea, Frank Wilcox, Jane Jones Trio, Harry Hollingsworth, Frank Mayo, Emory Parnell, Billy Wayne, Philip Morris, Maurice Costello, John St. Clair. *Prod:* Warner Bros. 104m. The film was originally titled *The World Moves On.*

THE FIGHTING 69TH (1940). Comedy-drama about a coward in the ranks of the "Fighting Irish," New York's celebrated Irish regiment in the First World War; as Jerry Plunkett, the "yellow" soldier. *Dir:* William Keighley. *Sc:* Norman Reilly Raine, Fred Niblo Jr., Dean Franklin. *With* Pat O'Brien, George Brent, Jeffrey Lynn, Alan Hale, Frank McHugh, Dennis Morgan, Dick Foran, William Lundigan, Guinn "Big Boy" Williams, Henry O'Neill, John Litel, Sammy Cohen, Harvey Stephens, DeWolfe (William) Hopper, Tom Dugan, George Reeves, John Ridgely, Charles Trowbridge, Frank Wilcox, Herbert Anderson, J. Anthony Hughe, Frank Mayo, John Harron, George Kilgen, Richard Clayton, Edward Dew, Wilfred Lucas, Emmett Vogan, Frank Sully, Joseph Crehan, James Flavin, Frank Coghlan Jr., George O'Hanlon, Jack Perrin, Trevor Bardette, John Arledge, Frank Melton, Edmund Glover, Frank Faylen, Edgar Edwards, Ralph Dunn, Arno Frey, Roland Varno, Robert Layne Ireland, Elmo Murray, Jacques Lory, Jack Boyle Jr., Creighton Hale, Benny Rubin, Eddie Acuff, Jack Mower, Nat Carr, Jack Wise. *Prod:* Warner Bros. 90m.

TORRID ZONE (1940). Comedy of romantic intrigue and trouble with a bandit-revolutionary set on a South American banana plantation; as Nick Butler, banana plantation trouble-shooter. *Dir:* William Keighley. *Sc:* Richard Macaulay, Jerry Wald. *With* Pat O'Brien, Ann Sheridan, Andy Devine, Helen Vinson, Jerome Cowan, George Tobias, George Reeves, Victor Kilian, Frank Puglia, John Ridgely, Grady Sutton, Paul Porcasi, Frank Yaconelli, Dick Boteler, Frank Mayo, Jack Mower, Paul Hurst, George Regas, Elvira Sanchez, George Humbert, Trevor Bardette, Ernesto Piedra, Manuel Lopez, Tony Paton, Max Blum, Betty Sanko, Don Orlando, Victor Sabuni, Paul Renay, Joe Molina. *Prod:* Warner Bros. 88m.

CITY FOR CONQUEST (1941). Boxing melodrama about a likeable, proletarian fighter who is blinded in the ring; as Danny Kenny, the good-natured trucker who follows his sweetheart's urging and embarks on an ill-fated career as a boxer. *Dir:* Anatole Litvak. *Sc:* John Wexley ("City for Conquest," the novel by Aben Kandel). *With* Ann Sheridan, Frank Craven, Donald Crisp, Arthur Kennedy, Frank McHugh, George Tobias, Elia Kazan, Jerome Cowan, Anthony Quinn, Lee Patrick, Blanche Yurka, George Lloyd, Joyce Compton, Thurston Hall, Ben Welden, John Arledge, Ed Keane, Selmer Jackson, Joseph Crehan, Bob Steele, Billy Wayne, Pat Flaherty, Sidney Miller, Ethelreda Leopold, Lee Phelps, Charles Wilson, Ed Gargan, Howard Hickman, Murray Alper, Dick Wessell, Bernice Pilot, Charles Lane, Dana Dale (Margaret Hayes), Ed Pawley, William Newell, Lucia Carroll. *Prod:* Warner Bros. 101m.

THE STRAWBERRY BLONDE (1941). Sweet turn-of-the-century semi-musical comedy about a correspondence school dentist who never quite conquers his crush on a "strawberry blonde"—until a stretch in prison gives him second thoughts; as Biff Grimes, the pugnacious self-taught dentist. *Dir:* Raoul Walsh. *Sc:* Julius J. Epstein, Philip G. Epstein ("One Sunday Afternoon," the play by James Hagan). *With* Olivia de Havilland, Rita Hayworth, Alan Hale, George Tobias, Jack Carson, Una O'Connor, George Reeves, Lucile Fairbanks, Edward McNamara, Herbert Heywood, Helen Lynd, Roy Gordon, Tim Ryan, Addison Richards, Frank Mayo, Jack Daley, Suzanne Carnahan (Susan Peters), Herbert Anderson, Frank Orth, James Flavin, George Campeau, Abe Dinovitch, George Humbert, Creighton Hale, Russell Hicks, Wade Boteler, Peter Ashley, Roy Gordon, Max Hoffman Jr., Pat Flaherty, Peggy Diggins, Bob Perry, Dorothy Vaughan, Richard Clayton, Ann Edmonds, Lucia Carroll, Harrison Green, Eddie Chandler, Carl Harbaugh, Frank Melton, Dick Wessell, Paul Barrett, Nora Gale. *Prod:* Warner Bros. 97m. The film is the second of three Hollywood versions of "One Sunday Afternoon"; besides the original by Paramount in 1933 with Gary Cooper, Warners re-made the property as a musical in 1948 with Dennis Morgan, Janis Paige and Dorothy Malone.

THE BRIDE CAME C.O.D. (1941). Comedy about an oil heiress abducted by an aviator who is promised by her father ten dollars per pound delivery—if he deposits her unmarried into daddy tycoon's arms; as Steve Collins, the flyer. *Dir:* William Keighley. *Sc:* Julius J. Epstein, Philip G. Epstein (the story by Kenneth Earl, M. M. Musselman). *With* Bette Davis, Stuart Erwin, Jack Carson, George Tobias, Eugene Pallette, Harry Davenport, William Frawley, Edward Brophy, Harry Holman, Chick Chandler, Keith Douglas, Herbert Anderson,

Left, with Alan Hale in THE STRAWBERRY BLONDE
Right, with Bette Davis in THE BRIDE CAME C.O.D.

DeWolfe (William) Hopper, William Newell, Charles Sullivan, Eddy Chandler, Tony Hughes, Lee Phelps, Jean Ames, Alphonse Martell, The Rogers Dancers, Peggy Diggins, Mary Brodel, Olaf Hytten, James Flavin, Sam Hayes, William Justice, Lester Towne, Richard Clayton, Garland Smith, Claude Wisberg, Lucia Carroll, Peter Ashley, John Ridgely, Saul Gorss, Jack Mower, Creighton Hale, Garrett Craig. *Prod:* Warner Bros. 92m.

CAPTAINS OF THE CLOUDS (1942). Drama concerning a cocky American bush pilot in Canada who joins the Royal Canadian Air Force; as Brian MacLean, who dies a hero's death in a skyfight with Nazi raiders. *Dir:* Michael Curtiz. *Sc:* Arthur T. Horman, Richard Macaulay, Norman Reilly Raine (the story by Arthur T. Horman, Roland Gillett). *With* Dennis Morgan, Brenda Marshall, Alan Hale, George Tobias, Reginald Gardiner, W. A. Bishop, Reginald Denny, Russell Arms, Paul Cavanagh, Clem Bevans, J. M. Kerrigan, J. Farrell MacDonald, Patrick O'Moore, Morton Lowry, O. Cathcart-Jones, Frederic Worlock, Roland Drew, Lucia Carroll, George Meeker, Benny Baker, Hardie Albright, Roy Walker, Charles Halton, Louis Jean Heydt, Byron Barr (Gig Young), Michael Ames (Tod Andrews), Willie Fung, Carl Harbord, James Stevens, Bill Wilkerson, Frank Lackteen, Edward McNamara, Charles Smith, Emmett Vogan, Winifred Harris, Miles Maner, Pat Flaherty, Tom Dugan, George Offerman Jr., Gavin Muir, Larry Williams, John Hartley, John Kellogg, Charles Irwin, Billy Wayne, Rafael Storm, John Gallaudet, Barry Bernard, George Ovey, Walter Brooks, Ray Montgomery, Herbert Gunn, Donald Dillaway, James Bush. *Prod:* Warner Bros. 113m. Technicolor,

YANKEE DOODLE DANDY (1942). Musical biography of Broadway showman George M. Cohan; as Cohan. *Dir:* Michael Curtiz. *Sc:* Robert Buckner, Edmund Joseph (story by Buckner). *With* Joan Leslie, Walter Huston, Richard Whorf, George Tobias, Irene Manning, Rosemary De Camp, Jeanne Cagney, S. Z. Sakall, George Barbier, Walter Catlett, Frances Langford, Minor Watson, Eddie Foy Jr., Chester Clute, Douglas Croft, Patsy Lee Parsons, Captain Jack Young, Audrey Long, Odette Myrtil, Clinton Rosemond, Spencer Charters, Dorothy Kelley, Marijo James, Henry Blair, Jo Ann Marlow, Thomas Jackson, Phyllis Kennedy, Pat Flaherty, Leon Belasco, Syd Saylor, William B. Davidson, Harry Hayden, Francis Pierlot, Charles Smith, Joyce Reynolds, Dick Chandlee, Joyce Horne, Frank Faylen, Wallis Clark, Georgia Carroll, Joan Winfield, Dick Wessel, James Flavin, Sailor Vincent, Fred Kelsey, George Meeker, Frank Mayo, Tom Dugan, Creighton Hale, Murray Alper, Garry Owen, Ruth Robinson, Eddie Acuff, Walter Brooke, Bill Edwards, William Hopper, William Forrest, Ed Keane, Dolores Moran, Poppy Wilde, Lorraine Gettman (Leslie Brooks). *Prod:* Warner Bros. 126m.

JOHNNY COME LATELY (1943). Whimsical comedy concerning the campaign by an elderly lady newspaper publisher and a vagabond journalist against a small town's corrupt politicians; as Tom Richards, the wandering newspaperman. *Dir:* William K. Howard. *Sc:* John Van Druten ("McLeod's Folly," the book by Louis Bromfield). *With* Grace George, Marjorie Main, Marjorie Lord, Hattie McDaniel, Edward

CAGNEY

McNamara, Bill Henry, Robert Barrat, George Cleveland, Margaret Hamilton, Norman Willis, Lucien Littlefield, Edwin Stanley, Irving Bacon, Tom Dugan, Charles Irwin, John Sheehan, Clarence Muse, John Miller, Arthur Hunnicutt, Victor Kilian, Wee Willie Davis, Henry Hall. *Prod:* William Cagney Production for United Artists. 97m.

BLOOD ON THE SUN (1945). Action drama set in Tokyo in the Twenties; as Nick Condon, an American reporter who learns of Baron Tanaka's plan for world conquest and tries to smuggle the incriminating documents out of Japan. *Dir:* Frank Lloyd. *Sc:* Lester Cole, Nathaniel Curtis (the story by Garrett Fort). *With* Sylvia Sidney, Wallace Ford, Rosemary De Camp, Robert Armstrong, John Emery, Leonard Strong, Frank Puglia, Jack Halloran, Hugh Ho, Philip Ahn, Joseph Kim, Marvin Miller, Rhys Williams, Porter Hall, James Bell, Grace Lem, Oy Chan, George Paris, Hugh Beaumont, Gregory Gay, Arthur Loft, Emmett Vogan, Charlie Wayne. *Prod:* William Cagney Production for United Artists. 98m.

13 RUE MADELEINE (1946). Taut documentary-style drama concerning the espionage missions of overseas American agents during World War II; as Bob Sharkey, heroic leader of the American spy group. *Dir:* Henry Hathaway. *Sc:* John Monks Jr., Sy Bartlett. *With* Annabella, Richard Conte, Frank Latimore, Walter Abel, Melville Cooper, Sam Jaffe, Marcel Rousseau, Richard Gordon, Everett G. Marshall, Blanche Yurka, Peter Von Zerneck, Alfred Linder, Ben Low, James Craven, Roland Belanger, Horace MacMahon, Alexander Kirkland, Donald Randolph, Judith Lowry, Red Buttons, Otto Simanek, Walter Greaza, Roland Winters, Harold Young, Sally McMarrow, Colby Neal, Karl Malden, Jean Del Val, Reed Hadley. *Prod:* 20th Century-Fox. 95m.

THE TIME OF YOUR LIFE (1948). Loving adaptation of William Saroyan's eccentric comedy-drama of life in a San Francisco waterfront saloon; as Joe, the barroom philosopher. *Dir:* H. C. Potter. *Sc:* Nathaniel Curtis (the play by William Saroyan). *With* William Bendix, Wayne

Left, with James Barton and William Bendix in THE TIME OF YOUR LIFE
Right, with Virginia Mayo in WHITE HEAT

Morris, Jeanne Cagney, Broderick Crawford, Ward Bond, James Barton, Paul Draper, Gale Page, James Lydon, Richard Erdman, Pedro De Cordoba, Reginald Beane, Tom Powers, John "Skins" Miller, Natalie Schafer, Howard Freeman, Renie Riano, Lanny Rees, Nanette Parks, Grazia Marciso, Claire Carleton, Gladys Blake, Marlene Aames, Moy Ming, Donald Kerr, Ann Cameron, Floyd Walters, Eddie Borden, Rena Case. *Prod:* William Cagney Picture for United Artists. 109m.

WHITE HEAT (1949). Savage drama about the criminal adventures of a homicidal, paranoiac "mama's boy" gangster; as Cody Jarrett, the bestial thug who is beset by violent, recurring headaches. *Dir:* Raoul Walsh. *Sc:* Ivan Goff, Ben Roberts (original story by Virginia Kellogg). *With* Virginia Mayo, Edmond O'Brien, Margaret Wycherly, Steve Cochran, John Archer, Wally Cassell, Mickey Knox, Fred Clark, C. Pat Collins, Paul Guilfoyle, Fred Coby, Ford Rainey, Robert Osterloh, Ian MacDonald, Marshall Bradford, Ray Montgomery, George Taylor, Milton Parsons, Claudia Barrett, Buddy Gorman, DeForrest Lawrence, Garrett Craig, George Spaulding, Sherry Hall, Harry Strang, Jack Worth, Sid Melton, Fern Eggen, Eddie Foster, Lee Phelps. *Prod:* Warner Bros. 114m.

WEST POINT STORY (1950). Shabby musical comedy about a brash Broadway musical director's struggle to mount the annual West Point cadet variety show; as Elwin Bixby, the theatrical magnate. *Dir:* Roy Del Ruth. *Sc:* John Monks Jr., Charles Hoffman, Irving Wallace (story by Wallace). *With* Virginia Mayo, Doris Day, Gordon MacRae, Gene Nelson, Alan Hale Jr., Roland Winters, Raymond Roe, Wilton Graff, Jerome Cowan, Frank Ferguson, Russ Saunders, Jack Kelly, Glen Turnbull, Walter Ruick, Lute Crockett, James Dobson, Joel Marston, Bob Hayden, DeWit Bishop. *Prod:* Warner Bros. 107m.

KISS TOMORROW GOODBYE (1950). Drama about a vicious gangster who tricks the crooked police of a big city into a payola scheme; as Ralph Cotter, the trickster. *Dir:* Gordon Douglas. *Sc:* Harry Brown (the novel by Horace McCoy). *With* Barbara Payton, Ward Bond, Luther Adler, Helena Carter, Steve Brodie, Rhys Williams, Barton MacLane, Herbert Heyes, Frank Reicher, John Litel, Dan Riss, John Halloran, William Frawley, Robert Karnes, Kenneth Tobey, Neville Brand, William Cagney, George Spaulding, Mark Strong, Matt McHugh, Georgia Caine, King Donovan, Frank Wilcox, Gordon Richards. *Prod:* William Cagney Production for Warner Bros. 102m.

COME FILL THE CUP (1951). Sombre drama of a newspaperman's fight against alcoholism and—coincidentally—the local underworld; as Lew Marsh, the drinking journalist. *Dir:* Gordon Douglas. *Sc:* Ivan Goff, Ben Roberts (the novel by Harlan Ware). *With* Phyllis Thaxter, Raymond Massey, James Gleason, Gig Young, Selena Royle, Larry Keating, Charlita, Sheldon Leonard, Douglas Spencer, John Kellogg, William Bakewell, John Alvin, King Donovan James Flavin, Torben Meyer, Norma Jean Macias, Elizabeth Flournoy, Henry Blair. *Prod:* Warner Bros. 113m.

STARLIFT (1951). Musical comedy about Hollywood film stars who visit Travis Air Force Base near San Francisco during the Korean

War; as himself. *Dir:* Roy Del Ruth. *Sc:* John Klorer, Karl Kamb (story by Klorer). *With* Doris Day, Gordon MacRae, Virginia Mayo, Gene Nelson, Ruth Roman, Janice Rule, Dick Wesson, Ron Hagerthy, Richard Webb, Hayden Rorke, Howard St. John, Ann Doran, Tommy Farrell, John Maxwell, Don Beddoe, Mary Adams, Bigelowe Sayre, Eleanor Audley, Pat Henry, Gordon Polk, Robert Hammack, Ray Montgomery, Bill Neff, Stan Holbrook, Jill Richards, Joe Turkel, Rush Williams, Brian McKay, Jack Larson, Lyle Clark, Dorothy Kennedy, Jean Dean, Dolores Castle, William Hunt, Elizabeth Flournoy, Walter Brennan Jr., Robert Karnes, John Hedloe, Steve Gregory, Richard Monohan, Joe Recht, Herb Latimer, Dick Ryan, Bill Hudson, Sarah Spencer, James Brown, Ezelle Poule, Gary Cooper, Virginia Gibson, Phil Harris, Frank Lovejoy, Lucille Norman, Louella Parsons, Randolph Scott, Jane Wyman, Patrice Wymore. *Prod:* Warner Bros. 103m. Cagney appears in a cameo role only.

WHAT PRICE GLORY? (1952). Semi-comical musical re-make of the First World War pacifist drama about two American army officers in France who must bulwark the front-line trenches with area villagers; as Captain Flagg. *Dir:* John Ford. *Sc:* Phoebe Ephron, Henry Ephron (the play by Maxwell Anderson, Laurence Stallings). *With* Corinne Calvet, Dan Dailey, William Demarest, Craig Hill, Robert Wagner, Marisa Pavan, Casey Adams, James Gleason, Wally Vernon, Henry Letondal, Fred Libby, Ray Hyke, Paul Fix, James Lilburn, Henry Morgan, Dan Borzage, Bill Henry, Henry "Bomber" Kulkovich, Jack Pennick, Ann Codee, Stanley Johnson, Tom Tyler, Olga Andre, Barry Norton, Luis Alberni, Torben Meyer, Alfred Zeisler, George Bruggeman, Scott Forbes, Sean McClory, Charles Fitzsimmons, Louis Mercier, Mickey Simpson. *Prod:* 20th Century-Fox. Technicolor. 111m.

A LION IS IN THE STREETS (1953). Drama of the grab for political power made by a Southern swamp peddler; as Hank Martin, the personable, self-taught lawyer who runs for governor. *Dir:* Raoul Walsh. *Sc:* Luther Davis (the novel by Adria Locke Langley). *With* Barbara Hale, Anne Francis, Warner Anderson, John McIntire, Jeanne Cagney, Lon Chaney Jr., Frank McHugh, Larry Keating, Onslow Stevens, James Millican, Mickey Simpson, Sara Haden, Ellen Corby, Roland Winters, Burt Mustin, Irene Tedrow, Sarah Selby. *Prod:* William Cagney Production for Warner Bros. Technicolor. 88m.

RUN FOR COVER (1955). Western drama about an innocent ex-con who goes West and becomes a small-town sheriff; as Matt Dow, the gun-handy lawman who befriends a treacherous youth. *Dir:* Nicholas Ray. *Sc:* Winston Miller (story by Harriet Frank Jr., Irving Ravetch). *With* Viveca Lindfors, John Derek, Jean Hersholt, Grant Withers, Jack Lambert, Ernest Borgnine, Ray Teal, Irving Bacon, Trevor Bardette, John Miljan, Gus Schilling, Emerson Treacy, Denver Pyle, Henry Wills. *Prod:* Pine-Thomas/Paramount. Technicolor and VistaVision. 92m.

LOVE ME OR LEAVE ME (1955). Hard-boiled musical biography of singer Ruth Etting and her stormy relationship with racketeer-sponsor Martin "The Gimp" Snyder; as Snyder. *Dir:* Charles Vidor. *Sc:* Daniel Fuchs, Isobel Lennart (story by Fuchs). *With* Doris Day, Cameron

Left, in WHAT PRICE GLORY? Right, in MAN OF A THOUSAND FACES

Mitchell, Robert Keith, Tom Tully, Harry Bellaver, Richard Gaines, Peter Leeds, Claude Stroud, Audrey Young, John Harding, Dorothy Abbott, Phil Schumacher, Otto Reichow, Henry Kulky, Jay Adler, Mauritz Hugo, Veda Ann Borg, Claire Carleton, Benny Burt, Robert B. Carson, James Drury, Richard Simmons, Michael Kostrick, Roy Engel, John Damler, Genevieve Aumont, Dale Van Sickel, Johnny Day, Larri Thomas, Patti Nestor, Winona Smith, Shirley Wilson, Robert Malcolm, Robert Stephenson, Paul McGuire, Barry Regan, Jimmy Cross, Henry Randolph, Chet Brandenberg. *Prod:* Metro-Goldwyn-Mayer. Cinemascope and Eastman Colour. 122m.

MISTER ROBERTS (1955). Comedy-drama about near-mutinous conditions aboard a Naval vessel in the Pacific caused by a bull-headed captain; as the Captain. *Dir:* John Ford, Mervyn LeRoy. *Sc:* Frank Nugent, Joshua Logan (the play by Logan and Thomas Heggen based on Heggen's novel). *With* Henry Fonda, Jack Lemmon, William Powell, Ward Bond, Betsy Palmer, Phil Carey, Nick Adams, Harry Carey Jr., Ken Curtis, Frank Aletter, Fritz Ford, Buck Kartalian, William Henry, William Hudson, Stubby Kruger, Harry Tenbrook, Perry Lopez, Robert Roark, Pat Wayne, Tige Andrews, Jim Moloney, Denny Niles, Francis Conner, Shug Fisher, Danny Borzage, Jim Murphy, Kathleen O'Malley, Maura Murphy, Mimi Doyle, Jeanne Murray-Vanderbilt, Lonnie Pierce, Martin Milner, Gregory Walcott, James Flavin, Jack Pennick, Duke Kahanamoko, Carolyn Tong, George Brangier, Clarence E. Frank. *Prod:* Orange Production for Warner Bros. CinemaScope and Warner-Color. 123m.

THE SEVEN LITTLE FOYS (1955). Semi-musical biography of vaudevillian Eddie Foy; as pal George M. Cohan, who stops by a Friars Club dinner to honour Foy. *Dir:* Melville Shavelson. *Sc:* Melville Shavelson, Jack Rose. *With* Milly Vitale, George Tobias, Angela Clarke, Herbert Heyes, Richard Shannon, Billy Gray, Lee Erickson, Paul De Rolf, Lydia Reed, Linda Bennett, Jimmy Baird, Tommy Duran, Lester Matthews, Joe Evans, George Boyce, Oliver Blake, Milton Frome, King Donovan, Jimmy Conlin, Marian Carr, Harry Cheshire, Renata Vanni, Betty Uitti, Noel Drayton, Jack Pepper, Dabbs Greer, Billy Nelson, Joe Flynn, Jerry Mathers, Lewis Martin. *Prod:*

Paramount. VistaVision and Technicolor. 93m. Cagney recreates his George M. Cohan role in a cameo appearance.

TRIBUTE TO A BAD MAN (1956). Western drama about a crusty Colorado horse rancher who will even resort to lynching to protect his land holdings against thieves and rustlers; as Jeremy Rodock, the ageing rancher. *Dir:* Robert Wise. *Sc:* Michael Blankfort (a short story by Jack Schaefer). *With* Don Dubbins, Stephen McNally, Irene Papas, Vic Morrow, James Griffith, Onslow Stevens, James Bell, Jeanette Nolan, Chubby Johnson, Royal Dano, Lee Van Cleef, Peter Chong, James McCallion, Clint Sharp, Carl Pitti, Tony Hughes, Roy Engel, Bud Osborne, John Halloran, Tom London, Dennis Moore, Buddy Roosevelt, Billy Dix. *Prod:* Metro-Goldwyn-Mayer. CinemaScope and Eastman Colour. 95m.

THESE WILDER YEARS (1956). Emotional drama about a middle-aged multi-millionaire who searches adoption homes for the son he illegitimately fathered in his youth; as Steve Bradford, the tycoon. *Dir:* Roy Rowland. *Sc:* Frank Fenton (a story by Ralph Wheelwright). *With* Barbara Stanwyck, Walter Pidgeon, Betty Lou Keim, Don Dubbins, Edward Andrews, Basil Ruysdael, Grandon Rhodes, Will Wright, Lewis Martin, Dorothy Adams, Dean Jones, Herb Vigran, Ruth Lee, Matt Moore, Jack Kenny, Harry Tyler, Luana Lee, William Forrest, John Maxwell, Emmett Vogan, Charles Evans, Tom Laughlin, Bob Alden, Michael Landon, Jimmy Ogg, Elizabeth Flournoy, Russell Simpson, Kathleen Mulqueen, Russ Whitney, Lillian Powell. *Prod:* Metro-Goldwyn-Mayer. 91m.

MAN OF A THOUSAND FACES (1957). Biography-drama of silent screen star Lon Chaney; as Chaney. *Dir:* Joseph Pevney. *Sc:* R. Wright Campbell, Ivan Goff, Ben Roberts (story by Ralph Wheelwright). *With* Dorothy Malone, Jane Greer, Marjorie Rambeau, Jim Backus, Robert J. Evans, Celia Lovsky, Jeanne Cagney, Jack Albertson, Nolan Leary, Roger Smith, Robert Lyden, Rickie Sorensen, Dennis Rush, Simon Scott, Clarence Kolb, Danny Beck, Philip Van Zandt, Hank Mann, Snub Pollard. *Prod:* Universal-International. CinemaScope. 122m.

SHORT CUT TO HELL (1957). Shoddy re-make of *This Gun for Hire;* Cagney directed. *Dir:* Cagney. *Sc:* Ted Berkman, Raphael Blau (the screenplay by W. R. Burnett from the novel "A Gun for Sale" by Graham Greene). *With* Robert Ivers, Georgann Johnson, William Bishop, Jacques Aubuchon, Peter Baldwin, Yvette Vickers, Murvyn Vye, Milton Frome, Jacqueline Beer, Gail Land, Dennis McMullen, William Newell, Sarah Selby, Mike Ross, Douglas Spencer, Danny Lewis, Richard Hale, Douglas Evans, Hugh Lawrence, Joe Bassett, William Pullen, Russell Trent, Joe Forte, Roscoe Ates, John Halloran. *Prod:* Paramount. 87m. The actor also appeared in a brief prologue to the film.

NEVER STEAL ANYTHING SMALL (1958). Musical comedy-drama concerning a crooked stevedore's union flack who muscles his way to power in the longshoreman's organisation; as Jake MacIllaney, the waterfront labour hoodlum. *Dir:* Charles Lederer. *Sc:* Charles Lederer ("Devil's Hornpipe," unproduced musical by Maxwell Anderson and

Rouben Mamoulian). *With* Shirley Jones, Roger Smith, Cara Williams, Nehemiah Persoff, Royal Dano, Anthony Caruso, Horace MacMahon, Virginia Vincent, Jack Albertson, Robert J. Wilke, Herbie Faye, Billy M. Greene, John Duke, Jack Orrison, Roland Winters, Ingrid Goude, Sanford Seegar, Ed (Skipper) McNally, Gregg Barton, Edwin Parker, Jay Jostyn, John Halloran, Harvey Perry, Phyllis Kennedy, Rebecca Sand, *Prod:* Universal-International. CinemaScope and Eastman Colour. 94m.

SHAKE HANDS WITH THE DEVIL (1959). Tight-knit drama about a skilled surgeon who aids the underground movement in Ireland— set during the Irish home rule struggle of the Twenties; as Sean Lenihan, the rebel doctor. *Dir:* Michael Anderson. *Sc:* Ivan Goff, Ben Roberts (adaptation by Marian Thompson of the novel by Reardon Conner). *With* Don Murray, Dana Wynter, Glynis Johns, Michael Redgrave, Sybil Thorndike, Cyril Cusack, John Breslin, Harry Brogan, Robert Brown, Marianne Benet, Lewis Carson, John Cairney, Harry Corbett, Eileen Crowe, Alan Cuthbertson, Donal Donnelly, Wilfred Dawning, Eithne Dunne, Paul Farrell, Richard Harris, William Hartnell, John Le Mesurier, Niall MacGinnis, Patrick McAlinney, Ray McAnally, Clive Morton, Noel Purcell, Peter Reynolds, Christopher Rhodes, Ronald Walsh, Alan White. *Prod:* Pennebaker for United Artists. 110m.

THE GALLANT HOURS (1960). Documentary-style drama of a five-week period in 1942 in the Pacific during a critical sea battle between American forces and Japanese forces, and the instrumental role of Admiral William F. "Bull" Halsey in the allied victory; as Halsey. *Dir:* Robert Montgomery. *Sc:* Beirne Lay Jr., Frank D. Gilroy. *With* Dennis Weaver, Ward Costello, Richard Jaeckel, Les Tremayne, Robert Burton, Raymond Bailey, Carl Benton Reid, Walter Sande, Karl Swenson, Vaughan Taylor, Harry Landers, Richard Carlyle, Leon Lontoc, James T. Goto, James Yagi, John McKee, John Zaremba, Carleton Young, William Schallert, Nelson Leigh, Sydney Smith, Herbert Lylton, Selmer Jackson, Tyler McVey, Maggie Magennio, James Cagney Jr., Robert Montgomery Jr. *Prod:* Cagney-Montgomery Production for United Artists. 115m.

ONE, TWO, THREE (1961). Cold-war comedy about the troubles of a company-climbing Coca-Cola executive in West Berlin; as C. P. MacNamara, the soft drink boss. *Dir:* Billy Wilder. *Sc:* Billy Wilder, I. A. L. Diamond (the one-act play by Ferenc Molnar). *With* Horst Buchholz, Pamela Tiffin, Arlene Francis, Lilo Pulver, Howard St. John, Hanns Lothar, Leon Askin, Peter Capell, Ralf Wolter, Karl Lieffen, Henning Schluter, Hubert Von Meyerinck, Lois Bolton, Tile Kiwe, Karl Ludwig Lindt, Red Buttons, John Allen, Christine Allen, Rose Renee Roth, Ivan Arnold, Helmud Schmid, Otto Friebel, Werner Buttler, Klaus Becker, Siegfried Dornbusch, Paul Bos, Max Buschbaum, Jasper Von Oertzen, Inga De Toro, Jacques Chevalier, Werner Hassenland. *Prod:* Mirisch/Pyramid for United Artists. Panavision. 108m.

ARIZONA BUSHWACKERS (1968). Western drama about Confederate prisoners assigned as soldiers to federal troops on the frontier;

as the narrator. *Dir:* Lesley Selander. *Sc:* Steve Fisher (story by Fisher and Andrew Craddock). *With* Howard Keel, Yvonne De Carlo, John Ireland, Marilyn Maxwell, Scott Brady, Brian Donlevy, Barton MacLane, James Craig, Roy Rogers Jr., Reg Parton, Montie Montana. *Prod:* A. C. Lyles for Paramount. 87m. Techniscope and Colour. Cagney narrated the opening of the film.

SHORT FILMS
His short subjects (incomplete listing) include: *Intimate Interview* (Talking Picture Epics, 1930, directed by Grace Elliott); *Practice Shots* (Number eleven of Bobby Jones' "How I Play Golf" series, directed by George Marshall, with Cagney as a learner who asks golf questions of pro Bobby Jones, 1931); *Hollywood on Parade #8* (Meet Cagney promotional short, also with Frankie Darro and Joe E. Brown, on the Warners lot); *Screen Snapshots #11* (Columbia, 1934, with Cagney as one of many Hollywood stars at a charity event); *The Hollywood Gad-About* (Skibo Productions Inc., an Educational Films Corporation of America Treasure Chest Short, with Cagney and an all-star cast in a skit about a missing necklace, 1934); *A Trip Through a Hollywood Studio* (Warner Bros., with Cagney in cameo as one of many Warners stars on the sets busy filming, 1935); *For Auld Lang Syne* (Warner Bros., directed by George Bilson, with Cagney as one of many stars giving tribute to Will Rogers, 1938); *Show Business At War* (Issue number ten, volume nine of "The March of Time," 20th Century-Fox, including Cagney as one of many film stars doing troop shows for servicemen, 1943); *You, John Jones* (Metro-Goldwyn-Mayer, directed by Mervyn LeRoy, with Cagney as an air-raid warden who demonstrates the procedure in America in case of attack, 1943); and *Battle Stations* (20th Century-Fox, a U.S. Coast Guard documentary short, narrated by Cagney and Ginger Rogers, 1944).
He also narrated longer documentaries on patriotic and agricultural themes later in his career, including: *Road to the Wall* (Produced by CBS for the Department of Defense, with Cagney as narrator, 1962), and *Ballad of Smokey the Bear* (Produced by General Electric Theatre in co-operation with U.S. Department of Agriculture, with Cagney as the voice of Big Brother Bear in the animated feature, 1966).

ADDITIONAL DATA
William Cagney's screen appearances include: *Ace of Aces* (1933), *Lost in the Stratosphere, Palooka, Flirting With Danger* (1934), and *Stolen Harmony* (1935), and *Kiss Tomorrow Goodbye* (1950).
Jeanne Cagney's screen appearances include: *All Women Have Secrets* (1939), *Golden Gloves* (1940), *Queen of the Mob* (1940), *Yankee Doodle Dandy* (1942), *The Time of Your Life* (1948), *Don't Bother to Knock* (1952), *Quicksand* (1950), *A Lion Is in the Streets* (1953), *Kentucky Rifle* (1955), *Man of a Thousand Faces* (1957), *Town Tamer* (1965).
Cagney Productions in which the actor did not appear include: *Only the Valiant* (directed by Gordon Douglas, starring Gregory Peck, in 1951) and *Bugles in the Afternoon* (directed by Roy Rowland, starring Ray Milland, 1952), both co-produced with Warner Bros.

Other Media Cagney

STAGE

His New York stage appearances (excepting touring vaudeville, summer stock and military shows) include: "Pitter Patter" (Longacre Theatre, book by Will M. Hough, lyrics and music by William B. Friedlander, staged by David Bennett, 1920); "Outside Looking In" (Greenwich Village Playhouse Inc., moving to 39th Street Theatre, written by Maxwell Anderson, directed by Augustin Duncan, 1925, 113 performances); "Broadway" (Broadhurst Theatre, staged by authors Philip Dunning and George Abbott, 1926–27); "Women Go On Forever" (Forrest Theatre, written by Daniel N. Rubin, staged by John Cromwell, 1927, 117 performances); "Grand Street Follies of 1928" (Booth Theatre, directed by Agnes Morgan, dances by Cagney and Michel Fokine, 1928, 144 performances); "The Grand Street Follies of 1929" (Booth Theatre, book and lyrics by Agnes Morgan, staged by Agnes Morgan, 1929, 53 performances); "Maggie the Magnificent" (Cort Theatre, written by George Kelly, staged by the author, 1929, 32 performances); and "Penny Arcade" (Fulton Theatre, written by Marie Baumer, directed by William Keighley, 1930, 24 performances).

RADIO AND TELEVISION

His radio and television work includes: national radio broadcasts of "Is Zat So?" (with sister-in-law Boots Mallory for "Lux Radio Theater" in 1936), "Ceiling Zero" (with Ralph Bellamy and Stuart Erwin for Lux in 1939), "Angels With Dirty Faces" (with Pat O'Brien and Gloria Dickson for Lux in 1939), "Revlon Revue" (with Gertrude Lawrence for Blue Network, later ABC), "Johnny Got His Gun" (1940), "Captains of the Clouds" ("Cavalcade of America" programme on NBC in 1942), "Yankee Doodle Dandy" (Screen Guild Players in 1942); and rare television appearances on "The Ed Sullivan Show" ("live" dramatic scene from *Mister Roberts*, with Henry Fonda and Jack Lemmon, on June 20, 1955), and "Robert Montgomery Presents" (Dramatic play, "Soldier From the Wars Returning," with Cagney as a cynical Army sergeant assigned to escort home the body of a soldier killed in the Korean war, directed by Peter Lafferty, September 10, 1956, NBC).

Bibliography

BOOKS

Agee, James, "Agee on Film," Boston, Beacon Press, 1966.

Arliss, George, "My Ten Years in The Studios," Boston, Little, Brown and Company, 1940.

Bergman, Andrew, "James Cagney," New York, Pyramid, 1973.

Bluen, A. William, Gen. Ed., "The Movie Business: American Film Industry Practice," New York, Hastings House, 1972.

Bromfield, Louis, "It Takes All Kinds," London, Harper and Bros., 1931.

Brown, Joe E., "Laughter Is A Wonderful Thing," as told to Ralph Hancock, New York, A. S. Barnes and Co., 1956.

Davis, Bette, "The Lonely Life," New York, G. P. Putnam and Sons, 1962.

Dickens, Homer, "The Films of James Cagney," New Jersey, Citadel Press, 1972.

Farber, Manny, "Negative Space," Praeger Publishers, New York, 1971.

Goodman, Ezra, "Bogey: The Good-Bad Guy," New York, Lyle Stuart, Inc., 1965.

Griffith, Richard, Ed., "The Talkies," Dover Publications, 1971.

Gussow, Mel, "Don't Say Yes Until I Finish Talking, The Biography of Darryl F. Zanuck," New York, Doubleday and Co., 1971.

Higham, Charles and Joel Greenberg, "The Celluloid Muse," New York, Angus and Robertson, 1969.

Hyams, Joseph, "Bogie," New York, New American Library, 1966.

Kanin, Garson, "Tracy and Hepburn: An Intimate Memoir," New York, Bantam, 1971.

Lahr, John, "Notes on a Cowardly Lion: The Biography of Bert Lahr," New York, Alfred A. Knopf, 1969.

Lawson, John Howard, "Film in the Battle of Ideas," New York, Masses and Mainstream, 1953.

LeRoy, Mervyn, "Take One: Mervyn LeRoy," New York, Hawthorn, 1974.

Levin, Martin, Ed., "Hollywood and the Great Fan Magazines," New York, Arbor House, 1970.

Madsen, Axel, "Billy Wilder," London, Secker and Warburg, 1968.

McBride, Joseph, "Focus on Howard Hawks," New Jersey, Prentice-Hall, 1972.

McCoy, Horace, "Kiss Tomorrow Goodbye," New York, Random House, 1948.

Miller, Don, "B Movies," New York, Curtis, 1973.

Moley, Raymond, "The Hays Office," New York, Bobbs-Merrill Co., 1945.

O'Brien, Pat, "The Wind At My Back," New York, Doubleday, 1964.

Offen, Ron, "Cagney," Chicago, Henry Regnery Company, 1972.

Reagan, Ronald, "Where's the Rest of Me?," with Richard G. Hubler, New York, Duell, Sloan and Pearce, 1965.

Rivkin, Allen, "Hello Hollywood," New York, Doubleday and Co., 1962.

Robson, E. W. and M. M., "The Film Answers Back: An Historical Appreciation of the Cinema," London, John Lane The Bodley Head, 1934.

Rosten, Leo C., "Hollywood," New York, Harcourt, Brace and Co., 1941.

Sarris, Andrew, "The American Cinema," New York, Dutton, 1968.

Sennett, Ted, "Warner Brothers Presents," New Rochelle, Arlington House, 1971.

Shipman, David, "The Great Movie Stars: The Golden Years," New York, Crown, 1970.

Tynan, Kenneth, "Curtains," New York, Atheneum, 1961.

Warner, Jack L., "My First Hundred Years in Hollywood," with Dean Jennings, New York, Random House, 1964.

Warshow, Robert, "The Immediate Experience: Movies, Comics, Theatre and Other Aspects of Popular Culture," New York, Doubleday, 1964.

Wilson, Robert, Ed., "The Film Criticism of Otis Ferguson," Philadelphia, Temple University Press, 1971.

Wood, Tom, "The Bright Side of Billy Wilder, Primarily," New York, Doubleday, 1970.

Zierold, Norman, "The Moguls," New York, Coward-McCann, Inc., 1969.

MAGAZINES, NEWSPAPERS AND OTHER

Boston Globe, May 20, 1973, "Cagney is Alive and Well and Living in Retirement," Charles Champlin, Los Angeles Times.

Closeup, April, 1930, "The Personality of the Player: A Phase of Unity," H. A. Potamkin.

———, September, 1931, "Notes from America," Herman G. Weinberg.

———, March, 1933, "The Year of the Eclipse," H. A. Potamkin.

Colliers, September 3, 1932, "Tough, By Request," Henry F. Pringle.

———, August 31, 1940, "Tough, On and Off," John Durant.

———, October 28, 1955, "Cagney," Cameron Shipp.

Coronet, November, 1955, "Gentle Tough of Martha's Vineyard," H. Benz.

Cosmopolitan, June, 1955, "Cagney's Year," Louella O. Parsons.

Esquire, July, 1972, "Hollywood," Peter Bogdanovich.

Films, Summer, 1940, "Unions in Hollywood," Robert Joseph.

Films and Filming, March, 1959, "James Cagney Talking."

———, February, 1967, "A Cutter at Heart: Anatole Litvak," interview.

Films in Review, August–September, 1958, "James Cagney," Don Miller.

Focus on Film, No. 7, Interview with Henry Hathaway.

Fortune, December, 1937, "Warner Brothers."

Literary Digest, April 7, 1934, "On the Current Screen."

Look, September 20, 1955, "The New Craze for Cagney," Laura Bergquist.

Movie, May, 1963, Interview with Nicholas Ray.

New Theatre and Film, December, 1935, "James Cagney," Forrest Clark.

Newsweek, April 22, 1968, "Yankee Doodle Dandy."

New York Herald Tribune, April 24, 1955, "James Cagney Lives Down on Two Farms," Thornton Delehanty.

New York Times, June 28, 1931, "James Cagney, Actor."

——, December 27, 1936, "James Cagney Dreams of O'Casey," John T. McManus.

——, September 5, 1943, "The Firm of Cagney Brothers, Inc.," Theodore Strauss.

——, March 6, 1955, "That's Cagney All Over," Barbara Beach Jamison.

"Notes on Film Noir," Paul Schrader, First Los Angeles International Film Exposition.

Read, February, 1944, "America's Most Lovable Bad Boy," J. Nelson Tuck.

Saturday Evening Post, October 2, 1943, "The Cantankerous Cagneys," H. Allen Smith.

——, January 7, 14 and 21, 1956, "How I Got This Way," James Cagney as told to Pete Martin.

Saturday Review, October 1, 1949, "Cagney Rides Again," John Mason Brown.

Screen, Winter 1972/73, "The American Photo League," Bill Nichols.

Sight and Sound, Winter, 1958, "James Cagney," Philip Oakes.

Village Voice, December 7, 1972, "Partners in Crime and Conversion," Molly Haskell.

Women's Home Companion, November, 1934, "They Toughened Him Up," Alva Johnston.

Much of the material for this book was garnered from *The Boston Globe* library, extensive *New York Times* clippings, the collected issues of *The Velvet Light Trap* and the vast, often-undated sources, including fan magazines and studio promo data, of the Wisconsin Center for Theatre Research at the University of Wisconsin in Madison. Only the principal, available sources are listed.

Index

239

DATE DUE

JUL 8 1976

JAN 1 1977

SEP 2 7 1984

MAR 2 5 1996

GAYLORD   PRINTED IN U.S.A.

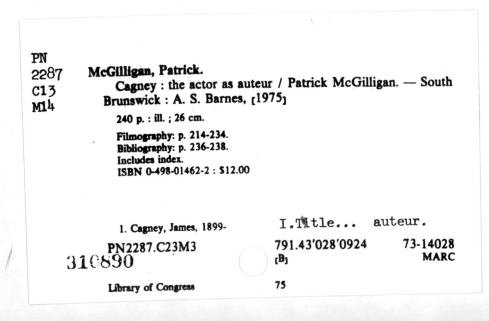